Qu[illegible]s

TO SM[illegible] BUSINESS
QUESTIONS

Quick answers

TO SMALL BUSINESS QUESTIONS

Alison Alsbury

series editor Ros Jay

Prentice Hall

London • New York • San Francisco • Toronto • Sydney • Tokyo • Singapore
Hong Kong • Cape Town • Madrid • Paris • Milan • Munich • Amsterdam

PEARSON EDUCATION LIMITED

Head Office:
Edinburgh Gate
Harlow CM20 2JE
Tel: +44 (0)1279 623623
Fax: +44 (0)1279 431059

London Office:
128 Long Acre, London WC2E 9AN
Tel: +44 (0)20 7447 2000
Fax: +44 (0)20 7240 5771
Website: www.business-minds.com

First published in Great Britain in 2001

ISBN 0 273 65326 1

British Library Cataloguing in Publication Data
A CIP catalogue record for this book can be obtained from the British Library.

10 9 8 7 6 5 4 3 2 1

Designed by Sue Lamble
Typeset by Northern Phototypesetting Co Ltd, Bolton
Printed and bound in Great Britain by Biddles Ltd, Guildford & King's Lynn

The Publishers' policy is to use paper manufactured from sustainable forests.

About the author

Alison Alsbury is Hereford City Promotions and Development Manager. She was previously Centre Manager at Salters Shopping Centre, Droitwich Spa. The focus of her present role is marketing; the shopping centre role included a substantial HR element. She is a fluent linguist. Highlights of her previous and highly varied career were interpreting at several international trade fairs, and running her own small business – a small translating company.

For nearly 15 years Alison has also worked as a freelance writer. She edited *Maw on Corporate Governance,* still a prescribed text on the subject. She interviews and writes regularly for recruitment and HR publications. Before her involvement with the *Quick Answers* series, she wrote *European Executive Training: A Handbook for Senior Managers* (Financial Times/Pitman, 1992). Her main 'hobby' has to be motherhood – solo parenting for four children for the past 13 years.

Contents

Acknowledgements

I would like to thank the following people and organisations for their help and contributions in putting together this book.

ACAS
The Advertising Association
Barclays Bank plc Small Business Services
British Chambers of Commerce
The British Franchise Association
The British Venture Capital Association
Chartered Institute of Marketing
The Citizens' Charter Unit
Clearlybusiness.com
Companies House
Confederation of British Industry (CBI)
Department for Education and Employment
Department of Trade and Industry
The Direct Mail Information Service
The Dryden Press
The Enterprise Panel
ESOMAR
The Federation of Small Businesses
Fit for the Future Campaign
The Forum of Private Business
The Franchise Business
The Health and Safety Executive
HMSO
HSBC Bank plc
IFF Research Ltd
Inland Revenue
The Insolvency Service
The Institute of Direct Marketing

Institute of Directors
Institute for Employment Studies
Institute of Management Foundation
Institute of Manpower Studies
Institute of Personnel and Development
Lloyds TSB Bank plc
MORI
NatWest Franchise Section
NatWest UK
The Policy Studies Institute
Small Business Research Trust
The Small Business Service
Social and Community Planning Research
Virgin Publishing

Pam Flynn
Miriam Fox
Lesley Mitchell
Nick Morris
Jo O'Driscoll
Graham Ross Russell
Juliet Russell
Julie Sullivan

Introduction

This is a business reference book with a difference. The information it contains is directly useful to you and your business. There's a lot of statistical material available, but it tends to be industry-specific or whole industry figures. It's not terribly helpful to know what's going on in the baked bean industry if you run a chain of travel agencies. And knowing what total small business turnover figures are each year tells you precious little about your own profits and cash flow.

This book will give you relevant – not industry-specific – business data, so it will apply to you whatever business you're in. It starts with the questions you might reasonably ask, and tries to answer them. When statistics are not the answer, the book brings you advice from nationally recognised sources. All the information in this book is relevant to the UK. Businesses overseas do some things very differently, and building their research information into the results would dilute the accuracy of the figures. The book gives you average data for the individual organisation, so you can see how they compare with yours.

You can use *Quick Answers to Small Business Questions* for four main purposes:

- **Benchmarking:** you'll find information about how other small firms conduct their business activities, and you can measure your performance against the average.
- **Planning:** before you launch into a new initiative, you can look through the relevant section to see which key factors you should consider. For example, if you're wondering whether to work from home or rent premises, you'll find that the relevant section of this book will tell you what problems you might encounter, and the main benefits of the two choices.
- **Decision making:** you'll find the answers to all sorts of questions here, to help you reach decisions. Suppose you're trying to work out

how to market a new product. The relevant section of this book will tell you how to research your market and how to plan your marketing campaign, and suggest which advertising media to use.

- **Supporting applications for finance and other proposals:** the information in this book comes from reliable and authoritative sources. Consequently you will find it invaluable for adding weight to your own arguments. Suppose you want to persuade the local bank manager to extend your overdraft. After referring to this book, you will be able to draw up an excellent business plan, and will be fully aware of the questions you're likely to be asked.

Quick Answers to Small Business Questions pulls together information on business topics from start-up to selling your business, tackling all the issues which growth brings in its wake, and calling in on staff recruitment, company formation, health and safety, IT, technology transfer, and many others along the way. It should quickly become one of the most well-thumbed books on your shelf.

The series

This book is one of the *Quick Answers* series. The other books in the series are *Quick Answers to Marketing Questions, Quick Answers to Key People Questions*, and *Quick Answers to Web Marketing Questions.* The original series which they replace, *The Essential Sourcebooks,* has proved immensely popular; that series has now been extended to cover other vital areas of business. Gurus – leading industry specialists – have also kindly contributed to the *Quick Answers* series, so they include a wealth of practical advice from people in the know.

You may find that certain topics you are interested in are included in the other books. Inevitably, *Quick Answers to Small Business Questions* gives an introduction to marketing and HR issues which are dealt with in more detail in the other books in the series. Where only one or two pieces of data overlap between the books, we have included them in both books to make it easier for you to find them. Comments in the text refer you to the other books in the series as necessary.

The data

In this series of books we have used only the most reliable data we could find. Clearly the methodology varies widely between studies, but if we included the full details of it each time there would be no room to include the findings. Each piece of data is clearly sourced where it appears in the text, and you will find a complete list of contact details at the back of the book (Appendix 2) should you wish to find out more.

We have studied the data ourselves, of course, and we have not included any material that we consider to be unreliable. In a few cases, we felt that the information available needed to be treated with a measure of caution. In these instances, we have made this view clear in the surrounding text. We took the view, however, that any information is more useful than none, as long as you are aware of the possible risks in treating it as gospel. Where we felt that data were seriously flawed or biased, we excluded them.

The research findings included in the series are the most up-to-date we could find, and in the vast majority of cases were published within the past three or four years. In a few cases the research is older than this, but often the reason no one has updated it is precisely because they do not expect it to have changed. We have not included any information that we consider to be unreliable because of its age.

The *Quick Answers* series is a comprehensive guide to useful UK business data and advice. But since the series is based on research data, we are obviously limited by the research that is available. We have found useful material on all the major areas of business, but it is possible that you may be interested in a particular aspect of one of these areas that you cannot find listed here. If this happens, it will be because (after months of research, and contact with hundreds of organisations) we have failed to track down any reliable data on the subject. If you know of any survey or other research data that are relevant to this series but which we have not included, we would be very pleased to hear from you so that we can include them in the next edition.

The contributors

The data in these books have been contributed by many of the most highly respected institutes and research organisations, by government departments, and by some of the top experts in various fields. We are very grateful to them for their co-operation.

Some of the reports from which we have taken extracts are publicly available from these organisations. In most cases, we have reproduced only a small part of the full research findings – the information we think will be of the widest interest. But if you have a special interest in any subject, you may well want to see the full report. A listing of surveys, reports, guides and fact sheets that are published by our contributing organisations appears at the front of the book. This listing not only includes the publications from which we have taken extracts but also gives details of any other reports and surveys that you might find interesting. Many of the contributing organisations provide excellent websites – without exception, they are worth visiting.

How to use the book

The book is divided into broad business topics (for example 'planning your business'), which are subdivided into more specific categories (such as 'legal and tax issues'). These are then divided further into areas within this (for example 'types of business'). Finally, the information in these sections has been split into individual subject areas, each headed with a question (e.g. What are the requirements of a partnership?).

We have presented each piece of data in the form which illustrates it most clearly. In many cases, this involves using charts, graphs, matrices and other things that make some people feel slightly unnerved and confused. If you're one of these people, you may find Appendix 1 helpful. It is a user-friendly guide to reading statistics which briefly explains each type of graph, chart and figure that you may come across while using the book. Let me reassure you that we have not tried to be clever, but have used only those graphics which are in relatively common usage.

Although we have designed the books to be functional, we were surprised when we put them together to find just how fascinating much of the material is, even when the subject matter is not immediately relevant. You should find it easy to track down the information you want; we hope, however, that you will find the book sufficiently interesting that you will not only use it for its primary purpose – as a reference book – but will also find it entertaining to browse through for general interest.

Surveys and reports, 2001

The following surveys, reports and publications are produced by the organisations that have contributed to this book. You will find listed many of the full reports from which we have reproduced extracts in this book, along with other relevant publications. If you would like to order any of the surveys, reports or other publications listed here, the contact details of the organisations are in Appendix 2.

About small businesses

The Role of the Small Firm in the UK Economy: Hot Stereotypes and Cool Assessments, James Curran, Small Business Research Trust Report, May 1999.

Small and Medium Enterprise (SME) Statistics for the UK, 1999, DTI Statistical News Release, 7 August 2000.

Starting up in Business, Barclays Research Review. Barclays Bank plc Small Business Services, 1999.

Secrets of success

Banking and Raising Finance – Finding the Right Bank for Your Business, www.clearlybusiness.com

Help for Your Business, NatWest Bank plc Small Business Services, October 2000.

Ready to Help You Succeed, Lloyds TSB Business Starter Pack, 2000.

Starting a Business – Taking a Closer Look, HSBC Bank plc Business Starter Pack, 1999.

Starting and Growing Your Own Business – Entrepreneurial Management, course notes for small business owners, Nick Morris and Bridget Rosewell, City University Business School.

Starting up in Business, Barclays Research Review, Barclays Bank plc Small Business Services, 1999.

Starting in Business, Barclays Research on Small Business Characteristics, Barclays Bank, 1995.

Start-Up Guide, NatWest Bank plc in conjunction with the Foundation for Small and Medium Enterprise Development, University of Durham, February 2000.

Thinking of Starting a Business?, Barclays Bank plc Business Starter Pack, 1998.

Planning your business

Company Formation, Companies House, 2000.

The Data Protection Act Explained, www.clearlybusiness.com

Planning to Keep One Step Ahead, Barclays Bank plc Small Business Services, 1996.

Setting up and Running Your Business, Barclays Bank plc Business Starter Pack, 2000.

A Step-by-step Guide to Your Business Plan, Lloyds TSB Bank plc Business Services, 1999.

Finance

Barclays Short-term Loan, Flexible Business Loans and *Loan Guarantee Scheme*, all from Barclays Information Pack, Barclays Bank plc Small Business Services, 1997.

Barclays Commercial Mortgage, Barclays Information Pack, 1997.

Behind the Veneer of Success: Propensities for UK Franchisor Failure, Small Business Research Trust, 1997.

Factoring, Barclays Information Pack, 1997.

Funding Your Business, Barclays Review, Barclays Bank plc Small Business Services, May 1997.

Kidsons Impey Small Business Tracking Survey XIV, prepared by Consensus Research Ltd and Critical Research Ltd, January 1995.

1997 NatWest/BFA Franchise Survey, NatWest UK and The British Franchise Association.

The NatWest Guide to Buying a Franchise, National Westminster Bank plc, August 2000.

Soft Loan Schemes and the Finance Gap – An Evaluation Study, James Curran, Robert Blackburn and Martina Klett-Davies, Small Business Research Centre, August 1994.

Sources of Finance, SBRT/Lloyds Report, September 2000.

The Two Partners of Franchising, Peter Stern, Franchise World Directory, 1998.

What are the Benefits of Franchising?, The Franchise Business Factsheet, November 2000, or see www.franchisebusiness.co.uk

What is Franchising?, The Franchise Business Factsheet, November 2000, or see www.franchisebusiness.co.uk

What Should I Look For in a Franchise?, The Franchise Business Factsheet, November 2000, or see www.franchisebusiness.co.uk

Marketing

Advertising Means Business – A Practical Guide to Advertising, The Advertising Association, 1997.

DMIS Intelligence Sector Reports, Direct Mail Information Service, 1997.

Innovation and Growth – Top Ten Tips on Market Research for Technology Businesses, www.clearlybusiness.com

International Prices Study, European Society for Opinion and Market Research (ESOMAR), 1994.

Journal of Marketing Management, The Dryden Press.

Marketing and The Small Firm, Barclays Bank plc Small Business Services, May 1997.

Manufacturing – The Marketing Solution, Chartered Institute of Marketing survey, 1995.

The Practitioner's Guide to Direct Marketing, The Institute of Direct Marketing, 1992.

Understanding Market Segmentation, DSS Research, August 2000.

Managing your business

Accounting and Tax – Make Sure You're Paid on Time, Accounting and Tax – How to Deal with VAT, Getting Online – IT for SMEs, Your Business – How to Run a Successful Family Business, all from www.clearlybusiness.com

Better Payment Practice – A Guide to Credit Management, Department of Trade and Industry, January 1998.

Finding the Time: A Survey of Managers' Attitudes to Using and Managing Time, Karen Cole, Institute of Management, 1995.

Information Technology, Barclays Review, 1996.

NatWest SBRT Quarterly Survey of Small Businesses in Britain, Vol. 16, No. 2, June 2000, Small Business Research Trust at the Open University Business School.

NatWest SBRT Quarterly Survey of Small Businesses in Britain, Vol. 16, No. 3, September 2000, Small Business Research Trust at the Open University Business School.

Quarterly Small Business Management Reports, Lloyds Bank/Small Business Research Trust.

Setting Up and Running Your Business, Barclays Bank plc Business Starter Pack, June 2000.

Managing growth

Best Practice Benchmarking, Department of Trade and Industry, 1995.

Bulletpoint, Sample Issue 2000, Bulletpoint Communications Ltd.

Fit for the Future, CBI Campaign Literature, October 2000.

Growing Success – Helping Companies to Generate Wealth and Create New Jobs Through Business Incubation, The Enterprise Panel, October 1996.

Internationalisation for World Class Strategies, Association of British Chambers of Commerce, 1995.

Quarterly Surveys of Small Firms, The Forum of Private Business.

Your business – how to attract a business angel, www.clearlybusiness.com

Innovation and Growth – Ten Tips on Finding Private Equity Finance, *Ten Tips on Intellectual Property Rights*, *Ten Top Tips on Technology Transfer* and *Interview with an Entrepreneur*, all from www.natwest.com

Staff

'Compliance Costs', *NatWest SBRT Quarterly Survey of Small Businesses in Britain*, Vol. 12, No. 1, March 1996.

Communication and Consultation, ACAS, 1990.

Counting Costs to Keep Competitive, Confederation of British Industry, 1994.

Cultural Change and the Small Firm, Barclays Review, Barclays Bank Small Business Services,1997.

Employee Involvement in Small Firms, Policy Studies Institute, 1997.

Employee Motivation and the Psychological Contract, IPD Employee Attitude Survey, 1997.

Employee Selection in the UK, Institute of Manpower Studies,1988.

Employers' Recruitment Practices, The 1992 Survey, Social and Community Planning Research, 1992.

Essentials of Health and Safety, The Health and Safety Executive, 2000.

Focus on Absence Survey, Confederation of British Industry and PPP Healthcare, CBI Publications, 2000.

From Absence to Attendance, Alistair Evans and Steven Palmer, Institute of Personnel and Development, 1997.

Garnishing the Corporate Carrot, Marketing Week, November 1990.

Health and Safety in Small Firms – An Introduction to Health and Safety, The Health and Safety Executive, October 1997.

'Introduction to personnel management', www.bizmove.com/personnel

IPD Survey of Performance Management Policies and Practices in the UK, Institute of Personnel and Development, 1997.

IPD Survey of Sickness Absence, Institute of Personnel and Development, 2000.

'Keeping it Legal: Company Directors – What do they actually do?'

'Keeping it Legal: The Minimum Wage – Are you paying enough?'

'Managing People: How to find the best staff for your business'.

The above three factsheets are from www.clearlybusiness.com

Mind the Gap. How to Fill the Skills Gap and Improve Your Recruiting – A Guide for Small Businesses, Department for Education and Employment, 2000.

Recruitment, Lloyds Bank/SBRT Quarterly Small Business Management Report, Vol. 5, No. 2, July 1997.

Sickness Absence Monitoring and Control – A Survey of Practice, IRS Employment Trends, September 1994.

Skills Needs in Great Britain and Northern Ireland, 1996, Public Attitude Surveys Ltd research for the Department of Education and Employment.

Skills Needs in Great Britain and Northern Ireland, 1998, IFF research for the Department of Education and Employment.

Team Working and Pay, Institute for Employment Studies, 1995.

Getting out

'Facts on family business in the UK', www.ffi.org

Liquidation and Insolvency, Companies House.

'Selling your business: the sales process', www.clearlybusiness.com.

'Selling your business: closing the deal', www.clearlybusiness.com.

Starting up in Business, Barclays Research Review, 1999.

Welcome to R3's 9th Survey of Business Recovery, 2000, www.insolvency.org

1

About small businesses

the questions

- How big a turnover do start-up businesses expect in their first year?
- Do small business owners seek advice before they set up?
- What advice do small business owners find the most helpful?

Established businesses / 9

- How many small business people work from home?
- What government support would small business owners most like to see provided?

About small businesses

the answers

Definition of a 'small' business

There is no UK official or universally accepted definition of the 'small firm'.

How does the government define a small business?

The government adopts a range of definitions, depending on the particular piece of legislation or policy.

- The DTI's discussion of the statistics employs the EU definitions (small firms employ fewer than 50, medium fewer than 250, and large are all firms with 250 or more employees) but stresses that there is no single definition.
- The main reason given for this variability is that business size distributions are sector-dependent. Oil refineries are likely to have higher capitalisation, numbers of employees and turnover than car repairers, so it is impossible to compare a 'small' oil refinery with a 'small' car repairer.
- The DTI includes in its statistics a 'size class zero' business – those made up of sole traders, or partners without employees.

(*Source: The Role of the Small Firm in the UK Economy: Hot Stereotypes and Cool Assessments*, James Curran, Small Business Research Trust Report, May 1999)

How helpful is the EU definition of a small business?

The main weakness is that there are very few 'large' UK businesses if size is defined by number of employees. Taking the EU definition above, fewer than 7,000 of the 3.7 million businesses in the UK employ 250 or more people.

Does it help to define small businesses by turnover?

Barclays Bank plc has undertaken substantial research into small businesses, and uses as its definition 'businesses with sales turnover of up to £1 million'. Other research organisations also use financial information to define 'small'.

How do academic researchers define small businesses?

Kingston University's Small Business Research Centre's programme on small service businesses (1989–1992) points out that other characteristics define a small business.

- The enterprise has to be legally independent (not a branch or establishment or subsidiary).
- A 'grounded' definition of small is required for each sector – achieved through interviews with trade representatives, owner-managers and others involved in the sector to establish perceptions of 'small'.
- Multi-dimensional definitions are more accurate – number of employees should be one factor, tied in with perceptions, turnover, and capitalisation. The definition of 'small' should then reflect sector-relevant criteria for each type of activity.

(*Source: The Role of the Small Firm in the UK Economy: Hot Stereotypes and Cool Assessments*, James Curran, Small Business Research Trust Report, May 1999)

How are small businesses defined in this book?

The definition of 'small' will depend on the source of the information used. When it is important to know how 'small' is defined by a survey, the relevant definition will be given in the text.

Is there a commonly accepted definition of 'small business'?

In reality, there is a broad consensus on what constitutes a 'small' business. The owners and managers of small businesses recognise that their firm falls within that category; members of the public see small businesses as firms that are not large.

Taking the DTI definition of 'small', 'medium' and 'large', only 7,000 companies in 1999 were 'large' (more than 250 employees); only 24,000 firms were 'medium' (50–249 employees). It is reasonable to define all the rest as small.

The impact of small firms

How many small businesses are there?

Of the 3.7 million businesses in 1999, more than 2.3 million were 'size class zero' – those made up of sole traders or partners without employees (see Table 1.1). Just over 1.3 million businesses were therefore employers – a large number employing between one and four staff.

Table 1.1 Number of businesses, employment and turnover by size of enterprise, start 1999

Size	Number			Per cent		
Number of employees	Businesses	Employment (000s)	Turnover (£m ex VAT)	Businesses	Employment	Turnover
None	2,324,340	2,708	90,463	63.2	12.5	4.7
1–4	963,615	2,395	221,986	26.2	11.0	11.4
5–9	201,835	1,459	123,029	5.5	6.7	6.3
10–19	109,280	1,533	149,451	3.0	7.1	7.1
20–49	46,995	1,462	147,505	1.3	6.7	7.6
50–99	14,450	1,011	102,860	0.4	4.7	5.3
100–199	8,165	1,131	116,638	0.2	5.2	6.0
200–249	1,570	349	38,633	—	1.6	2.0
250–499	3,220	1,121	149,275	0.1	5.2	7.7
500+	3,515	8,576	804,039	0.1	39.4	41.4
All	3,676,940	21,746	1,943,880	100	100	100
All with employees	1,352,600	19,038	1,853,417	36.8	87.5	95.3

(*Source: Small and Medium Enterprise (SME) Statistics for the UK, 1999 –* DTI Statistical News Release, 7 August 2000)

What contribution do small firms make to the economy?

Chart 1.1 illustrates the proportion of businesses, employment and turnover in small, medium and large firms at the start of 1999. Whatever the definition of 'small' business used (in this case it is defined by number of employees), it is clear that small businesses make a vital contribution to the national economy.

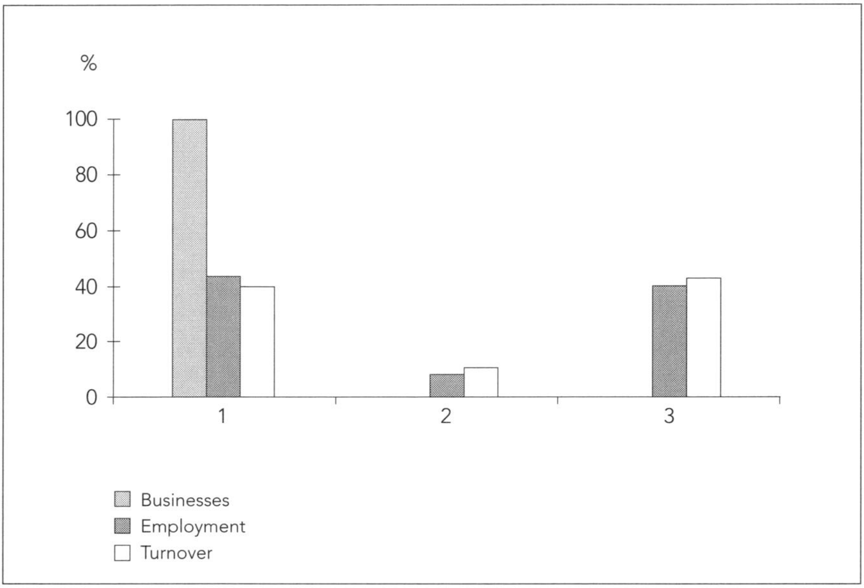

Chart 1.1 Proportion of businesses, employment and turnover in small, medium and large firms, start 1999

(*Source: Small and Medium Enterprise (SME) Statistics for the UK, 1999* – DTI Statistical News Release, 7 August 2000)

The small business sector

Start-ups

Who makes up the small business sector?

Around half a million businesses are set up each year. So what sort of person takes the plunge and enters the world of self-employment? The average first-time small business owner is a male, in his thirties, running his business on a full-time basis.

- 72% of small business start-ups are run by men.
- 66% of people starting up for the first time are 25–44 years old.
- 91% of owners run their business on a full-time basis.

(*Source: Starting up in Business*, Barclays Research Review, 1999)

What are typical small business characteristics?

- The typical small business start-up is a sole trader, operating in the distribution sector, using separate premises.
- The average turnover is £100,000.
- The average employment figures are three full-time employees and three on part-time contracts.
- Sole trader is the most popular legal form of small business – 51% start this way.
- Partnerships account for only 18% of the market.

By far the greatest percentage of start-ups are in the distribution sector (which includes retailing, wholesale and hotels). Business services and leisure are the next largest sectors for start-ups, representing a further 14% and 11% of the market respectively.

(*Source: Starting up in Business*, Barclays Research Review, 1999)

How big a turnover do start-up businesses expect in their first year?

While the average anticipated turnover of a small business is around £100,000, 6% expect to turn over in excess of £500,000 in their first year (see Chart 1.2).

Those that set up as a limited company expect a higher turnover, with almost a quarter (24%) anticipating turnover of more than £250,000 compared with only 7% of partnerships and 1% of sole traders.

Do small business owners seek advice before they set up?

Given that two-thirds of owners have not run a business in the past, and four out of ten are entering a different line of work, how many feel the need to undergo training or seek help? A quarter undertook technical training specific to the business; 12% went on a management or 'how to run a business' course.

In fact, two-thirds of inexperienced owners seek some form of advice before they set up – 74% of those with no experience sought advice, compared with 40% of those with experience. Chart 1.3 illustrates their sources of help and advice.

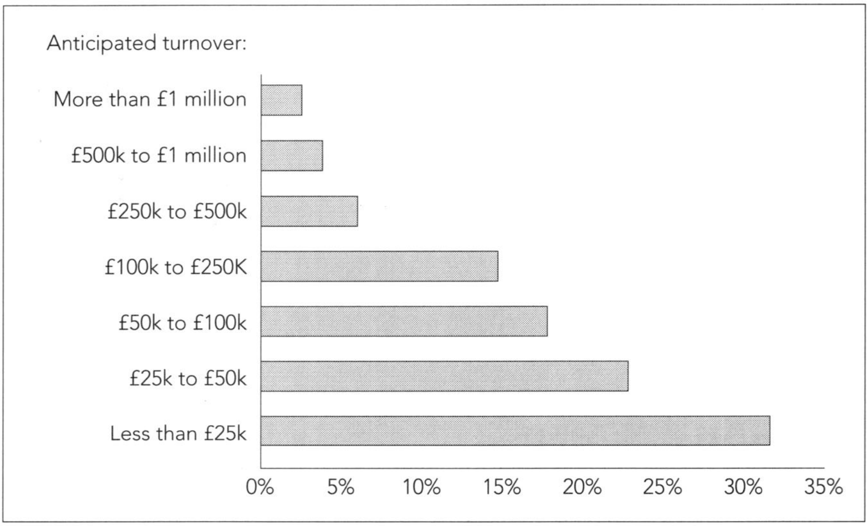

Chart 1.2 Anticipated turnover in first year

(*Source: Starting up in Business*, Barclays Research Review, 1999)

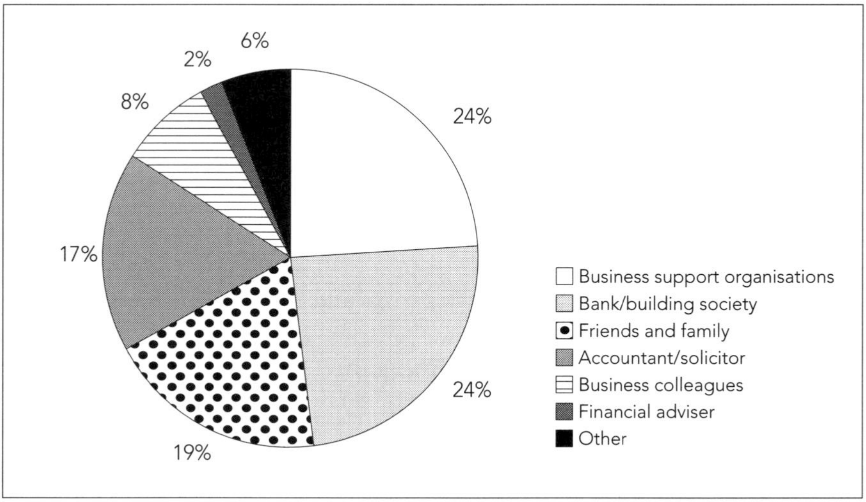

Chart 1.3 Sources of help and advice for start-ups

(*Source: Starting up in Business*, Barclays Research Review, 1999)

What advice do small business owners find the most helpful?

Small business owners were asked to look back at the advice they received, and decide which sources they found helpful.

- 85% appreciated the advice from their friends and family.
- 84% found Business Links a useful source of advice.
- 79% found Enterprise Agencies useful.

Established businesses

How many small business people work from home?

While most small business owners work from business premises (78%), women are more likely to work from a home base, with three times as many (19%) working from home most of the time, and a further 12% using their home as a work base. This suggests that many women are trying to juggle domestic responsibilities with those of work (see Chart 1.4).

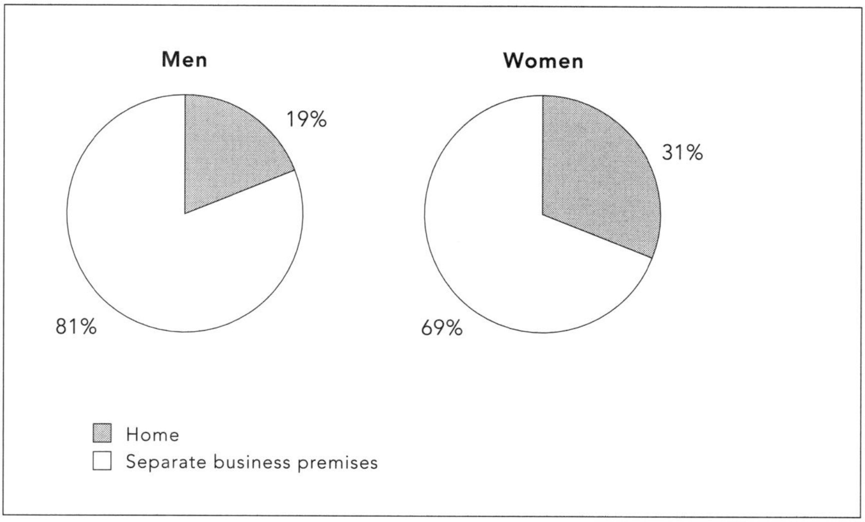

Chart 1.4 Where the business is based by gender

(*Source: Starting up in Business*, Barclays Research Review, 1999)

What government support would small business owners most like to see provided?

Small business owners are calling for specific support from the government with the focus inevitably on financial help. The government's Competitiveness White Paper has begun to address these issues, but it is interesting to see what concerns small businesses most (see Table 1.2).

Table 1.2 Support requested from government

Support requested	Percentage
Provision of grants and loans	58
Reduction in taxes	43
Greater availability of advisory bodies	15
Reduction in red tape	10
Offering training schemes	9
Maintenance of economic stability	3
More support for inventions	3
Make other companies pay on time	1

(*Source: Starting up in Business*, Barclays Research Review, 1999)

2

Secrets of success

the questions

- What is Shell LiveWIRE?
- What about government-sponsored business consultancy services? How do these work?
- How do you find the right bank for your business?

Secrets of success

the answers

An entrepreneur is:

Someone who bites off more than he can chew, hoping that one day he'll learn to chew it.

(*Source:* Casey Stench, baseball manager)

Success or failure – what makes the difference?

Two facts are worth remembering.

- All large companies started small.
- In a dynamic economy, most businesses at any one time are small.

(*Source: Starting and Growing Your Own Business – Entrepreneurial Management,* Nick Morris and Bridget Rosewell, City University Business School)

What do successful companies teach us?

British Petroleum was founded in 1901 by William Know D'Arcy, an English lawyer who made his first money from Australian gold. He followed a hunch about oil at Masjid-i-Suleiman (Persia) and it took seven years to find. After the Amoco merger, BP is the third largest oil company and the tenth largest company, in the world.

Compaq was founded by Rod Canion, Jim Harris and Bill Murto. It raised $20 million capital from US technology financier Ben Rosen and had a national dealer network in a year, and first-year sales topped $100 million. It behaved like a seasoned company from the start.

Hewlett-Packard was founded by William Hewlett and David Packard. Based in a garage, they had tried out many electronic products including a foot-fault indicator and a harmonica tuner. Their first successful product was the Audio Oscillator, priced at $54.50. Their approach included very little market research – just 'suck it and see'.

It's easier to develop a new idea without too much bureaucracy – the incentives are much stronger and many people prefer being their own boss.

(*Source: Starting and Growing Your Own Business – Entrepreneurial Management,* Nick Morris and Bridget Rosewell, City University Business School)

What do the most successful small business leaders have in common?

A common characteristic of British high-growth medium-sized businesses is the presence of entrepreneurial leaders. The majority are what can be described as 'professional entrepreneurs'. Their key characteristics are:

- they were *professionally trained* (usually in a large multinational company);
- they have a *'theory of the business'* – a recipe for success;
- they can provide a *clear vision of the future* for the business, but the vision is seldom expressed on paper as a formal mission statement;
- they maintain *'bus ticket' controls* – key management ratios which allow them quickly to check the health of the business;
- they are committed to *success through continuous change and innovation*;
- they *understand their market* and have a strong desire to grow the business and compete successfully;
- they are *totally dedicated* and identify closely with the business;
- they have a *strong commitment to the people in the organisation.*

(*Source: Starting and Growing Your Own Business – Entrepreneurial Management,* Nick Morris and Bridget Rosewell, City University Business School)

What characteristics does a business need for survival?

Given the high failure rate of small businesses, it surely helps to understand the attributes of success. Strong ability to manage the business, together with a commitment to quality, seem to be the most important characteristics, although good staff and adaptability also came high on the list (see Table 2.1).

Table 2.1 Attributes of success

Characteristic	% considering it necessary for survival
Ability to manage the business	93
Better quality products/services than competitors	90
Good quality staff	86
Ability to adapt quickly to changes in the market	85
Well capitalised	68
Lower costs than competitors	67
High investment back into the business	58

(*Source: Starting up in Business*, Barclays, 1999)

What about personal characteristics?

Barclays asked 400 nationally representative small business owners to identify their main strengths in running their firms (Table 2.2). Interpersonal skills topped the list.

Table 2.2 Small business owners' main strengths

Characteristic	% considering it a strength
Being able to get on with customers and staff	90
Motivation	88
Resilience – 'sticking to the job'	84
Being competitive	83
Being decisive	81
Thinking through decisions	78
Sound business acumen	69
Knowing when to seek advice	68

(*Source:* Starting up in Business, Barclays, 1999)

The onus to do well is particularly important for nearly two-thirds of business starters, as they provide their families' only or main source of income.

Are men better business starters than women?

This question was put to 500 members of the general public and three-quarters refused to generalise about whether men or women were better business starters. However, on closer examination, the differences are more apparent (see Charts 2.1 and 2.2).

Whatever the difference between the sexes, starting up in business is seen as a great opportunity for anyone who believes enough in themselves and has the will and determination to succeed.

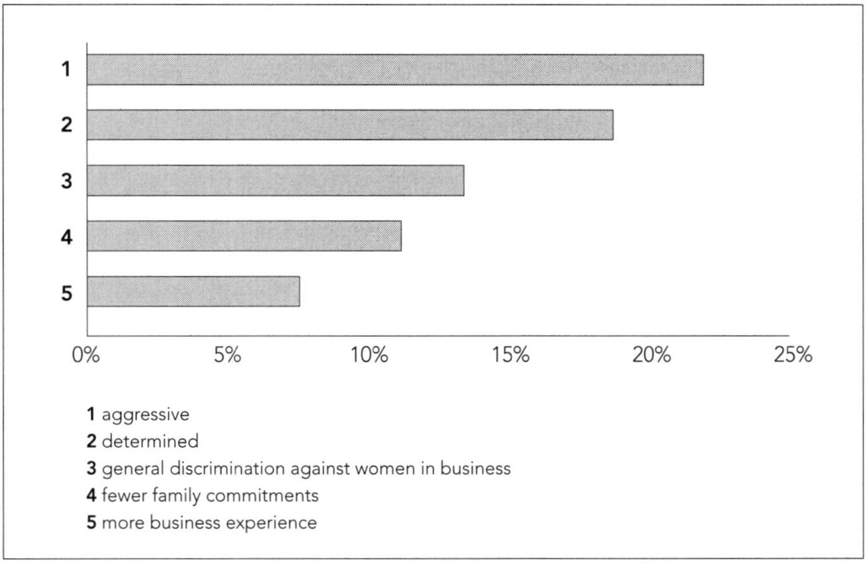

Chart 2.1 What the general public think makes *men* better business starters

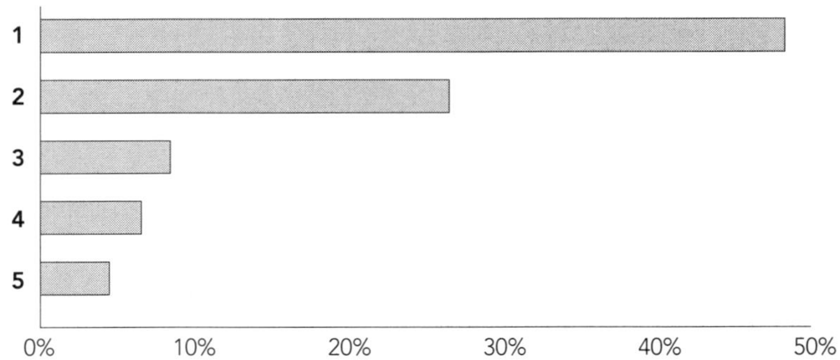

1 Determined
2 Natural organisers
3 Work harder/more conscientious
4 Better with people
5 Shrewd

Chart 2.2 What the general public think make *women* better business starters

(*Source: Starting up in Business*, Barclays, 1999)

Will you be able to go it alone?

It is all too easy to suppose that you have *all* the right personal attributes for running a successful business. HSBC Bank plc, which advises thousands of small businesses, suggests that you take a long hard look at yourself. To help you understand your strengths, the bank offers a quick questionnaire.

(*Source: Starting a Business – Taking a Closer Look*, HSBC 1999)

Questionnaire

Please circle the statements that best match your outlook:

1 Are you a self-starter?

- a *'I use my initiative. I don't need anyone to tell me what to do.'*
- b *'Once someone's told me what to do, I get on with it.'*
- c *'I only put myself out when I want to.'*

2 How do you get on with other people?

- a *'I make sure I get on with everybody.'*
- b *'I have a close circle of friends. I don't need other people.'*
- c *'I'm never at ease in company.'*

3 Can you lead and motivate others?

a *'Most people follow my lead.'*

b *'I'm good at giving orders once I know exactly what's required.'*

c *'I'll join in once something is already started.'*

4 Can you take responsibility?

a *'I like to take charge and see things through.'*

b *'I'll take over if I have to but I'd prefer someone else to be responsible.'*

c *'There's always an eager beaver waiting to show off. I'll leave them to it.'*

5 Are you a good organiser?

a *'I like devising a plan. I'm usually the organiser.'*

b *'I'm OK when everything goes to plan. I get confused when things go wrong.'*

c *'I take things as they come.'*

6 How conscientious a worker are you?

a *'I'll go the extra mile for something I really want.'*

b *'I work hard for a while. But when I've had enough that's it.'*

c *'Why push myself? People take it easy and still get by.'*

7 Can you make decisions?

a *'I often make snap decisions. They usually work out well.'*

b *'If I have time to think about them.'*

c *'I prefer others to make decisions.'*

8 Can people believe what you say?

a *'I always say what I mean.'*

b *'I try to be honest, but sometimes it's too difficult or complicated to explain everything in detail.'*

c *'Sometimes I say what I think other people want to hear.'*

9 Can you stay the course?

a *'Once I have a goal, nothing will stop me achieving it.'*

b *'I usually finish what I start.'*

c *'If it doesn't go right first time, I lose interest.'*

10 Do you consider it important to take care of your health?

a *'I am fighting fit. I look after myself, so I'll stay that way.'*

b *'What will be, will be.'*

c *'It's my mind, not my body, that's the main thing.'*

11 What experience do you have in your proposed area of business?

a *'I've been in the trade for years.'*

b *'I need to learn new skills. I plan to go on training courses.'*

c *'Experience isn't that important.'*

12 Do you have the support of your family and friends?

a *'My family know the risks. They are happy to get by on reduced income for a while.'*

b *'They're not sure what's involved, but think it's worth a try.'*

c *'My family and social life are all important.'*

Total up the number of a's, b's and c's. If you mainly circled a's, you've probably got what it takes to make it by yourself. You are motivated, decisive, and good with people. If you ticked mainly b's and c's, think again about going it alone. Setting up with someone whose talents complement your own could be an option. The vital thing is to be clear about your personal goals, and those for your business. Vision, drive and passion are as important as experience and knowledge if a business is to prosper.

Q What personal qualities will you need?

The most important personal qualities are:

- self-sufficiency – as a sole trader or owner-manager, you will have to draw deeply on your experience and character. The big decisions are now yours not someone else's;
- initiative – you will have to be a self-starter, spotting opportunities and acting on your own without external support;
- resilience – unless you are very lucky, your business will not always run smoothly; sometimes it will be like running a marathon;
- responsibility – there's no one else to blame: the buck stops with you;
- imagination – you'll need to anticipate your customers' needs and motivate your staff. You'll need to find innovative ways round challenges. You'll need to keep a cool head in a crisis. And you must be willing to learn.

(*Source: Thinking of Starting a Business?*, Barclays, 1998)

What skills will you need?

You don't need to be an expert at everything, but you do need to be able to see the whole management picture. The following skills are vital:

- management – the ability to keep control of your business and to know what resources and skills you need to achieve that;
- financial – understanding and controlling the finances of your business is vital;
- marketing – you need to understand your customers and how your product or service meets their needs. One key aspect is pricing – how to sell at a price which will encourage your customers to buy and still make a profit for you;
- production and distribution – it's important to produce a product or a service efficiently, and to deliver it effectively to the customer or the retailer;
- technical or specialist knowledge and expertise – if you have something that few others in your chosen market have, you are more likely to succeed.

(*Source: Thinking of Starting a Business?*, Barclays, 1998)

Why will you succeed?

The conventional view is that your business is more likely to succeed if it fulfils three criteria.

1. The people involved realistically assess their own strengths and weaknesses, and try to overcome shortcomings. This is the most important criterion.
2. The idea and the market for your business have the necessary growth potential, and you have experience in that market.
3. Financing is sufficient to cover the shortfall of working capital, especially in the early days.

(*Source: Starting and Growing Your Own Business – Entrepreneurial Management,* Nick Morris and Bridget Rosewell, City University Business School)

Why might you fail?

You will fail if your operation does not match up to the three criteria mentioned above.

Some more specific examples of likely causes of failure are:

- overestimating sales and underestimating how long it takes to achieve them;
- underestimating costs;
- failing to control costs ruthlessly;
- losing control over cash, carrying too much stock, allowing customers too long to pay, paying suppliers too promptly;
- failing to identify your market because of inadequate market research;
- failing to adapt your product to meet customer needs and wants;
- lacking sufficient skills in one of the following areas – selling and marketing, financial, production, technical;
- failing to build a team which is compatible and complementary when your business needs to grow;
- taking unnecessary risks;
- underpricing.

(*Source: Starting and Growing Your Own Business – Entrepreneurial Management,* Nick Morris and Bridget Rosewell, City University Business School)

Reasons for running your own business

What is the main reason for starting a small business?

What role does the prospect of making more money play? It appears that the main motivations are personal rather than financial. When asked about the timing of their decision to start a business, respondents identified particular factors for starting a business – see Table 2.3. Most people, however, make the decision to start a business to change their lifestyle or gain more control – see Table 2.4.

Table 2.3 Reasons for starting a business

Reason	Total	Men	Women
Left job/redundancy	30%	32%	23%
Increasing demand in the market	13%	14%	10%
Necessary funding/capital found	12%	10%	17%
Overall confidence in the economy	10%	11%	6%
Saw a gap in the market	7%	7%	8%

(*Source: Starting up in Business*, Barclays, 1999)

Table 2.4 More personal reasons for starting a business

Reason for starting business	%
Greater satisfaction from being your own boss/frustrated at work	25
Desire for more independence	17
Saw an opportunity that was too good to miss	14
Better financial prospects	12
No real alternative	10
Possibilities of earning money for doing something you like	6

(*Source: Starting up in Business*, Barclays, 1999)

Is it silly to leave a secure job?

Barclays research shows that on average a self-employed person works 9.5 hours a day, six days a week. Yet despite the greater risk of financial insecurity, the majority of entrepreneurs Barclays questioned left a secure job to start a business (see Chart 2.3).

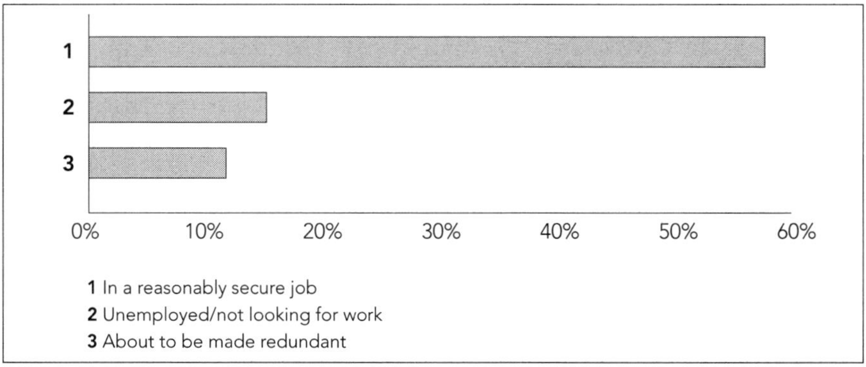

Chart 2.3 Employment situation at the time of start-up

(*Source: Starting up in Business*, Barclays, 1999)

Being an entrepreneur

What is entrepreneurship?

Entrepreneurship is a process of personal and organisational renewal which brings social benefit and economic vitality to our society.

Entrepreneurship captures an attitude and a way of behaving whereby individuals take ownership of their own development, accept responsibility for the impact of their efforts and are willing to accept and create change if it will lead to individual, economic and social benefits.

(*Source:* Durham University Business School – MA in Entrepreneurship, 1999)

What makes a good entrepreneur?

I can honestly say I have never gone into any business purely to make money. If that is the sole motive, then I honestly believe that you are better off not doing it. A business has to be involving; it has to be fun, and it has to exercise your creative instincts.

(*Source: Losing My Virginity*, Richard Branson, Virgin Publishing, 1998)

Are you decisive?

Self-assessment questionnaire

Please answer Yes or No to the following questions.

1 'I often feel I'm the victim of outside forces I cannot control.'
2 'I often work later than planned.'
3 'Some days seem to go by without my having achieved a thing.'
4 'Given a bad situation, I'll always try to get something out of it.'
5 'I think a well ordered pattern of life with regular hours suits me best.'
6 'I'm much happier not having to rely on other people.'
7 'I'm prepared to take risks only when I've carefully thought through all the consequences.'
8 'There's no point starting something unless you're going to see it through.'
9 'People often tell me how good I am at seeing things from their point of view.'
10 'I tend not to be too ambitious to avoid being disappointed.'
11 'It's very important to me that people recognise my success.'

12 'When I find myself talking to a telephone answering machine, I usually hang up.'
13 'I've never been one to follow the crowd.'
14 'All that matters is how much I earn, regardless of how hard I work to get it.'

Score 2 points if you answered Yes to questions 2, 4, 7, 8, 9, 11 and 13 and zero points for questions 1, 3, 5, 6, 10, 12 and 14. Score 2 points if you answered No to questions 1, 3, 5, 6, 10, 12 and 14, and zero points for questions 2, 4, 7, 8, 9, 11 and 13. The maximum score is 28 points. The higher your score, the better equipped you are likely to be to solve problems and make decisions.

(*Source: Thinking of Starting a Business?*, Barclays Bank plc, 1998)

Is starting and growing a business right for you?

An important part of your self-analysis should be motivation. It may be a helpful exercise to sit down and note what your aims are under the following headings.

- *Money.* How much? When? In what form? As much as possible? Enough to live on?
- *Working hours.* Number of hours? Amount of holiday? Flexibility?
- *Risks.* Like a gamble? Only low risk acceptable? Prefer calculated risks?
- *Stress.* Looking for lower levels of stress? Can you cope with stress?
- *Type of work.* Want to concentrate on what you're good at – to achieve your full potential? Want to be able to do the work you like, and choose which work to leave for others?
- *Independence.* Fed up with being told what to do? No longer wish to explain your actions to your superiors? Think you can do better than your boss?
- *Achievement.* Want to set yourself standards to achieve? To see if you can do it where others fail?
- *Power.* Looking for the sense of power which being the boss can give? Want to enhance your reputation or status? Want to do better than someone else?

- *Personal relations.* Happier on your own, away from irritating workmates?

(*Source: Starting and Growing Your Own Business – Entrepreneurial Management*, Nick Morris and Bridget Rosewell, City University Business School)

A viable proposition

Do you need a specific idea?

There are a number of ways of getting into business.

1. *Starting from scratch.* No matter how carefully you research your market, you are never going to be sure how good the idea is until you are actually up and running. An entirely new business may be the best way to take advantage of a gap in the market, and there will be no price to pay for 'goodwill'.
2. *Improving on a current business.* This requires studying an existing business's methodology, improving on its methods, and setting up in competition.
3. *Buying a business.* Take professional advice before committing yourself to buying an existing business.
4. *Becoming a franchisee.* A franchise is when you buy the right and the trading name and system of a business that is already running.

(*Source: Start-up Guide*, NatWest Bank plc in conjunction with the Foundation for Small and Medium Enterprise Development, University of Durham, February 2000)

How important is the business idea?

You may have the best idea in the world for a business, you might even have a product or service nobody has thought of before, but a good idea will not guarantee you success. Before you begin to make plans to develop your idea, there are five key questions you should ask yourself.

1. Are there people who will want what you have to sell?
2. Who are they?
3. How will you market your idea to them?
4. What will you charge them?
5. Will it earn you a living?

(*Source: Thinking of Starting a Business?*, Barclays Bank plc, January 1998)

How do you get your business from mind to paper?

There are several stages.

1 *Why do I want to start a business?*

Are you going into business to make more money? Do you want to be involved in something that interests you? Do you want independence? Whatever your reasons for starting up, be clear about your business and personal aims, and set yourself goals.

(*Source: Start-up Guide,* NatWest Bank plc in conjunction with the Foundation for Small and Medium Enterprise Development, University of Durham, February 2000)

2 *The business mission*

The key aims of a business are known as 'the business mission statement'. If you have a firm idea of your aims and where you want to go, you are more likely to succeed. These are some examples of the points you might make in a business mission statement:

- to offer a first-class business and personal minicab service throughout Anytown;
- to be the leader in the business and at the top end of the personal minicab market, and to have high-profile local business within two years;
- to make 40% profit on the money used to start the business;
- to expand the business from five cars to ten within three years.

(*Source: Start-up Guide,* NatWest Bank plc in conjunction with the Foundation for Small and Medium Enterprise Development, University of Durham, February 2000)

3 *Fact-finding*

Time and money spent proving the viability of your proposition before you 'open for business' are time and money well spent. If you are planning to launch a new product or service, or you are setting up in a new location, make sure the market is there for what you are offering. If you are setting up in competition with other businesses, make sure you are offering a better deal. If you are buying an existing business or becoming a franchisee, study the facts and figures closely. Always ask why, if a business is so successful, someone is trying to get out of it.

(*Source: Starting a Business – Taking a Closer Look,* HSBC Bank plc, September 1999)

4 *Talk about it*

The Small Business Service is charged by the government to deliver a comprehensive service to small businesses. It has a pilot National Call Handling Service – 08456 045678 – which will put you in touch with your local business support service – Business Links in England, Small Business Gateways in Lowland Scotland, Business Information Source in Highland Scotland, Business Connect in Wales, and LEDU in Northern Ireland. Its website (www.businessadviceonline.org) provides online links to a wide range of other organisations that may be useful sounding boards at this preliminary stage.

In addition, the high street banks all provide small business advisors, who offer advice about how to get started.

5 *Write it down*

Thinking your idea through carefully can help you decide if you're on the right lines. So write down answers to the following questions.

- *Is it a new idea?* Very few businesses are truly innovative, so try to work out why no one has done it before. Ruthless analysis may reveal a flaw in your thinking before it's too late.
- *Can you improve on an old idea?* You need to give people a very good reason to switch allegiance to you, so what are the new/unique advantages and benefits?
- *Have you considered franchising?* This is not a risk-free option – you could be buying into more costs than you anticipated. But you do buy the right to use an existing format and trading name, and an established brand image – and you get training, advice and marketing campaigns.
- *Who will you be competing against?* Use market research to find out who your competitors are – look through *Yellow Pages*, trade magazines, or be a customer and study leaflets and price lists.
- *Have you identified your customers?* Unless you know who you're selling to, you're not really in business. How many potential customers are there for your product or service?
- *How many customers will want to buy at a price you need to set in order to make a profit?* Be realistic – charging too little can be just as big a mistake as charging too much.

(*Source: Ready to Help You Succeed*, Lloyds TSB Business, 2000)

Have you identified your market?

The main aim of research is to ask the right questions and obtain accurate answers. When conducting your research prior to starting a business, you should be aiming to produce an indicator of the likely market for your product or service. It is helpful to identify:

- the size of the market you aim to supply;
- the share of the market you can realistically capture;
- how much that market share is worth.

If the value of the market is low, your business may not be able to make enough money.

(*Source: Starting a Business – Taking a Closer Look*, HSBC Bank plc, September 1999)

Do you know enough about your market?

The sort of questions you need to answer includes the following.

1 *Customers*

a What type of person or business will buy your product or service?

b What qualities will they expect in your product or service?

c How many potential customers can you realistically expect?

d How do you let these customers know what you have on offer?

e How much spending power do these customers have?

f Will their spending power increase or decrease?

2 *Competitors*

a Do other businesses offer similar products or services to yours?

b What do they charge?

c Are there any gaps in the market which you could fill?

d How do they make and sell their products?

e Do they have an established reputation?

f How easy would it be for someone else to enter this market if you make a success of it?

(*Source: Starting and Growing Your Own Business – Entrepreneurial Management*, Nick Morris and Bridget Rosewell, City University Business School)

Will you be able to compete?

Are there opportunities in the market for your business? Test your market plan by answering these ten questions:

1. Is my market getting smaller, growing or staying the same?
2. Who are my main competitors?
3. How will the competition react to my business?
4. If I am selling to just one or two major buyers, have I checked that they are financially reliable?
5. If they fail, are there other buyers I can sell to?
6. Will my suppliers meet my needs?
7. If not, are there other suppliers I can use?
8. What turnover am I hoping for in the first year?
9. Is this realistic?
10. Do I know how much I have to sell to break even?

(*Source: Start-up Guide*, NatWest Bank plc in conjunction with the Foundation for Small and Medium Enterprise Development, University of Durham, February 2000)

Learning from the experts

What are the main sources of business advice and support?

The Small Business Service, Business Links, Training and Enterprise Councils, Enterprise Agencies, Chambers of Commerce, the Federation of Small Businesses, the Forum of Private Business, and Shell LiveWIRE for 16–30-year-olds. The government also sponsors business consultancy services in certain specialist subject areas.

(*Source: Help for Your Business*, NatWest Bank plc Small Business Services, October 2000)

What are Business Links?

Business Links are managed by the Small Business Service and provide a single point of access for all business support services. They are a national network of 89 local partnerships between Training and Enterprise Councils, Chambers of Commerce, Enterprise Agencies, local authorities, the Department of Trade and Industry, other providers of business support and local business representatives.

Business Links are known by that name in England; they are called Small Business Gateways in Lowland Scotland, the Business Information Source in Highland Scotland, Business Connect in Wales, and LEDU (the Local Economic Development Unit) in Northern Ireland.

(*Source: Help for Your Business*, NatWest Bank plc Small Business Services, October 2000)

What kind of help is available from Business Links?

Business Links provide access to the kind of help that really counts:

- how to raise money for growth;
- how to get into markets – from local to export;
- what grants are available;
- how to source the most suitable training packages;
- how to manage change;
- how to locate suppliers;
- regulatory information;
- impartial IT help.

(*Source: Help for Your Business*, NatWest Bank plc Small Business Services, October 2000)

What services do Business Links offer?

Business Links' key services for small businesses include:

- comprehensive business information providing detailed and specific research;
- personal, reliable, all-round advice from personal business advisors (PBAs);
- events, promotions, conferences, seminars and networking opportunities where businesses can work and meet other business people;
- specialist advice and services;
- help for start-up and micro-businesses;
- diagnostic help.

Not all services are run by Business Links themselves. An important feature is the informed referral to other services provided by Business Link partners and other business support organisations. For further information, call the Business Link Signpost Line on 0345 567 765.

(*Source: Help for Your Business*, NatWest Bank plc Small Business Services, October 2000)

What help can a personal business advisor offer?

There are many reasons for seeking the help of a PBA. You may need help drawing up a business plan, or the business could be in trouble or on the verge of rapid growth. You may just need to deal with a particular problem. A PBA can provide:

- objectivity – a new pair of eyes, as you may be too close to your business;
- business concepts and methods, introducing you to the tools of business analysis that help you make decisions;
- contacts and local knowledge through their clients and fellow advisors;
- experience – business management principles apply widely, so advisors can often ask the right questions to help you think round a problem;
- access to resources – grants, loans, training courses, premises, etc.

(*Source: Working With Your Business Advisor*, HSBC, January 1998)

What will a PBA expect from you?

- Commitment and genuine enthusiasm, including some clear ideas of how to make your business work.
- Preparation and action – prepare carefully for your first meeting; outline the issue clearly. The sessions will have value only if they result in action.
- Openness – do not pretend to understand things when you don't. Ask for clarification. Be frank. And take constructive criticism.

Useful tips when working with a PBA

1. Give your relationship a chance to work – as with any working relationship, you may experience difficulties.
2. Do not hesitate to ask your advisor informally about their background and qualifications. It will help you to understand how best to use their advice.
3. Don't let the advisor undermine your opinions. They can only offer advice – they won't have all the answers.
4. Different agencies will be able to offer different levels of advice. It may be useful to contact a number of organisations before committing to an advisor.

(*Source: Working With Your Business Advisor,* HSBC, January 1998)

What are Training and Enterprise Councils (TECs)?

The network of TECs in England and Wales was created to foster economic growth and contribute to regeneration. Their special focus is strengthening the skill base, and assisting local enterprises to expand and compete effectively.

(*Source: Help for Your Business,* NatWest Bank plc Small Business Services, October 2000)

What programmes do TECs run?

TEC programmes are designed at local level to meet the needs of businesses in the area they cover. Examples of the type of services available include:

- short enterprise awareness events to help people involved in working for themselves understand what is involved in setting up and running a business;
- help with business planning for managers who want to learn how to develop a business and training plan;
- seminars to improve business skills in bookkeeping, marketing, management and other skills;
- low-cost consultancy to help established companies develop their management team, or develop new training arrangements to meet future skill needs.

(*Source: Help for Your Business,* NatWest Bank plc Small Business Services, October 2000)

What are Enterprise Agencies?

Enterprise Agencies are not-for-profit organisations which provide advice, counselling, information, training and practical help to small businesses and to people who are planning to start up in business.

- Training seminars are offered in a range of subjects, either free of charge or for a nominal fee.
- Many agencies have soft loan funds, and some may have grants available to help with start-up costs.
- Other services include help for innovators, managed workshops, information on importing and exporting, and help with raising equity finance.

(*Source: Help for Your Business*, NatWest Bank plc Small Business Services, October 2000)

How do Chambers of Commerce help?

The British Chambers of Commerce (BCC) is a network of around 60 approved Chambers of Commerce, with more than 110,000 member businesses. The main services they provide include:

- *A national voice for local business* – approved chambers act with the BCC on their members' behalf and represent their interests to local and central government, MPs, and all other relevant bodies.
- *Business Intelligence* – chambers offer information services for members covering legislation affecting business, product sourcing, retailing and European affairs. They also hold information about members' products and services. In 1997, approved chambers dealt with more than 62,000 business information enquiries per month.
- *The exporter's friend* – approved chambers promote members' products and services overseas, and help them develop trading opportunities. They provide a whole range of international trade services, including payment advice and information on the shipping of goods, methods of payment, documentation and marketing. They are authorised to issue EC Certificates of Origin.
- *Training and business skills* – chambers provide details of suitable training courses, from skills courses to consultancy, in-company training and government-driven initiatives. The BCC is the largest independent training network in the UK.

- *The UK's biggest business network* – approved chambers collectively represent more than 110,000 UK businesses and organise a wide range of conferences and events. All approved chambers are linked through a nationwide intranet, looked after by the BCC.

(*Source: Help for Your Business*, NatWest Bank plc Small Business Services, October 2000)

What is the Federation of Small Businesses (FSB)?

The FSB is the largest campaigning pressure group, promoting and protecting the interests of the self-employed and owners of small firms. Formed in 1974, it has more than 112,000 members over 31 UK regions. Led by its Westminster parliamentary office, it applies pressure on MPs, government and Whitehall, and also lobbies politicians in their constituencies. It has the funds to take major test cases of importance to small businesses through the courts.

(*Source: Help for Your Business*, NatWest Bank plc Small Business Services, October 2000)

How can the FSB help?

The FSB provides legal and professional insurance of up to £1 million to protect business activities against:

- Inland Revenue investigations;
- VAT tribunals and appeals;
- industrial tribunal costs;
- employment disputes;
- statutory sick audits;
- PAYE audits.

It also provides defence against prosecution in connection with:

- The Health and Safety at Work Act;
- The Consumer Protection Act;
- The Food Safety Act;
- The statutory licence;
- The damage to property;
- The Data Protection Act;
- personal injury.

In connection with jury service it gives up to £100 per day for loss incurred by an owner or an employee.

General help includes:

- telephone helplines;
- export information and guidance;
- legal assistance, business and personal, 24 hours a day, 365 days a year;
- advice on taxation, VAT, DSS, PAYE, employment law, health and safety, and general insurance.

(*Source: Help for Your Business*, NatWest Bank plc Small Business Services, October 2000)

What is the Forum of Private Business (FPB)?

Founded in 1977, the FPB serves its 24,000+ member firms as a non-partisan, non-profit-making organisation. Its unique referendum system gives independent businesses direct influence on the laws and policies affecting them.

The quarterly FPB oral survey of private business owners' opinions provides regular evidence of current and anticipated concerns to the decision makers in European, national and local government, and financial institutions. The FPB is also engaged in lobbying for fairer rents and rates, and is developing a self-audit process for issues such as health and safety, crime prevention, etc.

(*Source: Help for Your Business*, NatWest Bank plc Small Business Services, October 2000)

What is Shell LiveWIRE?

LiveWIRE is a UK-wide Shell investment programme which aims to develop and manage programmes that improve opportunities for young people who wish to start or develop their own businesses.

The Outreach Programme:

- aims to act as a gateway to youth enterprise support;
- provides information for any 16–30-year-old who wants to start a business, and links to free local advice and support;
- provides each enquirer with a 'start your own business' booklet, showing how to turn ideas into reality;

- will appoint a suitable advisor, if requested;
- provides, through advisors, LiveWIRE support materials.

Business Start-Up Awards:

- provide an annual celebration of the nation's most promising young business people – entrants to the competition must be 16–30 years of age, and have been trading for less than three months and not more than 18 months; they send their business plan to the local co-ordinator;
- offer awards of more than £200,000 and support 'in kind' which are presented at the award ceremonies. A major cash award is presented to the most promising young UK business annually.

(*Source: Help for Your Business*, NatWest Bank plc Small Business Services, October 2000)

What about government sponsored Business Consultancy Services? How do these work?

There are six initiatives which are managed by specialist professionals – the Institute of Marketing, the Design Council, the Production Engineering Research Association (PERA) and 3i Enterprise Support Ltd.

Consultancy projects of between 5 and 15 man-days are undertaken, charged at half the cost (the DTI pays the balance). In assisted and urban programme areas, only one-third of the cost is charged. A specialist consultant visits the firm, providing advice on one of the following:

- *marketing* – strategy, pricing, competition, distribution, future development, exports;
- *design* – innovation, production, materials, packaging, and point-of-sale material;
- *quality* – standards maintenance, production and profitability improvements;
- *manufacturing and services systems* – modern technology, computer designing, robotics, flexible manufacturing;
- *business planning* – development of business plans with benefits to cost control and profitability;
- *financial and information systems* – information systems, budget and financial control, computer needs.

(*Source: Help for Your Business*, NatWest Bank plc Small Business Services, October 2000)

For contact details of all the above bodies, please see Appendix 2.

How do you find the right bank for your business?

Banks are a natural place to seek expertise. Personal banking and small business banking are very different, so you may find that a new bank bringing more specialised services could bring you advantages. Consider these key points as you look around.

1. Check out the written material – do they provide a start-up guide?
2. Is the bank online? This will save time.
3. Do they offer free banking? Most do while a business gets started.
4. How close is the bank to the office?
5. Do they offer overdraft/loan facilities? How much credit are they likely to offer you?
6. Is there a small business advisor at your branch?
7. Will your bank assign a particular person to you? A name and a face always help.
8. How many company credit cards will be allowed? Will you be eligible immediately? Look out for fees, transaction charges – and any card perks.
9. Where is the value-added service? Can the bank offer advice on VAT, tax, recruitment issues, health and safety, insurance?
10. Is the bank likely to keep you up to date? Does it offer seminars or follow-up services, or a monthly review?

(*Source:* www.clearlybusiness.com, 'Banking and Raising Finance – Finding the Right Bank for Your Business')

3

Planning your business

the questions

Planning your business

the answers

Choosing location and premises

Where will you set up your business?

When Conrad Hilton was asked to give the three most important factors for the success of a hotel, he is reported to have answered 'Location, location and location'.

Location is usually the most important part of a retail business, and it can be very important in some other businesses, too. Even if you are working from home, you will have to think about things such as planning permission and access.

If you intend to lease or buy a retail outlet, check the location thoroughly. Look at the number and kind of shoppers, and facilities such as car parking. Ask the police about the crime rate in the area.

(Source: *Start-Up Guide*, NatWest Bank plc in conjunction with the Foundation for Small and Medium Enterprise Development, University of Durham, February 2000)

Have you chosen an appropriate workplace?

Where you run your business from will contribute greatly to its success. It must be pleasant for you and any employees to work in. It must be welcoming to customers. Most importantly, you must be able to afford the premises.

Ten points to consider

1. What is required? A shop, an office, a workshop or a factory? A room at home?
2. Size – will it be big enough if the business grows?
3. Location – particularly if you rely on passing trade.
4. Availability of gas, water, electricity supplies.
5. Rent, lease or buy the freehold?
6. Security requirements.
7. Car parking.
8. Maintenance and running costs.
9. Rates.
10. Fitting-out costs, including telephones, fax machines, office equipment and furniture.

(*Source: Starting a Business – Taking a Closer Look,* HSBC Bank plc, 1999)

What are the advantages of working from home?

Working from home is convenient. It reduces travel costs and business overheads. A certain proportion of running costs, such as maintenance, heating and lighting, may be tax deductible.

But beware of setting aside any part of your home to be used exclusively for business. While you may be able to claim tax relief against income tax, and recover part of the VAT in your domestic gas and electric bills, you may become liable for uniform business rate and capital gains tax on the part of your home used for business.

Before you start, check that the tenancy or legal title to the property allows you to run a business there. If in doubt, consult a solicitor. Make sure that your house insurance is adequate. It might need to be extended to cover business activities and equipment.

(*Source: Starting a Business – Taking a Closer Look,* HSBC Bank plc, 1999)

How do you find serviced offices?

Some Local Enterprise Agencies provide managed workshops, studies and offices for small businesses. You are not usually locked into a long-term lease, and can occupy on a month-by-month basis.

Further information is available from your local authority's Economic Development Unit, estate agents, local press, science parks and Local Enterprise Agencies.

(*Source: Starting a Business – Taking a Closer Look*, HSBC Bank plc, 1999)

Legal and tax issues

Types of business

Is there more than one type of business?

One of the first decisions you have to make is the most suitable type of business under which to trade. There are three general types – sole trader, partnership and limited company. Whichever route you choose, you must notify the Inland Revenue and the DSS as soon as you start trading.

(*Source: Starting a Business – Taking a Closer Look*, HSBC Bank plc, 1999)

What are the requirements of setting up as a sole trader?

This is the most straightforward option. As a sole trader, you are self-employed and will be taxed under the new self-assessment system. Your income tax bill will be calculated after your legitimate business expenses have been deducted. Your income will fall under 'Schedule D' and you will have to pay income tax twice a year, in January and July.

You will also have to pay Class 2 National Insurance contributions. These are charged at a flat weekly rate. If your profits exceed specific limits set by the Inland Revenue, Class 4 contributions are also payable half yearly in arrears.

As a sole trader, you are personally liable for the debts of your business. Unless you employ staff or make alternative arrangements, the business comes to a halt when you are ill or on holiday.

(*Source: Starting a Business – Taking a Closer Look*, HSBC Bank plc, 1999)

What are the requirements of a partnership?

In a partnership, two or more people own the business. Each partner is subject to income tax on their share of the profits. National Insurance contributions are also payable, as for a sole trader.

Partners share the workload, and bring additional capital and expertise into the business. All partners are individually and collectively responsible for the total debts of the business. Partners should be chosen with care.

(*Source: Starting a Business – Taking a Closer Look*, HSBC Bank plc, 1999)

What should a partnership agreement contain?

Always employ a solicitor to draw up a formal partnership agreement. The rights and obligations of each partner should be clearly laid out. These include:

- voting rights;
- how the business will be wound up if necessary.

Make plans for the future of the partnership in the event of the ill health or death of a partner. Take out life assurance and critical illness cover.

(*Source: Starting a Business – Taking a Closer Look*, HSBC Bank plc, 1999)

Forming a company

Is there more than one type of company?

There are four main types of company:

- private company limited by shares – members' liability is limited to the amount unpaid on shares they hold;
- private company limited by guarantee – members' liability is limited to the amount they have agreed to contribute to the company's assets if it is wound up;
- private unlimited company – there is no limit to the members' liability;
- public limited company (PLC) – the company's shares may be offered for sale to the general public, and members' liability is limited to the amount unpaid on shares held by them.

(*Source: Company Formation*, Companies House, 2000)

Who can form a company?

The Companies Act generally allows one or more persons to form a company for any lawful purposes by subscribing to its Memorandum of

Association. However, a public company or an unlimited company must have at least two subscribers.

(*Source: Company Formation*, Companies House, 2000)

How do you form a company?

Ready-made companies are available from company formation agents – details in *Yellow Pages*. If you incorporate a company yourself, you will need to send the following documents, together with a registration fee (see below), to the Registrar of Companies:

- a Memorandum of Association;
- Articles of Association or 'Table A' (obtainable from Companies House);
- Form 10;
- Form 12.

These documents are explained below.

(*Source: Company Formation*, Companies House, 2000)

What is a Memorandum of Association?

A Memorandum of Association sets out:

- the company's name:
- where the registered office of the company is situated (in England, Wales or Scotland);
- what it will do (its objects). The object of a company may simply be to carry on business as a general commercial company.

Other clauses to be included in the memorandum depend on the type of company being incorporated. The form of memorandum for each type of company is set out in a set of tables called The Companies (Tables A to F) Regulations, 1985. The company's memorandum delivered to the Registrar must be signed in front of a witness who must attest the signature.

(*Source: Company Formation*, Companies House, 2000)

What are Articles of Association?

The Articles of Association comprise the document that sets out the rules for running the company's internal affairs. Model articles are provided in the Tables mentioned above.

A company limited by shares which has adopted the whole of Table A without modification does not need to deliver a copy for registration. However, you must attach a letter to your application saying this. If Table A is adapted, you must deliver the articles for registration.

All companies that are limited by guarantee or unlimited must register articles. These should be in accordance with, or as near to that form as circumstances permit, the following tables:

- Company limited by guarantee without share capital — Table C.
- Company limited by guarantee with share capital — Table D.
- Unlimited company with share capital — Table E.

The company's articles delivered to the Registrar must be signed by each subscriber in front of a witness who must attest the signature.

(*Source: Company Formation*, Companies House, 2000)

What is Form 10?

Form 10 gives details of the first director(s), secretary and intended address of the registered office. The company's directors must give their names and addresses, dates of birth, occupation, and details of any other directorships held in the last five years. Each officer appointed and each subscriber must sign and date the form. The same person can be both director and company secretary, provided that there is another director.

(*Source: Company Formation*, Companies House, 2000)

What is Form 12?

Form 12 is a statutory declaration of compliance with all the legal requirements relating to the incorporation of a company. It must be signed by a solicitor who is forming the company, or by one of the people named as director or company secretary on Form 10. It must be signed in the presence of a commissioner for oaths, a notary public, a justice of the peace or a solicitor.

(*Source: Company Formation*, Companies House, 2000)

What is a registered office?

It is the address of a company to which Companies House letters and reminders will be sent. It must be an effective address for delivering documents to the company. Any change of address must be notified to Companies House.

(*Source: Company Formation*, Companies House, 2000)

What is the minimum number of officers a company requires?

Each company must have formally appointed company officers at all times. A private company must have at least:

- one director, and
- one secretary. The secretary need not be formally qualified; the company's sole director cannot also be the company secretary.

A public company must have at least:

- two directors, and
- one secretary, who must be formally qualified.

All company officers have wide responsibilities in law. The key requirements are contained in the Companies House booklet *Directors and Secretaries Guide*.

(*Source: Company Formation*, Companies House, 2000)

What changes must be notified to Companies House after incorporation?

- The appointment of a new officer – use Form 288a.
- An officer's resignation from the company – Form 288b.
- Changes in an officer's name or address, or any other details registered on Form 10 – use Form 288c.

(*Source: Company Formation*, Companies House, 2000)

Can anyone be a director?

In general terms, yes, but there are some rules. You cannot be a company director if:

- you are an undischarged bankrupt, or disqualified by a court from holding a directorship;
- in the case of PLCs and their subsidiaries, you are over 70 years of age.

There is no minimum age limit for a director in England and Wales, although they must be able to consent to their appointment. In Scotland, a director must be at least 16 years old.

Some people not of British nationality are restricted as to the type of work they can take while in Britain. This can be checked with the Home Office Immigration and Nationality Department.

(*Source: Company Formation*, Companies House, 2000)

Can I choose any name I want for my company?

No. There are some restrictions on your choice of company name. Companies House produces a booklet, *Company Names*, explaining these restrictions.

Company name checks

Check that the name you want is acceptable to Companies House before you complete the company formation documents. It will not be acceptable if:

- you register the same name as another company;
- you use certain words which are restricted;
- you wish to use a name which is likely to cause offence.

Check that your chosen name is not too similar to names already on the register. If your chosen name is like another, an objection can be made within 12 months and you could be directed by the Secretary of State to change the company's name.

(*Source: Company Formation*, Companies House, 2000)

How much does Companies House charge for registration?

The standard registration fee is £20. A premium service (costing £100) provides incorporation on the same day as Companies House receives the formation documents, as long as they arrive before 3 p.m.

Same-day applications

Posted, couriered and other sealed same-day applications must be clearly marked on the envelope 'for the attention of the New Companies Section' and 'Same-day Incorporation'.

(*Source: Company Formation*, Companies House, 2000)

Where can you obtain forms to incorporate a company?

Forms 10 and 12 are available free of charge from Companies House. Specimens of Memoranda and Articles of Association can be obtained from accountants, solicitors, company formation agents or legal stationers.

(*Source: Company Formation*, Companies House, 2000)

Compliance with regulations

When is it worth registering for VAT?

If your annual turnover is greater than the limit specified each year in the Budget, you are required to register for VAT with HM Customs and Excise.

VAT is charged on certain business products and services. If you register, you will have to collect any VAT on goods and services you sell, deduct any VAT you pay on purchases, and pay or claim the difference from HM Customs and Excise on either a quarterly or a yearly basis.

If your turnover falls below the specified limit, it could still be to your advantage to register, either if most of your customers are registered or if you have heavy start-up costs on which VAT could be reclaimed.

(*Source: Starting a Business – Taking a Closer Look*, HSBC Bank plc, 1999)

What about tax and National Insurance (NI)?

If you employ one or more people, you will need to deduct tax from their earnings under the PAYE scheme. You may also have to deduct your employees' NI contributions and pay them at the same time as you pay your own NI contributions. The Contributions Agency, based at the local Social Security Office, should be able to advise on NI.

You will need to keep detailed financial records so that you can complete tax and VAT returns accurately. A tax return will need to be submitted at the end of each financial year.

(*Source: Starting a Business – Taking a Closer Look*, HSBC Bank plc, 1999)

How do you set up accurate records?

- Record every sale and purchase.
- Consider using a personal computer and software, or employing a part-time bookkeeper if the accounts are likely to be complicated.
- Keep back-up records, such as invoices, bank statements and paying-in slips, to show where the income came from.
- Make 100% certain that you separate your business from your personal expenses.

(*Source: Starting a Business – Taking a Closer Look*, HSBC Bank plc, 1999)

How long do you have to keep financial records for?

You must retain your records for at least five years from the latest date for sending back your tax return – approximately six years in total (*source: Starting a Business – Taking a Closer Look*, HSBC Bank plc, 1999).

What trading regulations are likely to affect the business?

1. Planning permission is sometimes required, such as for change of use.
2. You may need a licence to trade (required for cinemas, amusement arcades, car hire firms, mobile traders, restaurants).
3. The property deeds of your premises may carry restrictions or local bye-laws may prohibit certain trades. Check these with your planning office.
4. Other trading regulations exist to protect the interests of buyers and sellers. They include:
   - health and safety at work;
   - hygiene, particularly in the preparation, handling and storage of food;
   - fire precautions.

Official inspectors have wide powers to investigate every business. Further information on these regulations can be obtained from your local Environmental Health Department, fire service or the Health and Safety Executive.

(*Source: Starting a Business – Taking a Closer Look*, HSBC Bank plc, 1999)

When will you need patents, copyrights and trade marks?

1 Patents are designed to prevent other businesses from using your inventions, designs and other original work. Contact the Patent Office or the Chartered Institute of Patent Agents for details.

2 Drawings, written works, and individual compositions such as songs or pieces of literature can also be protected, by copyright.

3 Trade marks provide registry and protection for the use of certain names and symbols. Contact the Institute of Trade Mark Agents for details.

(*Source: Starting a Business – Taking a Closer Look,* HSBC Bank plc, 1999)

Do you need to register under the Data Protection Act?

The Data Protection Act is concerned about data on individuals. The information need not be particularly sensitive – it may be an address. Under the Act, individuals have the right to access any information held about them within 40 days. Notification costs £35 a year.

Exemptions

If you use data for core business purposes only, including staff administration, accounts and records, advertising, marketing and PR, you are unlikely to need to notify the Data Protection Commissioner. You are also exempt from the Act if you process data for personal, family or recreational use.

Non-exempt purposes

You will not be exempt if you use data on computer for, among other things, trading and sharing personal information, legal services, private investigation, crime prevention and the prosecution of offenders, health and education, research, pastoral care, consultancy or advisory services, and the provision of financial services.

General rules

The information kept must be accurate, relevant and not excessive. You must keep it no longer than necessary, and must have appropriate security to protect it. If the information held is sensitive, you must have the individuals' explicit consent to hold it. Sensitive data includes information on racial or ethnic origins, medical records, religious beliefs, trade union membership, sexual life or criminal records.

(*Source:* www.clearlybusiness.com – 'The Data Protection Act Explained.')

The business plan

Advice

Where can you go for advice?

For many people, the whole process of starting a small business seems like trying to run through a minefield. And the only safe way through a minefield is to find someone who knows where the mines are. So who can you turn to? Barclays Bank asked a sample of starters who they turned to. Their answers are outlined in Table 3.1.

Table 3.1 Where starters turn for advice

Advisor	Percentage of starters seeking advice
Bank	30
Business Link/TECs	16
Friends/relatives	15
Enterprise agency	12
Account	11

(*Source: Starting in Business*, Barclays Research on Small Business Characteristics, Barclays Bank plc, 1995)

The value of planning

How many businesses plan?

Business planning appears to be a misunderstood discipline; the majority of small business owners do not make a formal plan. Only three in ten businesses have a formal plan. Well over one third have no plan at all (see Chart 3.1).

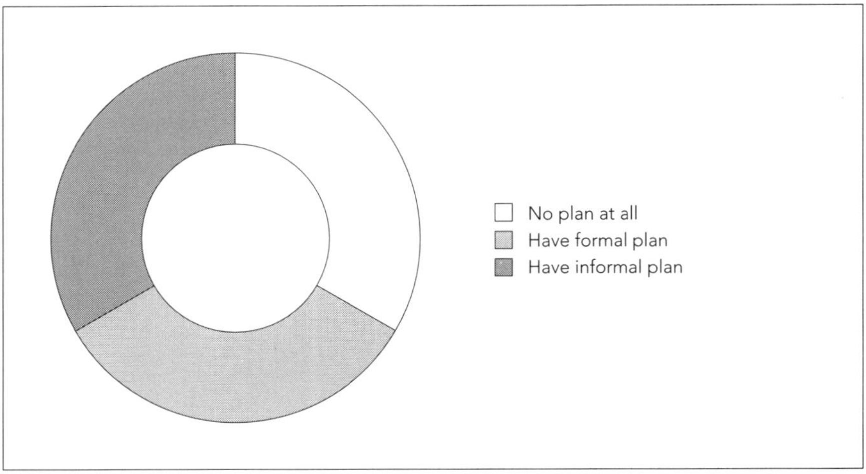

Chart 3.1 How many businesses plan?

(*Source: Planning to Keep One Step Ahead*, Barclays, 1996)

Why plan?

Businesses produce a formal plan for several reasons:

- tracking business performance and viability;
- securing finance;
- expansion;
- to formalise strategy.

Barclays asked a nationally representative sample of 400 businesses with a turnover of up to £1 million what was the main reason for developing a business plan. It appears that very few businesses use a formal plan to prepare for the future; the majority of plans concentrate on historical information (see Chart 3.2).

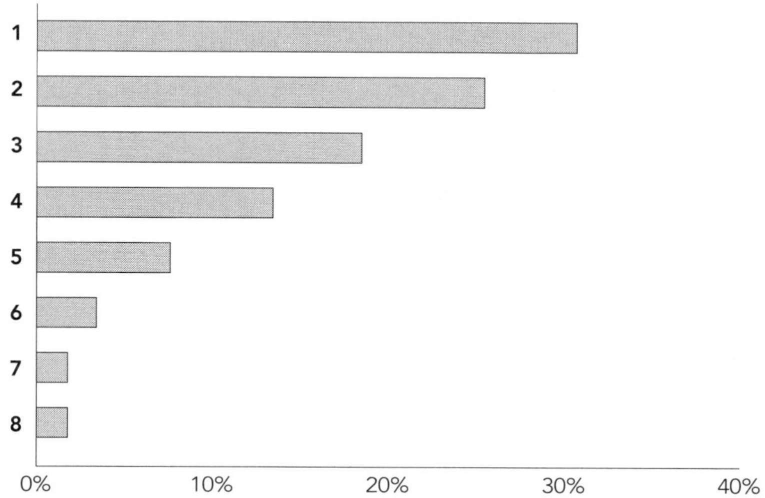

1 To monitor business performance against targets
2 To secure finance
3 To establish the business's viability
4 To formalise ideas and objectives
5 To formalise marketing strategy
6 To establish a pricing policy
7 To take on new partners
8 To establish control

Chart 3.2 Main reason for developing a business plan

(*Source: Planning to Keep One Step Ahead*, Barclays, 1996)

How should you use the plan?

The effectiveness of a business plan will depend on the time and resources businesses invest in it. Nearly half of all small businesses may be failing to get the most out of their formal plans because they devote less than 5% of management time to the process. Those who get the most out of their business plans are owners who use planning to help make decisions about where they are heading – and to manage change effectively.

(*Source: Planning to Keep One Step Ahead*, Barclays, 1996)

How often should the business plan be updated?

A business plan should be seen as a working document that is regularly updated to take into account changing internal and external factors that might affect the business situation. Almost half of small businesses with a formal plan review it every six months, which suggests that it is an integral part of the way they do business (see Chart 3.3).

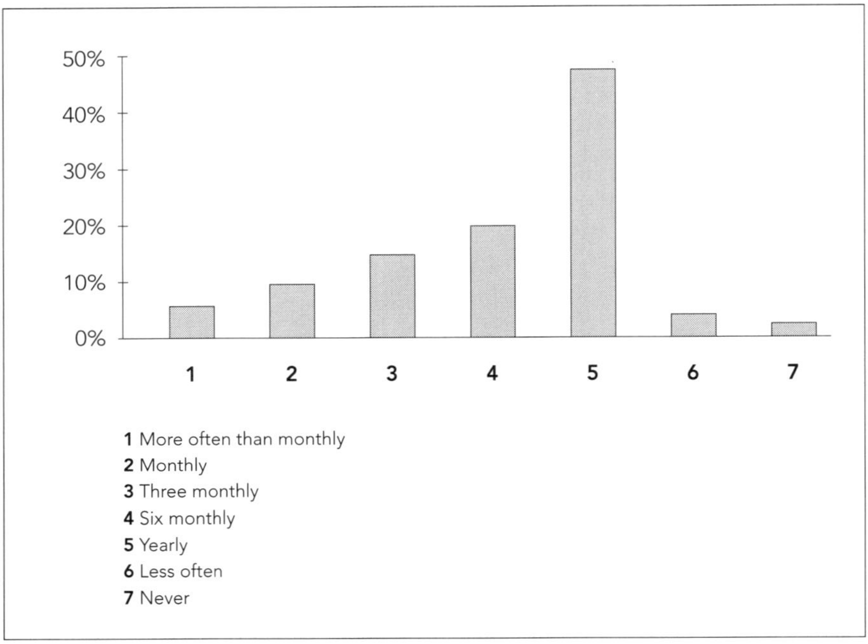

Chart 3.3 Regularity of business plan updates

(*Source: Planning to Keep One Step Ahead*, Barclays, 1996)

Preparing a business plan

How detailed does a business plan need to be?

There are no set guidelines. The level of detail will depend entirely on the nature of your business. A business plan sets out your objectives, estimates and financial forecasts. It will help you establish where you are, where you are going, and how you intend to get there.

(*Source: Starting a Business – Taking a Closer Look*, HSBC Bank plc, 1999)

Business plans of 8–10 pages seem to be the norm, but whatever size the plan is, keep it concise. Add extra information as appendices. Try to find a balance between too much and too little. The more money you are looking for, the more comprehensive you will need to be.

(*Source: Starting and Growing Your Own Business – Entrepreneurial Management,* Nick Morris and Bridget Rosewell, City University Business School)

What should the business plan contain?

- A cover page, with the business name and the names and addresses of the proprietors.
- A summary – write this last.
- A description of the business – history, performance, achievements, records if relevant.
- A description of your product(s) or service(s) and their advantages. Include details of patent or copyright if appropriate. Discuss competitive products.
- Details of the market: who are your target customers? Analyse the competition.
- A marketing plan – target market, predicted market share, pricing policy, promotion, selling and distribution. Give details of orders, or interest by potential customers.
- Management and organisation – give CVs, highlight strengths and training needs.
- Operations – equipment needed, the process, possible competitive advantage, personnel requirements.
- Financial information – give start-up or expansion costs, costing and pricing, cashflow forecasts, profit and loss projections, balance sheet projections. Focus on the breakeven point. Include details of investment, and a personal survival budget. Specify loans or grants needed. Give details of any assets available as security.

(*Source: Starting and Growing Your Own Business – Entrepreneurial Management,* Nick Morris and Bridget Rosewell, City University Business School)

Which financial forecast should you complete first?

You will need to decide on your *gross profit margin*. This is the amount of profit you will make. It's the key measure of how profitable your venture is likely to be.

You can set this figure either as a total, or for each product or item, calculating it after taking into account your *cost of sales*. These costs are known as *direct* or *variable* costs because they go up and down with the volume of production. They usually include such elements as:

- raw materials;
- packaging;
- staff commission.

But they do not include your overheads, which are known as *indirect* or *fixed* costs as they remain constant whether production goes up or down.

Fairly small fluctuations in gross profit can have a major effect on your bottom line. So the terms your suppliers give you, or the discounts you offer your customers, can make a big difference. It's usual to show gross profit as a percentage of sales.

Gross profit margin

$$\text{Gross profit margin} = \frac{\text{Gross profit} \times 100\%}{\text{Sales}}$$

You can work it out as a total, or for each product or item:

$$\text{Gross profit margin} = \frac{\text{Mark-up}}{\text{Selling price (cost of item + mark-up)}} \times 100\%$$

(*Source: A Step-by-step Guide to Your Business Plan*, Lloyds TSB Business, 1999)

Do you need start-up funding?

Many businesses start and prosper without borrowing money. Others need outside finance. If you need funds, you will need to clarify your requirements and to identify the most appropriate source of finance.

(*Source: Setting Up and Running Your Business*, Barclays Bank plc, 2000)

More details of sources of finance, for start-up or growth, can be found in Chapter 4.

How do you present the case for borrowing?

The first question you will have to resolve is how much you need. If you need to purchase equipment or premises to start your business, you should be able to assess these costs accurately. Build the costs of repaying any loan into the estimates of costs for your business.

The work you have done on your business will prove invaluable. The strength of your business idea will be important in building confidence. Lenders will want to be reassured on a number of points:

- what the money is for;
- how much you will be investing yourself;
- the amount you need to borrow;
- when you need it;
- how and when you will repay it;
- what security (if any) you can offer.

(*Source: Setting Up and Running Your Business*, Barclays Bank plc, 2000)

How do you calculate overheads?

Overheads are basically what it costs you to work for yourself. You have to pay them even if you produce, supply or sell nothing. However, they may not go up (or go up only a little) when you increase production and sales.

Overheads

Figures should be based on a 12-month period, and might include the following:

If you have business premises:

- rent repayments;
- rates;
- services (electricity, gas, telephone, water rates);
- buildings insurance.

Other elements to consider:

- legal and professional fees;
- equipment;
- business liability insurance;
- depreciation (what you deduct from an item to reflect the fact that it is wearing out);

- employee costs (salaries, NI contributions);
- bank/finance charges and interest;
- personal living expenses – the minimum your household needs to survive.

Smaller items:

- travelling costs;
- stationery.

(*Source: A Step-by-step Guide to Your Business Plan*, Lloyds TSB Business, 1999)

How do you calculate net profit margin?

The net profit margin takes the gross profit margin one stage further, by working out the profit after deducting the cost of sales and overheads.

Net profit margin

The formula is:

$$\frac{\text{Sales less costs of sales + overheads (net profit)}}{\text{Sales}} \times 100$$

To work out the net profit margin per item, use the same formula as for the gross profit margin, except that the cost of sale per item will include a figure per item for overheads.

(*Source: A Step-by-step Guide to Your Business Plan*, Lloyds TSB Business, 1999)

How do you prepare a breakeven analysis?

The breakeven analysis is a vital calculation, as it helps you work out if you have set your prices correctly. You'll need to include a breakeven analysis in your business plan, particularly if you expect to make losses to begin with.

The breakeven analysis is a calculation that shows when the *gross profit* or *volume of sales* will be enough to cover the overheads. The breakeven point can be worked out overall, or per item.

Breakeven analysis

The formula is:

$$\frac{\text{Overheads}}{\text{Gross profit margin}} \times 100 = \text{Breakeven level of sales (turnover figure for the year}$$

(This assumes the gross profit margin remains the same.)

From this figure, it is easy to work out how many individual items must be sold to break even:

$$\frac{\text{Breakeven sales}}{\text{Unit price}} = \text{Number of units per year required}$$

(*Source: A Step-by-step Guide to Your Business Plan,* Lloyds TSB Business, 1999)

What can you learn from a breakeven analysis?

Having calculated your breakeven point, it's time to look at your earlier calculations again – particularly sales and pricing, and overheads. Be prepared to rethink your figures if necessary. For example:

1. Have you over/underestimated likely sales?
2. Do your market research and customer analyses support your theoretical sales projections?
3. Are your pricing levels correct, or should you look to low-cost suppliers?
4. If reducing costs means lower quality, will this be acceptable in your business?
5. Can you reduce your fixed costs without harming the business? Perhaps by letting out part of your floor space that you will not require?

Once you have reviewed all these points, you are ready to complete cash flow and profit and loss forecasts.

(*Source: A Step-by-step Guide to Your Business Plan,* Lloyds TSB Business, 1999)

How do you prepare a profit and loss forecast?

This will summarise the sales and costs you expect each month over the next year. Blank forms are provided by all the high street banks in their start-up guides. Not all the headings apply to each business, so tailor them to suit your purposes.

Preparing a profit and loss forecast

Fill in the following for each month – budget and actual costs in two separate columns:

Period covered: April 2001–March 2002

	Month: April		Month: May, etc	
	Budget	Actual	Budget	Actual
Sales (net of VAT) (*a*)	*	*	*	*
Less: Direct costs	*	*	*	*
Cost of materials	*	*	*	*
Wages	*	*	*	*
Gross profit (b)	*	*	*	*
Gross profit margin (*b*/*a* x 100%)	*	*	*	*
Overheads	*	*	*	*
Salaries	*	*	*	*
Rent/rates/water	*	*	*	*
Insurance	*	*	*	*
Repairs/renewals	*	*	*	*
Heat/light/power	*	*	*	*
Postage/printing/stationery	*	*	*	*
Motor and travel	*	*	*	*
Telephone	*	*	*	*
Professional fees	*	*	*	*
Interest charges	*	*	*	*
Bank charges	*	*	*	*
Other	*	*	*	*
Total overheads (*c*)	*	*	*	*
Trading profit – (*b*) – (*c*)	*	*	*	*
Less: depreciation	*	*	*	*
Net Profit before tax	*	*	*	*
Cumulative Net Profit (running total per month)	*	*	*	*

(*Source: Setting Up and Running Your Business*, Barclays Bank plc, 2000)

Why do you need a cash flow forecast?

Cash flow is vital for the day-to-day survival of your business. Even if your business is profitable, delays in collecting money could mean that your cash dries up and your business is in jeopardy. Producing a cash flow forecast is a step in preventing this situation by helping you set out all the relevant figures.

Most cash flow forecasts cover a period of 12 months. If it is hard to look that far ahead, complete one for the first six months, and complete the forecast for the next six months about halfway through the first period. Cash flow forecasts, like profit and loss forecasts, have spaces for you to enter budget and then actual figures month by month. You can then check actual figures against projections, giving you an early indication of significant discrepancies, and enabling you to take corrective action.

(*Source: Starting a Business – Taking a Closer Look*, HSBC Bank plc, 1999)

How do you prepare a cash flow forecast?

When completing a cash flow forecast, make sure that:

- receipts for sales appear in the same month as projected sales. If you give credit, the amount must be shown under debtors in the month of receipt, not in the month of sale. For example, sales in month one, where two months' credit has been given, will be shown as a receipt in month three;
- cash payments are shown in the same month as the purchase. If you are given credit by your suppliers, the payment should be shown in the month that you make the payment, not the month of purchase;
- separate lines are used to indicate the purchase or sale of capital items such as plant, equipment, land and buildings that do not form part of your normal trading activities.

(*Source: Starting a Business – Taking a Closer Look*, HSBC bank plc, 1999)

Preparing a cash flow forecast

Fill in the following for each month – budget and actual costs in two separate columns:

Period covered: April 2001–March 2002

(Figures rounded to £s)	Month: April Budget	Month: April Actual	Month: May, etc Budget	Month: May, etc Actual
Receipts				
1 Sales (inc. VAT) – cash	£*	£*	£*	£*
2 – debtors	£*	£*	£*	£*
3 Other trading income	£*	£*	£*	£*
4 Loans you have received	£*	£*	£*	£*
5 New capital	£*	£*	£*	£*
6 Selling of assets	£*	£*	£*	£*
7 Other receipts	£*	£*	£*	£*
a **Total receipts**	£*	£*	£*	£*
Payments				
1 Cash for goods you have bought	£*	£*	£*	£*
2 Payments to creditors	£*	£*	£*	£*
3 Owner or directors' withdrawals	£*	£*	£*	£*
4 Wages and salaries (net)	£*	£*	£*	£*
5 PAYE/NI	£*	£*	£*	£*
6 Capital items (e.g. vehicles, equipment)	£*	£*	£*	£*
7 Transport and packaging	£*	£*	£*	£*
8 Rent and/or rates	£*	£*	£*	£*
9 Services (electricity, gas, water, phone)	£*	£*	£*	£*
10 Loan repayments	£*	£*	£*	£*
11 Hire or leasing repayments	£*	£*	£*	£*
12 Interest	£*	£*	£*	£*
13 Bank or finance charges	£*	£*	£*	£*
14 Professional fees	£*	£*	£*	£*
15 Advertising	£*	£*	£*	£*
16 Insurance	£*	£*	£*	£*

Period covered: April 2001–March 2002

(Figures rounded to £s)	Month: April Budget	Month: April Actual	Month: May, etc Budget	Month: May, etc Actual
17 VAT	£*	£*	£*	£*
18 Income tax and corporation tax	£*	£*	£*	£*
19 Dividends	£*	£*	£*	£*
***b* Total payments**	£*	£*	£*	£*
c **Net cash flow (*a* – *b*)**	£*	£*	£*	£*
20 Opening bank balance				
***d* Closing bank balance (*c* + 20)**	£*	£*	£*	£*

Basic assumptions: Average credit time your creditors give you to pay = ****

Average time you give your debtors to pay = ******

(*Source: Start-up Guide*, NatWest Bank plc in conjunction with the Foundation for Small and Medium Enterprise Development, University of Durham, February 2000)

4

Finance

the questions

Finance

the answers

Funding start-ups

Is access to funding easy?

Barclays Bank plc reviewed business funding in May 1997, using a sample of 400 nationally representative firms with a turnover of less than £1 million. This research found that:

- the average cost of setting up in business is around £11,000. Around one third of this cost is funded externally;
- the average time taken for a small business to raise external funding is around one month, with almost half (45%) receiving funding within a week;
- two-thirds of small businesses (67%) are happy with their experiences and would use the same methods again.

(*Source: Funding Your Business*, Barclays Review, May 1997)

What is start-up finance mainly used for?

The same research shows that demand for external funding is most likely to come from firms wishing to finance business premises (29%) and stock (21%). It is least likely that borrowed cash will be put towards wages or recruiting staff (2%). This suggests that loans are used for investment purposes, rather than to support day-to-day running costs (see Chart 4.1).

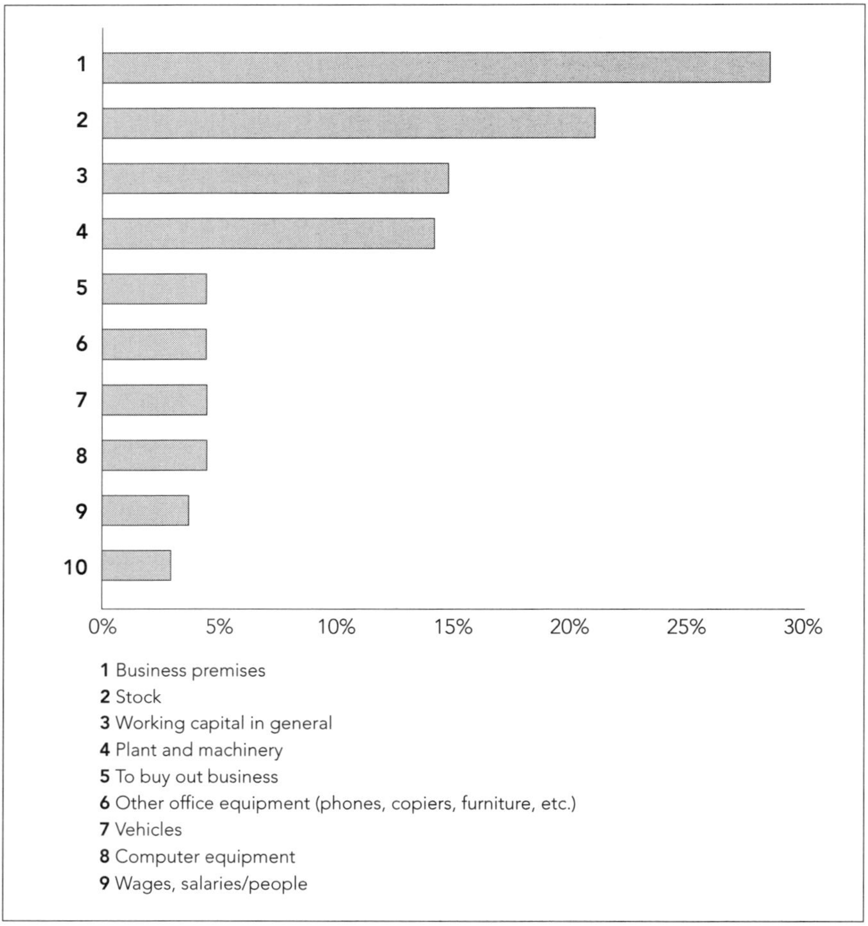

Chart 4.1 What was finance mainly used for?

(*Source: Funding Your Business*, Barclays Review, May 1997)

What is the main source of external finance?

The main source of external finance for both start-up (72%) and established businesses (82%) is overwhelmingly the banks. However, Barclays research also suggests that the level of awareness of other sources of finance remains low. Only half of businesses surveyed researched the funding options available to them before starting up; only 22% examined whether they were eligible for EU or government grants. Raising finance through factoring debts or sales invoices was considered by only one in ten businesses (see Table 4.1). For more details of all these forms of finance, see later in this chapter.

Table 4.1 Main sources of external funding for start-up businesses

Main sources of external funding	Total	Retail	Leisure	Business and professional	Production
Bank/building society	72%	86%	71%	71%	53%
Friends and family	4%	11%	20%	5%	19%
Borrowed on finance/loan company	4%	2%	3%	5%	6%
Personal savings/own money	3%	—	—	10%	6%
Business 'angel' (private investor)	1%	—	3%	—	3%
Government or EU grant	1%	—	3%	—	3%

(Source: Funding Your Business, *Barclays Review, May 1997)*

What are the other types of finance?

Businesses are usually financed by equity, debt, grants or a combination.

- *Equity* can be profits that you retain in the business, or new investment by you, your family and friends. It can also be investment from external sources, such as venture capital, provided by professional investors, by individuals investing as 'business angels', or as an investment in your firm by another business (this is known as 'corporate venturing'). External equity involves raising money by selling shares in your business in exchange for giving someone else a proportion of your profits and the future value of the business.
- *Debt* can be bank lending or overdrafts, or it can be based on the assets of your firm, such as factoring or invoice discounting, or hire purchase and leasing. The debt is usually secured against the assets of the business, or else is guaranteed by you or others. Your business must be able to generate enough cash to pay the interest on the money you borrowed.
- *Grants* may be available to you in certain parts of the country, or for certain types of business projects. They are usually 'one-off' payments. They often provide a percentage of costs for specific purposes, e.g. refurbishing premises or capital for equipment. Start-up grants are often a specific sum. Local authorities, the government, the European Union and some trusts provide these grants.

- *Awards* usually recognise specific achievements; they are either local or national. Prizes for such competitions can be cash, and can be in kind. The attendant publicity is an added bonus. The SMART awards are an obvious example. Run by the DTI, they help small and medium enterprises improve their competitiveness by developing new products and processes.

(Source: *Financing Your Business and Controlling Your Money: What Finance is Right for Your Business?*, Small Business Services Business Topics – Finance, 10 August 2000, www.businessadviceonline.org)

What are the most common methods of financing a business?

Retained profits head the list at 66%, followed by bank overdrafts (59%). The use of bank overdrafts varies by sector – 68% for manufacturing, but only 47% for business services. Stark differences are also apparent in the use of leasing/hire purchase, used by 48% of manufacturing firms but by only 21% of retail/distribution firms.

Table 4.2 Most commonly used methods of financing a business

Method	Percentage of firms using this method
Retained profits	66%
Bank overdrafts	59%
Bank loans	41%
Owner(s)' capital	39%
Leasing/hire purchase	36%

(Source: *Sources of Finance*, SBRT/Lloyds Report, September 2000)

How well do small businesses understand different sources of finance?

Although 77% claimed to have a good understanding of bank overdrafts, only 16% of small businesses have a good understanding of government grant aid.

Table 4.3 Levels of understanding regarding different sources of finance

Source of finance	Percentage of firms claiming a good level of understanding
Bank overdraft	77%
Bank loans	66%
Leasing/hire purchase	53%
Factoring/invoice discounting	43%
Share (equity) capital	34%
Government grant aid schemes	16%

(*Source: Sources of Finance*, SBRT/Lloyds Report, September 2000)

What are the main sources of financial support?

1. The Department of Trade and Industry: the Small Firms Loan Guarantee Scheme, and help in areas such as technology, research and development, export, etc.
2. Training and Enterprise Councils in England and Wales, Local Enterprise Companies in Scotland, and the LEDU in Northern Ireland.
3. Regional Development Agencies: these provide grants towards the redevelopment of redundant rural buildings for commercial purposes.
4. The Prince's Youth Business Trust (PYBT) helps unemployed people aged 18–29 to start up in business.
5. Shell LiveWIRE also provides start-up awards in cash or kind for owner-managers aged 16–30 in their first year of trading.

Chart 4.2 will help guide you to the most suitable form of finance.

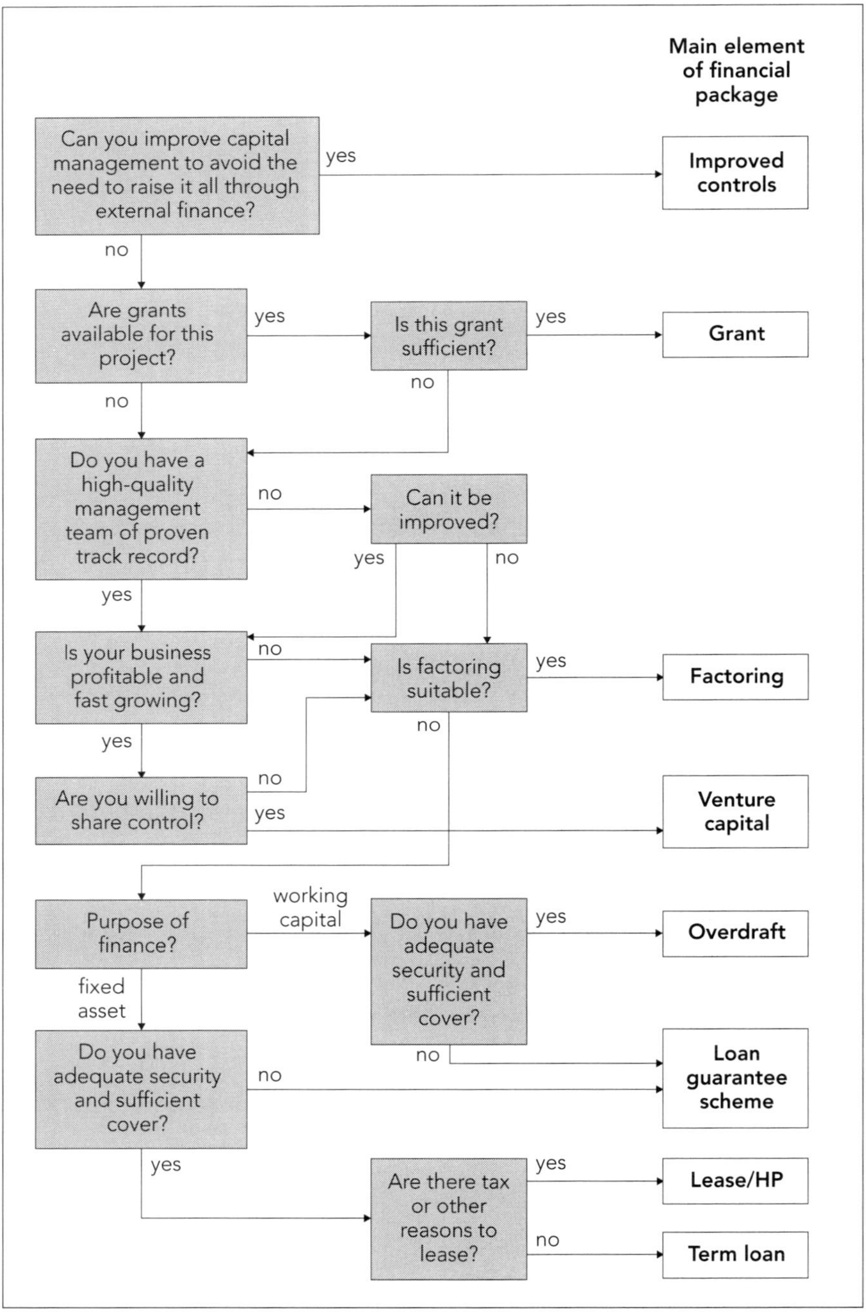

Chart 4.2 Finding the most suitable form of finance

(Source: *Financing Your Business and Controlling Your Money: What Finance is Right for Your Business?* Small Business Services Business Topics – Finance, 10 August 2000, www.businessadviceonline.org)

Franchising

What is franchising?

In simple terms, franchising is where a successful business format is replicated. This involves the franchisor's setting down in an operations manual proven and successful systems and procedures. Anyone joining the franchise will then be expected to operate the business exactly as set out in the manual.

When you hear the word 'franchise' you probably think of fast-food restaurants such as Burger King, McDonald's or Wimpy. In reality, there are franchises available in almost every business area that you can think of, and in most price ranges.

(*Source: What is Franchising?*, The Franchise Business Factsheet, November 2000, or see www.franchisebusiness.co.uk)

Why choose franchising?

Starting up a new business carries risk; a franchise reduces that risk. This is because it enables you, as the franchisee, to use the proven business system of your franchisor. The important factor from your point of view is that the franchisor's income is tied to that of your business. The franchisor can succeed only if you succeed.

(*Source: The NatWest Guide to Buying a Franchise*, National Westminster Bank plc, August 2000)

How successful are franchisees?

Since 1984, NatWest has sponsored an annual survey of franchising in the UK for the British Franchise Association. The survey has consistently shown that the failure rate of franchisees, who lose their business for financial reasons, is as low as 7%.

(*Source: The NatWest Guide to Buying a Franchise*, National Westminster Bank plc, August 2000)

The 1999 survey showed the overall turnover of the franchising industry to be in excess of £6 billion, with the number of business format franchising systems growing to 541, an increase of 30% since 1994.

The 27,000 individual franchised units in the UK provide more than 250,000 jobs. This makes franchising larger than the whole energy sector, and almost as big as the whole of the armed forces.

(*Source: What are the Benefits of Franchising?*, The Franchise Business Factsheet, November 2000, or see www.franchisebusiness.co.uk)

What should you look for in a franchise?

When you take up a franchise you are entering into a long-term partnership with the franchisor. It is therefore vitally important to check the background and business performance of your business partner.

The keys to a successful franchise relationship are:

- Does the product or service interest you and fire you with enthusiasm?
- Does the company have name awareness (a successful brand)?
- Has sufficient market research been carried out?
- Does it have a successful operation and marketing system?
- Is it a viable proposition?
- Do you understand the role you will play?
- Can you work with the franchisor and his team?

Above all, make sure you talk to franchisees who are already operating the business. They will normally be only too pleased to help as they were once in your situation.

(*Source: What are the Benefits of Franchising?*, The Franchise Business Factsheet, November 2000 or see www.franchisebusiness.co.uk)

How do you choose the right type of business franchise?

The first question to answer is 'What type of franchise can you afford?' To assess your price range, a very rough rule of thumb is to add up your available capital and multiply by three (e.g. if you have savings of £20,000, you could expect to be able to finance a franchise with start-up costs of around £60,000).

The second question to consider is what type of business would best suit you. You need to choose a business in which you will be happy to work day after day, and preferably one in which you have some aptitude, affinity or perhaps even some experience.

Finally, you should consider some marketing questions. Is the franchise serving an established market, or has that market yet to be developed? Is the market expanding or declining? Is it seasonal? Does it depend on trading from highly specialised sites? Is the franchise competitive in its market? What share of the market does it hold?.

(*Source: The NatWest Guide to Buying a Franchise*, National Westminster Bank plc, August 2000)

How do you choose the right franchise?

There are many questions that can be asked to assess the quality of the franchisor, but most fall into the following fields.

- Has the franchise been sufficiently tested and are its franchisees successful?
- Do the initial fee and continuing fees (or product mark-up) represent good value for money?
- Do the on-going fees (or product mark-up) still leave the product or service competitive in the marketplace, and provide sufficient profit for both franchisor and franchisee to make the business worthwhile?
- Has the franchisor got sufficient financial and management resources to deliver his promises? Is he fair and ethical in his business conduct?
- Is the franchisor a member of the British Franchise Association, whose members are required to abide by a code of practice?
- In the event of the franchisor's failure, are there alternative suppliers?

(*Source: The NatWest Guide to Buying a Franchise*, National Westminster Bank plc, August 2000)

How widespread is franchising?

If you're thinking of getting into franchising, it's worth knowing how mainstream it is nowadays.

- Annual sales relating to franchising in the UK total £6.4 billion.
- 541 business-format franchisors have created 26,800 separate businesses, and more than 264,000 people are employed in franchising.
- 94% of franchisees claim profitability.

(*Source: 1997 NatWest/BFA Franchise Survey*, NatWest UK and the British Franchise Association)

What characteristics do franchisors look for in franchisees?

What do the experts think are the most important characteristics for success in a prospective franchisee? Franchisors increasingly do not specify any age or gender preferences for potential franchisees, but they consider experience and attitude especially to be important. Table 4.4 shows percentage of franchisors who thought certain aspects mattered.

Table 4.4 The characteristics for success in franchising

Characteristics for success	All franchisors		
	1994	1995	1996
Experience			
Selling and marketing	32%	42%	51%
Other aspects of business	27%	30%	45%
This industry	24%	19%	28%
Self-employment	17%	16%	25%
Don't specify	39%	41%	28%
Attitude			
Self-motivated	88%	98%	95%
Financially aware	73%	86%	84%
Hard worker	84%	91%	91%
Hands on/owner operator	69%	77%	73%
Don't specify	4%	1%	4%

(*Source: 1997 NatWest/BFA Franchise Survey*, NatWest UK and the British Franchise Association)

The franchisee

What quality of relationship do franchisees have with their franchisors?

This is a crucial ingredient in a successful and stress-free franchise operation. An encouraging 92% of franchisees consider their relationship with their franchisor to be at least mainly satisfactory; what's more, this figure is gradually on the increase (see Table 4.5).

Table 4.5 The relationship between franchisors and franchisees

Quality of relationship	All franchisees		
	1994	1995	1996
Definitely satisfactory	44%	47%	55%
Mainly satisfactory	46%	39%	37%
Total satisfactory	**90%**	**86%**	**92%**
Mainly not satisfactory	7%	7%	4%
Definitely not satisfactory	3%	7%	5%
Total unsatisfactory	**10%**	**14%**	**9%**

(Source: *1997 NatWest/BFA Franchise Survey*, NatWest UK and the British Franchise Association)

How often should you review your franchise agreement?

If you want to remain competitive, and keep pace with changing markets, you need to keep the key functions of your business under constant review. For franchisors, this must include their standard franchise agreement. Franchisors were asked when, if ever, they last had a major review of their franchise agreement (see Table 4.6).

Table 4.6 Reviewing the franchise agreement

Time of last review	All franchisors	
	1995	1996
Never/no major review	18%	23%
Within the last year	52%	49%
1–2 years ago	15%	18%
3–5 years ago	7%	7%
6+ years ago	2%	1%
Don't know	6%	1%

(Source: 1997 NatWest/BFA Franchise Survey, NatWest UK and the British Franchise Association)

Are franchisees likely to renew their contracts?

One of the best measures of success is whether, when the contract expires, the franchisee wants to come back for more. Those franchisees with three years or less of their contract to run were asked whether or not they wished to renew (see Table 4.7).

Table 4.7

Franchisees' wishes	1995	1996
Wish to renew	72%	77%
Do not wish to renew	8%	6%
Undecided	20%	16%

- 25% of franchisors report that they charge a fee for contract renewal, a figure which has steadily decreased since 1991 (22%).

(*Source: 1997 NatWest/BFA Franchise Survey,* NatWest UK and the British Franchise Association)

What are the advantages of franchising for the franchisee?

Ten advantages for the franchisee

1. Proven business know-how of the franchisor.
2. Established brand names.
3. Large-scale advertising of brand name and business.
4. Training on product and business skills.
5. Full support during start-up.
6. Detailed operations manual.
7. On-going advice and guidance.
8. Agreed area of operation.
9. Rights and obligations clearly defined.
10. Commitment by franchisor to maximise franchisee's development – because their income depends on it.

(*Source: The Two Partners of Franchising,* Peter Stern, Franchise World Directory, 1998)

What should you check about a franchise?

If you are considering a franchise, what should you look out for? Are there ways of checking the soundness of the investment? Look carefully at:

- the business track record;
- the management and franchise experience of its principals;

- the total cash input, including working capital.

(*Source: The Two Partners of Franchising*, Peter Stern, Franchise World Directory, 1998)

What should potential franchisees avoid?

Any of these might indicate danger:

- the hard sell;
- a heavy initial franchise fee;
- the absence of a pilot operation;
- pyramid selling.

(*Source: The Two Partners of Franchising*, Peter Stern, Franchise World Directory, 1998)

Do failure rates vary by sector?

The simple answer is yes. Health care seems a stable option. Over an 11-year period, surveying 1,658 franchising firms, only 25% of health care firms had ceased franchising. The same survey recorded a wide difference in failure rates in other sectors (see Table 4.8).

Table 4.8 Franchise failure rates by sector

Sector	Failure rate, 1984–95
Health care	25%
Print and publishing	41%
Hotel and catering	57%
Miscellaneous sector	93%

(*Source: Behind the Veneer of Success: Propensities for UK Franchisor Failure*, Small Business Research Trust, 1997)

For the franchisor's perspective, see Chapter 7.

On-going finance

Choices

What types of equity scheme are there, and which are small businesses most likely to consider?

Are you aware of the different forms of equity finance schemes? There are a variety of equity schemes available, as the statistics in Table 4.9 show. In a *Kidsons Impey Small Business Tracking Survey,* small businesses were asked about their equity choices. A substantial 55% said they would consider venture/development capital.

Table 4.9 Would you consider the following choices of equity finance?

Choice	Percentage answering 'yes'
Venture/development capital	55
Personal equity purchase by existing shareholders	52
Personal equity purchase by new shareholders	52
Enterprise investment schemes	41
Corporate venture schemes	41
Venture trusts	24
Debenture issues	24
The Alternative Investment Market (AIM)	21
Business angels	14

(*Source: Kidsons Impey Small Business Tracking Survey XIV,* prepared by Consensus Research Ltd and Critical Research Ltd, January 1995)

Which types of debt are small businesses most likely to consider?

It may help you to know where other businesses go to borrow. The same survey asked small businesses about their borrowing preferences (for more details on the costs and benefits of various forms of loans, see below) – 72% said they would consider an overdraft (more than one response was allowed) (see Table 4.10).

Table 4.10 Would you consider the following forms of debt?

Choice	Percentage answering 'yes'
Overdraft	72
Loans	56
Leasing	39
HP	34
Invoice discounting	7
Factoring	6
Other	2

(*Source: Kidsons Impey Small Business Tracking Survey XIV*, prepared by Consensus Research Ltd and Critical Research Ltd, January 1995)

Venture capital

What is venture capital?

Venture capital provides long-term, unsecured, committed, risk-sharing capital which helps unquoted companies grow and compete. The ability to provide capital *and* experience sets venture capital apart from other sources of capital. Although venture capital requires the owner to sell some shares and sometimes to give the venture backer a non-executive board position, it seeks to increase the value to the owner, *without* taking control. Unlike a conventional lender, an equity investor makes returns from the growth and profitability of the business. A venture capital investor's returns are dependent on the profitability of the business.

(*Source:* British Venture Capital Association)

What are the advantages of venture capital?

Venture capital is a less familiar route than approaching a bank, so why use it? The real advantages of venture capital finance over other forms of finance are:

- it provides a solid capital base for the future – to meet your growth and development plans;
- there is no repayment during the term of the investment and no interest costs, therefore no detrimental impact on cash flow (unless the equity risk includes preference shares which pay a fixed

dividend and may also have redemption terms, or if the debt is not included in the package);

- the venture capitalist is a true business partner, sharing in your risks and rewards;
- there will be no charges on your business assets and no personal guarantees will be required;
- flexibility: there is a wide range of sources, types and styles of venture capital organisations to meet many different needs.

(*Source:* British Venture Capital Association)

What do you need in order to raise venture capital?

If you want to raise venture capital, what will you need? The British Venture Capital Association stresses the importance of your track record, reporting that you will need:

1. A business with high growth potential.
2. An experienced and ambitious management team.
3. A business with a proven product or service.
4. A market where your company has, or can gain, a protected position.
5. A complete management team of proven marketing, production and finance specialists with an effective team leader – to make things happen as planned.
6. A business plan which covers the above areas and demonstrates succinctly why your business should be given the finance and how you will deliver attractive returns for your investors.

(*Source:* British Venture Capital Association)

How much can you raise from venture capitalists?

This varies with the stage of investment, but few investments are made of less than £100,000. If you are looking for less than £100,000, there are seed funds, both independent, government-sponsored and part of larger venture capital organisations.

(*Source:* British Venture Capital Association)

At what stage of the business can you raise venture capital?

The British Venture Capital Association defines the various stages as follows:

1 *Seed:* financing provided to allow a business concept to be developed.
2 *Start-up:* financing provided for use in product development and initial marketing.
3 *Other early stage:* financing provided to companies that have not yet completed the product development stage and require further funds to initiate commercial manufacturing and sales.
4 *Expansion:* capital provided for the growth and expansion of an established company.
5 *Management buy-out:* funds provided to enable current management and investors to acquire an existing product line or business.
6 *Management buy-in:* funds provided to enable a manager or group of managers from outside the company to buy into a company.
7 *Secondary purchase:* purchase of existing shares in a company from another venture capital firm or from another shareholder or shareholders.

While finance can be raised at any stage of business development, venture capital companies tend to invest at the expansion stage. Funds at this stage may be used to finance increased production capacity, and/or provide additional working capital. Capital provided for turnaround situations is also included in this category, as is the refinancing of bank debts. There is less investment in smaller, earlier-stage companies, mainly owing to the additional risk associated with these investments.

(*Source:* British Venture Capital Association)

Business angels

What is a business angel? When can they help?

If you're not familiar with the whole concept of a business angel, it may help to understand a little of the background. The Enterprise Investment Scheme allows businesses to raise up to £1 million per tax year. Individuals are encouraged to invest £100,000 per tax year in a company by receiving tax relief on that sum. Investors previously unconnected with the company can become paid directors. The aim of these provisions is to encourage 'business angels' – wealthy people with extensive business experience – to provide finance and expertise.

Business angels operate in much the same way as venture capital companies, but they are always individuals, not corporations. Most regions of the UK now have business angel matching services, which encourage local investment and mentoring on a smaller scale. The National Business Angels Network matches investors with small businesses requiring £10,000 to £250,000 on a national scale, and is sponsored by several banks. For more information, contact the National Business Angels Network on 0207 329 2929.

Midland Enterprise Funds are regional venture capital funds managed by enterprise fund and equity venture organisations throughout England and Wales. They provide equity finance from £10,000 to £150,000. The funds usually invest in businesses that have good sales and profit-making potential.

(*Source:* www.natwest.com, 'Innovation and Growth – Equity Finance')

How do small businesses feel about external equity investment?

The issues of control and autonomy emerged strongly as concerns when the subject of external equity finance was broached by the Small Business Research Trust.

- Nearly two-thirds of respondents were worried about the central issue of 'loss of control'.

However, a number of additional issues were highlighted, for instance of 'finding prospective investor(s)', 'evaluating the right investor', and 'achieving an acceptable exit route'.

(*Source: Sources of Finance*, SBRT/Lloyds Report, September 2000)

For more details on finding and evaluating investors, see Chapter 4.

The alternative investment market

If companies are too small, unprofitable and/or young for flotation on the Official List of the London Stock Exchange, and they do not want to use venture capital or banks, then they can turn to the Alternative Investment Market – AIM.

Launched in 1995, AIM was introduced to provide companies with another means of raising equity finance. It was specifically designed to meet the needs of smaller, growing companies which might not meet the full criteria for listing, or for which a more flexible regulatory environment is more appropriate. It is open to companies with a shorter track record, regardless of where they are incorporated.

How many companies are quoted on AIM?

If you are considering approaching AIM for listing, are you one among many, or one of a select few? In February 2001, 545 companies were quoted on AIM, and more than £6.5 billion had been raised. The number of companies quoted does not give the full picture, however, as companies often use AIM as a 'stepping stone' on the way to becoming listed on the Stock Exchange.

(*Source:* www.londonstockexchange.com/ai)

What are the benefits of AIM?

Perhaps your company is still in the early stages, and does not have the kind of track record that listing requires. If you are considering turning to the AIM, the benefits include:

1. Access to public finance.
2. A reduction in the reliance on debt finance at a later date, and with greater ease.
3. Credibility and public profile for your company.
4. Scope for long-term stability.
5. Potential for sustained growth.
6. Confidence in the company for bankers, suppliers and customers.
7. For tax purposes, AIM companies are regarded as unquoted, which is an advantage.

(*Source: Kidsons Impey Small Business Tracking Survey XIV*, prepared by Consensus Research Ltd and Critical Research Ltd, January 1995)

Factoring

What is factoring?

A means of releasing money tied up in your sales ledger to provide working capital and fund business growth. Factoring agents will give you a proportion of the total of your invoices immediately. The balance is paid, less commission, when the customer pays the factor.

Summary of features and benefits

- As sales grow, the amount of cash available increases.
- Up to 80% of invoice value advanced, with the balance paid on collection.
- Funds advanced against new invoices within 24 hours if required.
- Factoring company takes on responsibility for sales ledger and credit management.
- Bad debt protection is available.
- Often provides more funds than a traditional overdraft.

The businesses most suited to using this service will be forecasting credit sales of at least £100,000 per annum, and will have a spread of debtors. You will be selling goods or services on normal credit terms, with no stage payments or contractual sales. Factoring is an expensive way of speeding up cash flow for small businesses, but larger businesses can reduce their costs of administration, and may find factoring economical.

(*Source: Factoring*, Barclays Information Pack, 1997)

What are the benefits of factoring?

This form of financing can help companies make better use of management time, and the money tied up in trade credit to customers. So if you are considering using a factoring company, you will benefit from the following services:

- immediate payment: the factoring company 'buys' your unpaid invoices as they arise;
- predictable finance: the factoring company provides finance of up

to 80% of the value of your invoices immediately, with the balance (less administration and finance charges) payable after a set period or when the invoice is paid;

- advice on credit risk;
- protection against bad debts.

Perhaps the main gain is the time period for payment of invoices. Companies which do not use factors and discounters wait on average 75 days for invoices to be paid. Companies which use factors get paid 80% immediately; the balance is paid on average only 58 days later.

(*Source: Association of British Factors and Discounters Annual Review*)

Does factoring offer a relatively low-cost option for raising finance?

Obviously, factoring has a cost – the credit company takes the risk, and expects to be paid for doing so, normally as a percentage of the bill you have sent out. If you are considering taking this path, it might help to know how other small businesses feel about factoring. Is the time saved chasing your own invoices a significant cost saving? The responses in Table 4.11 were obtained to 'Is this a relatively low-cost option?'

Table 4.11 Is factoring a relatively low-cost option for raising finance?

Response	Percentage of respondents
Strongly agree	5
Agree	24
Neither agree nor disagree	14
Disagree	31
Strongly disagree	27

(Source: *Kidsons Impey Small Business Tracking Survey XIV*, prepared by Consensus Research Ltd and Critical Research Ltd, January 1995)

Loans

Bank borrowing

How do small businesses feel about bank borrowing?

Only one in five (19%) of respondents felt that bank borrowing was something to be studiously avoided. Against that, 56% felt that it was a 'business tool for cash flow management', and a further 13% felt it was an 'inescapable fact of business life'.

Respondents in the business services sector had the most definite views – they were both the most likely to regard bank borrowing as a 'business tool for cash management' and the most likely group to feel that it was 'something to be avoided'. They were the least likely group to agree that it was an 'inescapable fact of business life'. Female respondents were clearly reconciled to the idea of bank borrowing.

(*Source: Sources of Finance*, SBRT/Lloyds Report, September 2000)

When is a short-term loan appropriate?

A short-term loan usually provides finance of between £25,000 and £250,000 for short-term requirements, such as the purchase of equipment or repairs and maintenance.

Summary of features and benefits

- Amount and timing to match requirements.
- Minimum £25,000, maximum £250,000.
- Available for any period up to 12 months.
- Choice of monthly, quarterly or bespoke repayment arrangements.
- Interest rate linked to base rate.
- Interest charged monthly.
- Subject to an arrangement fee – declared when loan agreed.

Short-term loans are essentially 'bridging finance' – for when you don't have the cash available but expect to be able to fund the expenditure from your income during the next year.

(*Source: Barclays Short-term Loan*, Barclays Information Pack, 1997)

What about other bank loans? How do they work?

Other loans are available to businesses looking for general finance between sums of £15,000 and £250,000.

Summary of features and benefits

- Available for capital projects or as working capital.
- Minimum £15,001, maximum £250,000.
- Any period up to 20 years.
- Choice of monthly or quarterly repayments.
- Endowment payment option.
- Capital repayment holiday available at the outset.
- Choice of interest rate structure (fixed or variable).
- Optional insurance cover for loan payments.

An endowment-linked option is also available, where interest and premiums only are paid throughout and capital payments are deferred to the end of the term.

(*Source: Flexible Business Loans*, Barclays Information Pack, 1997)

When is a commercial mortgage appropriate?

Commercial mortgages are available to businesses for the purchase, extension or renovation of owner-occupied commercial property.

Summary of features and benefits

- Minimum £15,000, maximum £250,000.
- 80% of the valuation or purchase price, whichever is lower.
- Any period up to 25 years.
- Choice of monthly or quarterly repayments.
- Choice of variable or fixed interest costs.
- Capital repayment holiday available at outset.
- Endowment and pension-linked repayment options.
- Optional insurance cover for mortgage repayments.

(*Source: Barclays Commercial Mortgage*, Barclays Information Pack, 1997

Loan guarantee scheme

What is the loan guarantee scheme?

This is a government-guaranteed loan scheme available to business customers.

Summary of features and benefits

- General-purpose finance for business lacking security or a track record.
- The government guarantees a proportion of each loan made under the scheme.
- Available for capital projects or as working capital.
- Minimum £5,000, maximum £250,000.
- Any period from 2 to 10 years.
- Choice of monthly or quarterly repayments.
- Capital repayment holiday available.
- A range of fixed and variable interest rates.
- Drawdown in lump sum or tranches.

The loan may be used for a wide range of business needs, from buying assets to funding working capital, subject to certain restrictions.

(*Source: Loan Guarantee Scheme*, Barclays Information Pack, 1997)

Soft loans

What is a 'soft loan' and are they easily available?

A soft loan provides finance for small businesses at below market rates, often combined with other support services, such as counselling. If you are unable to afford interest rates, or are deemed by normal lenders to be too risky, where can you turn for loans? How many soft loan schemes are there, and how available are they?

A study undertaken for the Small Business Research Centre found that:

- there are 82 soft loan schemes in the UK;
- public bodies sponsoring soft loans included local authorities and Enterprise Agencies;

- private-sector sponsors ranged from merchant bank Kleinwort Benson to Chorus and Shell UK;
- other bodies offering soft loans included the Mercers' Company, a City livery company, and the Royal British Legion.

(*Source: Soft Loan Schemes and the Finance Gap – An Evaluation Study*, James Curran, Robert Blackburn and Martina Klett-Davies, Small Business Research Centre, August 1994)

How do soft loan schemes operate?

Supposing you are considering a soft loan. The crucial question is, how do they work? The rules are slightly different for each scheme, so perhaps the easiest answer is to examine some schemes in detail. The high street banks are commonly involved as sponsors of soft loan schemes. The Small Business Research Trust considered eight soft loan schemes run by HSBC (then Midland Bank). The study covered 63 applications, of which 47 applied successfully, 15 were refused and one declined the offer of a loan.

- Each scheme had highly individual characteristics. Most had come into existence in a fairly ad hoc fashion, through the activities of particular individuals.
- The size of the schemes varied enormously. One had £10,000 at its disposal, enough for three or four loans at most; the largest had just under £1 million.
- The emphasis of the schemes was start-ups; about one-third of the loans were to established businesses.
- The average loan given was £6,700. The largest was £25,000.

(*Source: Soft Loan Schemes and the Finance Gap – An Evaluation Study*, James Curran, Robert Blackburn and Martina Klett-Davies, Small Business Research Centre, August 1994)

Were there write-offs?

Overall, write-offs had affected 17.3% of the businesses which had received loans from the schemes surveyed up to the time of the interviews. Of the businesses interviewed, the average amount written off was considerably less than £6,700, the average size of the loan, indicating that these were smaller loans and/or that some businesses were able to repay part of the loan before defaulting (*source: Soft Loan Schemes and the Finance Gap – An Evaluation Study*, James Curran, Robert Blackburn and Martina Klett-Davies, Small Business Research Centre, August 1994).

5

Marketing

the questions

- How well does your company perform in each part of the marketing process?
- How much effect does each marketing process have on business success?

Marketing strategy / 105

- Does your small firm plan its marketing strategy?
- Do other small firms get their marketing strategy right?
- Are other small firms good at marketing?
- How do other small firms promote their products?
- How do other businesses target existing customers?
- What help can you get in putting together your marketing strategy?
- What sort of information do you need for effective strategic planning?
- Is your strategic planning effective enough? And if not, what can you do about it?
- What makes a good strategic plan?
- How long does it take to plan and execute a campaign effectively?

The marketing mix / 111

- What is the marketing mix?

Product / 112

- What do people need to know about your product?
- How do you make your product appealing?

Price / 113

- Are your prices right?

Promotion / 115

Customer service / 120

Marketing effectiveness / 121

Marketing

the answers

Market segmentation

What is market segmentation?

Market segmentation describes the division of a market into homogeneous groups which will respond differently to promotions, communications, advertising and other marketing mix variables. Each group, or 'segment', can be targeted by a different marketing mix because the segments are created to minimise inherent differences between respondents within each segment and maximise differences between each segment.

Market segmentation was first used in the 1950s, when product differentiation was the primary marketing strategy used. In the 1970s and 1980s, market segmentation began to take off as a means of expanding sales and obtaining competitive advantages. By the 1990s, target or direct marketers were using many sophisticated techniques, including market segmentation, to reach potential buyers with highly customised offerings.

(*Source: Understanding Market Segmentation*, DSS Research, August 2000)

Why use market segmentation?

There are many good reasons for dividing a market into smaller segments. The three primary reasons are:

1 *Easier marketing*. It is easier to address the needs of smaller groups of customers, particularly if they have many characteristics in common (e.g. have the same income, are the same age, gender, etc.).

2 *Finding niches*. Helps identify under-served or unserved markets. Using 'niche marketing', segmentation can allow a new company or new product to target less contested buyers and help a mature product seek new buyers.

3 *Efficiency*. Market segmentation helps efficient use of marketing resources by focusing on the best segments for your offering – product, price, promotion, and place (distribution). Segmentation can help you avoid sending the wrong message or sending your message to the wrong people.

(*Source: Understanding Market Segmentation*, DSS Research, August 2000)

When should you use market segmentation?

Any time you suspect there are significant, measurable differences in your market, you should consider market segmentation. Identified segments must be:

- big enough – your market must be large enough to warrant segmenting. Don't try to split a market that is already very small;
- different – differences must exist between members of the market and these differences must be measurable through traditional data collection approaches (i.e. surveys);
- responsive – once the market is segmented, you must be able to design marketing communications that address the needs of the desired segments. If you can't develop promotions and advertising that speak to each segment, there is little value in knowing that those segments exist;
- reachable – each segment must be reachable through one or more media. You must be able to get your message in front of the right market segments for it to be effective. If one-eyed, green aliens are your best marketing opportunity, make certain there is a magazine, cable programme or some other medium that targets these people (or be prepared to create one);
- interested in different benefits – segments must not only differ on demographic and psychographic characteristics: they must also

differ on the benefits sought from the product. If everyone ultimately wants the same things from your product, there is no reason to segment buyers. However, this is seldom the case. Even commodities such as sugar and paper plates can benefit from segmentation.

- profitable – the expected profits from expanding your markets and more effectively reaching buyer segments must exceed the costs of developing multiple marketing programmes, redesigning existing products and/or creating products to reach those segments.

(*Source: Understanding Market Segmentation*, DSS Research, August 2000)

What criteria should you use to segment your market?

Almost any demographic, geographic, psychographic or behavioural variable can be used to classify people into segments. The most commonly used are:

- *demographic variables* – age, gender, income, ethnicity, marital status, education, occupation, household size, length of residence, type of residence, etc.
- *geographic variables* – city, county, postcode, mobility and changes of location, region, metropolitan or rural location, population density, climate, etc.
- *psychographic variables* – attitudes, lifestyle, hobbies, risk aversion, personality traits, leadership traits, magazines read, television programmes watched, etc.
- *behavioural variables* – brand loyalty, usage level, benefits sought, distribution channels used, reaction to marketing factors, etc.

(*Source: Understanding Market Segmentation*, DSS Research, August 2000)

What are the benefits of market segmentation?

There are five key benefits of market segmentation for your business:

1. You understand your customers' requirements better.
2. You can market more effectively.
3. You increase your understanding of the competition, and learn how to compete more effectively.

4 You are in a better position to develop new products or product variations.

5 You gain insights into possible new markets.

(*Source: Starting and Growing Your Own Business – Entrepreneurial Management*, Nick Morris and Bridget Rosewell, City University Business School)

Market research

What part does market research play in a small business?

Market research is vital to business planning. If you're serious about starting or growing a business, you should know who your potential customers are, how much they will pay for a product or service, and who your competitors are and what they offer.

Market research is equally crucial to existing businesses – it should shape your approach to every business process. Research helps you track changes in your customer base, and it helps you measure how changes in economic circumstances or in the behaviour of your competitors are affecting your business.

(*Source: Starting and Growing Your Own Business – Entrepreneurial Management*, Nick Morris and Bridget Rosewell, City University Business School)

What do you need to know?

The sort of questions you need to be able to answer includes the following:

1 *Customers:*
   a What type of person or business will buy your product or service?
   b What do they want from your product or service?
   c How many potential customers are there?
   d How do you let them know what you have on offer?
   e How much spending power do they have?
   f Will spending power rise or fall?

2 *Competitors:*
   a Are there any businesses offering similar products or services to yours?
   b What do they charge?
   c Are there any gaps in the market?

d What equipment and methods do they use?
e Are they seen to be good at it?
f Is anyone else likely to try to enter this market (e.g. if you make a success of it)?

3 *Operations:*
a What special skills are needed?
b What equipment is needed?
c What special regulations cover this business?
d How much do you need to charge?
e How much can you charge?
f What funding do you need and where can it be found?

(*Source: Starting and Growing Your Own Business – Entrepreneurial Management*, Nick Morris and Bridget Rosewell, City University Business School)

What types of research are there?

Market research is normally split into two types:

1 *Primary (field) research.* This is where you do not have any existing information, and have to arrange a way of collecting and interpreting the information yourself, e.g. a questionnaire.

2 *Secondary (desk) research.* Involves the use of published sources of information. 'Desk' is perhaps the wrong word because you have to visit libraries and other sources of public information to find the publications you want.

The way you carry out the research can be formal or informal. Formal research is highly organised and based on sound statistical methods. Informal research includes talking to trade associations, business contacts etc. to get their opinions of trends in the industry.

(*Source: Starting and Growing Your Own Business – Entrepreneurial Management*, Nick Morris and Bridget Rosewell, City University Business School)

What does it cost to commission market research?

If you need some market research into an area of business, can you afford to commission it? Or can you afford to do it yourself cost-effectively? Clearly it depends on the nature of the research. But the first thing you'll need to know is the respective costs of different types of market research commissions. A 1994 study asked research institutes to give quotations for six different research projects, and then calculated the average cost of each project to provide ballpark figures. Table 5.1 gives an outline of each project and the average cost of commissioning.

Table 5.1 Cost of commissioning research projects

Project 1	**A national usage and attitude study** on a chocolate confectionery product conducted via face-to-face interviewing among a quota sample of 750 adults (including 6 copies of a 45-page report).	£21,164
Project 2	**A national telephone tracking study** on washing powders among a quota sample of 500 housewives.	£10,307
Project 3	**An in-home product usage test** among an initial sample of 200 adult regular users of a dairy food product.	£9,981
Project 4	**Four group discussions among consumers** who are regular users of certain banking services.	£8,572
Project 5	**Twenty depth interviews with consumers** who are regular users of certain banking services.	£7,552
Project 6	**A business-to-business telephone survey** comprising 200 interviews with executives responsible for authorising the purchase/ acquisition of office photocopiers.	£11,280

(*Source: International Prices Study*, European Society for Opinion and Marketing Research (ESOMAR), 1994)

How do you make sure your market research is efficient?

Financiers require quantified facts on the viability of your business. Although the banks provide business profiles for established business types, specific market data are often not available for innovative businesses. You may therefore have to undertake the research yourself, usually by talking to potential buyers. So how do you make sure that the research you undertake is accurate and efficient?

Top ten tips on market research

1. Allow sufficient time and resources – people as well as cash! – and prepare well before every interview.
2. Set objectives – what do you need to know? Aim for market understanding, not just facts.
3. Do you need to protect your idea (with patents, etc.) before divulging it to potential customers?
4. Talk to the relevant people – find the person who will make the decision to buy.
5. Buyers want a product, not a technology. Promote the unique benefits of your product.
6. Don't confuse expressions of interest with a commitment to buy.
7. Market trends are more important than snapshots. Is the market static or growing? What is its size? Is it global?
8. Investigate competitors – don't ignore alternative ways of achieving the same result.
9. The price is part of the product offering. Develop a provisional pricing structure to make your discussions meaningful.
10. Check sales and distribution methods. What will work – and what won't?

(*Source:* www.clearlybusiness.com, 'Innovation and Growth – Top Ten Tips on Market Research for Technology Businesses')

Marketing processes

What aspects of marketing should you plan?

This is the first question to ask when you start to look at any marketing operation. But how do you go about answering it? One good way to start is by looking at what other businesses do. The Chartered Institute of Marketing's report *Manufacturing – The Marketing Solution* surveyed 44 manufacturing companies across the UK. One of its aims was to develop a valid framework that UK manufacturing companies can use to benchmark their performance through marketing. The survey identified seven separate marketing processes:

1 Marketing strategy.
2 Quality strategy.
3 Innovation.
4 Customer development.
5 Branding.
6 Supply chain management.
7 Manufacturing strategy.

The survey then developed a series of objective yes/no questions for each process that could be used to give each company an objective score of its performance.

(*Source: Manufacturing – The Marketing Solution*, Chartered Institute of Marketing Survey, 1995)

How well does your company perform in each part of the marketing process?

Having divided marketing into these seven processes, how much does performance vary between each? You could be really hot on manufacturing strategy but hopeless when it comes to branding. (If this is the case, you're not alone.) The surveyed companies performed far better in some areas than others. On average, the companies were best at manufacturing strategy, and noticeably poorest at branding. Each company was marked on a scale of 1 (poor) to 5 (excellent) for each of the seven processes (see Table 5.2).

Table 5.2 Performance in each part of the marketing process

Business process	1	2	3	4	5	Average score
Marketing strategy	9%	30%	32%	23%	7%	2.9
Quality strategy	18%	16%	20%	23%	23%	3.1
Branding	66%	16%	14%	4%	—	1.5
Innovation	14%	20%	29%	20%	16%	3.0
Customer development	9%	25%	23%	32%	11%	3.1
Supply chain management	14%	20%	29%	18%	18%	3.0
Manufacturing strategy	9%	20%	25%	23%	23%	3.3

(*Source: Manufacturing – The Marketing Solution*, Chartered Institute of Marketing Survey, 1995)

How much effect does each marketing process have on business success?

Does it really make much difference to the bottom line how well you do in all these areas? The survey measured which of the seven marketing processes were related to business success, which was measured in terms of return on sales. It found that performance in five of these areas correlated significantly with business success:

1 Marketing strategy.

2 Innovation.

3 Customer development.

4 Branding.

5 Supply chain management.

(*Source: Manufacturing – The Marketing Solution*, Chartered Institute of Marketing Survey, 1995)

Marketing strategy

Does your small firm plan its marketing strategy?

If it does, the outlook is positive. Barclays researched 400 small businesses, looking at the issue of business planning. The research showed that businesses which plan are more optimistic about the future and more ambitious than those that don't. They are also more likely to take advice, more likely to undertake training, and, as a result, more likely to achieve profitable growth (*source: Planning to Keep One Step Ahead*, Barclays Bank plc Small Business Services, September 1996).

Do other small firms get their marketing strategy right?

If you are experiencing problems with your marketing strategy, are you alone? Not according to Mike Davis of Barclays Bank:

Research among small business shows that loss of market and lack of sales are two of the main problems they face. Many of the half a million small businesses which close every year may do so because entrepreneurs have neither identified their markets properly, nor researched the competition, especially at the crucial early stage prior to starting up.

(*Source:* Mike Davis, Small Business Services Director, Barclays Bank plc)

Are other small firms good at marketing?

So how are your competitors faring? Do other small firms have a good track record in marketing? It would appear that the answer is no.

- Small businesses spend on average £1,500 a year on marketing, yet fewer than 4 in 10 measure the effectiveness of the activities undertaken.
- 8 out of 10 small businesses spend less than five hours a week promoting their business.
- 7 out of 10 entrepreneurs do not carry out market research prior to starting up, and, over time, even less planning activity is done.
- Only a quarter of small businesses properly calculate what they should charge to cover their costs.
- 7 out of 10 small businesses keep a database of existing customers, but only 1 in 10 uses it to secure future business.
- Over two-thirds of small businesses do not see the need to change their approach to marketing in the future.

(*Source: Marketing and The Small Firm*, Barclays Bank plc Small Business Services, May 1997)

How do other small firms promote their products?

Promotion plays an important part in shaping a business's image. It need not be expensive – good public relations can be undertaken in-house, and can rely on an investment of time rather than money. However, nearly two-thirds of businesses still rely on word of mouth or reputation rather than considering the wider range of promotional tactics available (see Table 5.3).

Table 5.3 Types of promotional activity undertaken

Word of mouth/reputation	60%
Advertising in business directories	30%
Advertising in local press	30%
Advertising in trade/business press	12%
Direct mail	11%
Brochures/leaflets/point-of-sale material	5%

Table 5.3 continued

Local radio advertising	4%
Posters/vehicle sides/branding	4%
National press/TV advertising	3%
Telephone contact/personal visits	5%
Sponsorship	2%
Seminars/conferences/exhibitions	4%
PR	1%

(*Source: Marketing and The Small Firm*, Barclays Bank plc Small Business Services, May 1997)

How do other businesses target existing customers?

Increasing sales from existing customers is often a better use of resources than targeting new ones. Nine out of ten entrepreneurs believe that the most appropriate way to target existing customers is to give the best possible service. But there are other low-cost ways to strengthen relationships – see Chart 5.1.

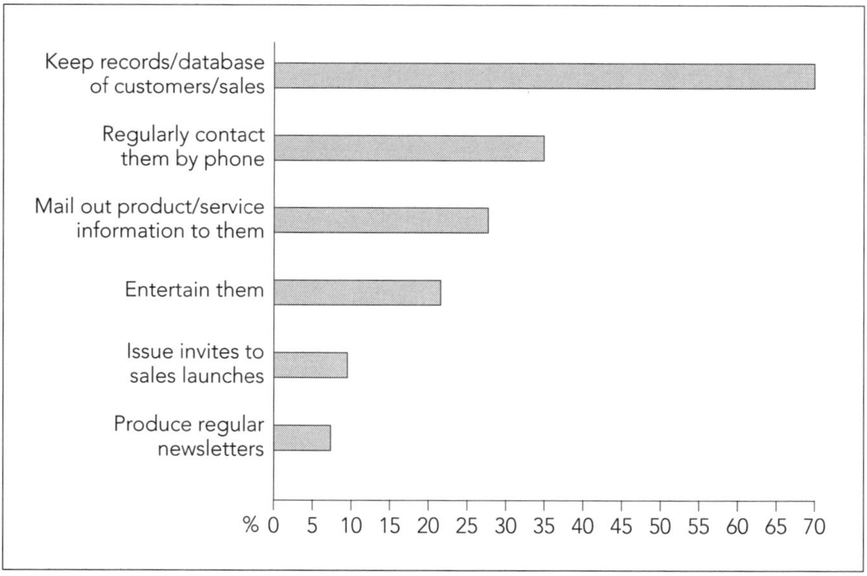

Chart 5.1 Activities used to target existing customers

(*Source: Marketing and The Small Firm*, Barclays Bank plc Small Business Services, May 1997)

What help can you get in putting together your marketing strategy?

There are various decision making methods you can use to help you draw up a strategic marketing plan. But do other companies really use these techniques? In their study *Marketing Planning Decision Making in UK and US Companies*, Gordon E. Greenley and Barry L. Bayus investigated which of these methods were being used. They also found out how many of the respondents regularly used each technique, and how many had tried but abandoned each one. The UK findings only are reproduced in Table 5.4.

Table 5.4 Decision-making methods

Decision	Regularly making use	Tried, no longer use	Heard of, never used	Heard of, appropriate	Never heard of method
SWOT analysis	54%	7%	14%	8%	12%
Portfolio analysis	42%	8%	21%	12%	11%
PLC analysis	51%	11%	20%	9%	5%
PIMS	5%	5%	30%	14%	42%
Perceptual mapping	12%	8%	25%	15%	36%
Conjoint analysis	5%	5%	20%	13%	53%
Qualitative judgement	55%	9%	13%	9%	9%

(Source: Journal of Marketing Management)

What sort of information do you need for effective strategic planning?

It depends on what exactly you're planning, of course. But are you feeding in all the information you could possibly need? Are you utilising as wide a range of data as, say, your competitors are using in their planning process? Greenley and Bayus asked their respondents what information they were inputting to four different aspects of marketing planning (see Table 5.5).

Table 5.5 Information going into four different aspects of marketing planning

Information input	Pricing products	Advertising budgets	Launching new products	Eliminating products
Focus groups	41%	35%	58%	48%
Internal data	90%	77%	76%	78%
Observation	70%	54%	73%	70%
Personal judgement	88%	87%	80%	75%
Surveys	33%	21%	59%	51%
Test marketing	29%	18%	68%	37%
Laboratory experiments	2%	2%	14%	7%
Panel data	17%	9%	18%	7%
Other syndicate data	20%	13%	23%	16%
Competitive data	88%	52%	86%	74%
Industry association data	48%	35%	50%	41%
Government data	31%	14%	44%	32%

(*Source: Journal of Marketing Management*)

Is your strategic planning effective enough? And if not, what can you do about it?

You may not feel that your strategic planning process needs any improvement (although you'd be in the minority if you did). But if it does, do you need different information or do you simply need better analysis of the data you already have? Greenley and Bayus asked this question in order to focus on the best way of improving the effectiveness of decision making in marketing planning (see Table 5.6).

Table 5.6 Different information or better analysis?

Decision	Improved analysis	Alternative data	No improvement needed
Pricing products	59%	43%	20%
Setting advertising budgets	65%	31%	21%
Launching new products	66%	45%	16%
Eliminating products	61%	35%	19%

(*Source: Journal of Marketing Management*)

What makes a good strategic plan?

Once you have gathered all your information and you're ready to put together your strategic plan, how can you be sure of making it as effective as possible? These are the criteria for a good strategic plan (the list was put together with reference to direct marketing, but it applies to any strategic marketing plan):

1 Easy to understand.

2 Precise but detailed, to avoid confusion.

3 Adaptable to change.

4 Realistic in application.

5 Covers all significant market factors.

6 Clearly identifies responsibilities.

(*Source: The Practitioner's Guide to Direct Marketing,* The Institute of Direct Marketing, 1992)

How long does it take to plan and execute a campaign effectively?

Are you one of those people who always find themselves wishing that they'd got started on each project earlier? If so, join the club. But why are most of us inclined to rush campaigns, at least to some extent? Often it's really not our fault. It's because we haven't a clue how long each stage should take and how early we should have started planning.

So here is a general guide to timescale for some of the more frequent marketing campaigns (see Chart 5.2).

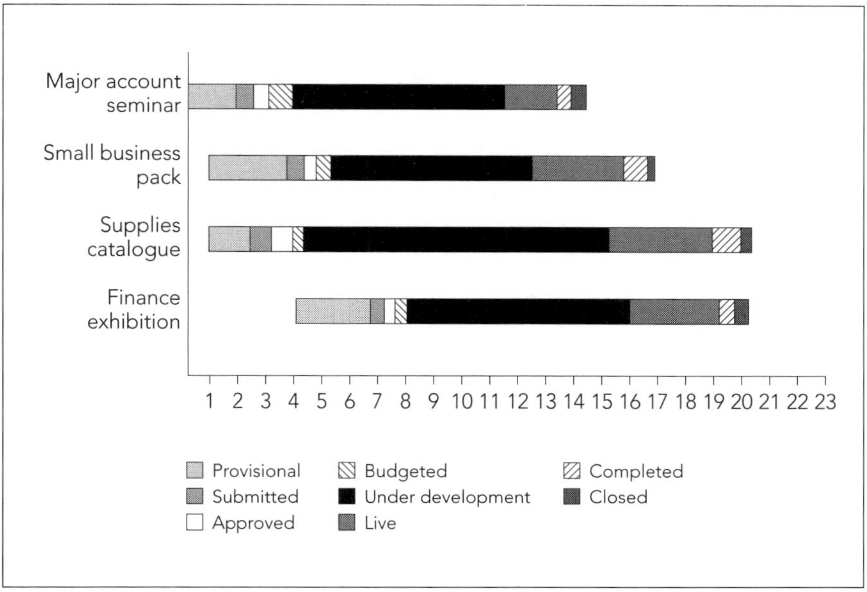

Chart 5.2 Marketing campaign timescales

(*Source: The Practitioner's Guide to Direct Marketing*, The Institute of Direct Marketing, 1992)

The marketing mix

What is the marketing mix?

As the previous sections have shown, market analysis, market research and market processes all have to be mixed and matched together if you are going to produce a successful marketing strategy. These elements have to combine with a host of other considerations, such as:

- How will you package the product?
- How will you organise sales and distribution?
- How will you develop the product to keep pace with the market?

To make it easier for the average businessperson, marketers talk about your 'marketing mix' – the way you combine all these variables to differentiate your product from that of your competitors and target your consumers. The experts split the variables into 'the four Ps' – product, price, place and promotion.

(*Source: Starting and Growing Your Own Business – Entrepreneurial Management*, Nick Morris and Bridget Rosewell, City University Business School)

Product

What do people need to know about your product?

People need to know:

- what you are selling;
- where you are;
- why they should buy from you rather than someone else.

Your advertising should create an image that attracts attention and is easy to associate with your business. An advertising agency is likely to be too expensive, but there are individuals or other small businesses that can help. Talk to them.

(*Source: Start-up Guide*, NatWest Bank plc in conjunction with the Foundation for Small and Medium Enterprise Development, University of Durham, February 2000)

How do you make your product appealing?

There are an enormous number of ways you can make your product different and more appealing. The sorts of factors you could consider are:

- looks – product and packaging;
- 'feel' – is it appropriate to the market?;
- functionality;
- does it have special features? Do they benefit the customer?;
- reliability;
- does it meet expectations in terms of quality/value for money?

(*Source: Starting and Growing Your Own Business – Entrepreneurial Management*, Nick Morris and Bridget Rosewell, City University Business School)

Price

Are your prices right?

To a large extent, your prices will depend on your market and costs. To make the most profit, you need to know what the customers will pay, what competitors charge and the costs of making each product. You will soon find out if you set the wrong prices. Set them too high, and people will not buy your products. Set them too low, and your product may look cheap and you will lose money.

You will probably have to change your first prices as you discover 'true costs' and the effect of price on your particular market. Remember that you need to make enough profit to pay all the costs of the business, including your own wages.

(*Source: Start-up Guide*, NatWest Bank plc in conjunction with the Foundation for Small and Medium Enterprise Development, University of Durham, February 2000)

An effective pricing policy will always take into account what customers are prepared to pay. One well known supermarket is currently charging substantially more for a packaged version of oven chips, onion rings, cooked chicken portions and a dip than for the component parts, describing it as an American banquet. You can charge a premium if you give the customer want they want.

(*Source: Starting and Growing Your Own Business – Entrepreneurial Management*, Nick Morris and Bridget Rosewell, City University Business School)

What pricing tactics should you use?

1 *Pricing tactics* can be important. It is more effective to mark prices clearly than to make customers ask.

2 *Price breaks* matter: it is better to break prices at 99p than to round them up to the pound. Study the pricing tactics of the big mail order catalogues and big stores – they never apply round prices.

3 *Other tactics* can also be effective. For example, the antique dealer who consults his record book before he states a price has a better chance of making a sale than someone who seems to pluck a figure out of thin air.

4 *Price cutting* is not normally a good idea for any business. If your profit margins are small, your cash will be tighter. It is better to sell

good products at a fair price and make a decent profit. Your customers have selective memories. They will forget the good price, but they will remember the bad product forever.

(*Source: Start-up Guide*, NatWest Bank plc in conjunction with the Foundation for Small and Medium Enterprise Development, University of Durham, February 2000)

How do you work out your prices?

Five steps to working out prices

1. Work out your household and personal overheads for one year.
2. Work out how much salary you need to pay yourself to cover your household and personal overheads.
3. Add all your business costs for the same year to your salary.
4. Divide the total by the estimated number of sales over the year. This will give you the cost per item.
5. Add on the profit you want to make for each unit.

Check what price your potential customers might pay. If they are not willing to pay your price, you may need to:

- reduce your costs; or
- highlight the difference between your product or service and your competitor's – to justify the higher price.

(*Source: Start-up Guide*, NatWest Bank plc in conjunction with the Foundation for Small and Medium Enterprise Development, University of Durham, February 2000)

Is there a link between price and cost?

There is one obvious link: businesses need to charge a price that will cover all their costs and generate a reasonable profit. Prices are usually the most that your customers will pay for your product, although a good pricing strategy includes promotional reductions. Profit is maximised only if prices are kept high and costs remain low. It's therefore vital to keep examining all the component parts of your costs to make sure that they stay as low as possible.

(*Source: Starting and Growing Your Own Business – Entrepreneurial Management*, Nick Morris and Bridget Rosewell, City University Business School)

Promotion

What role does promotion play?

Promotion can take many forms: advertising, direct mail, telesales, exhibiting, face-to-face selling, sponsorship, websites, point-of-sale material. The common thread that unites them all is the communication of information. In every case, the prospective customer needs not only to be aware of but also to understand the benefits of your product or service.

Once the customer is aware of your product, or has bought your product once, the role of promotion changes subtly. Its primary role then becomes to raise awareness or to increase customer loyalty.

(*Source: Starting and Growing Your Own Business – Entrepreneurial Management,* Nick Morris and Bridget Rosewell, City University Business School)

What information should companies provide?

Special deals and discounts are the most important elements of any direct marketing. Consumers like to be given product information, especially about food and drink brands. This tends to be more important than price details (see Chart 5.3).

Is direct mail an effective method of promoting your product?

The best way to answer this question is to look at how effectively direct mail influences a decision to purchase. Direct mail's influence on likelihood to purchase varies between sectors from one quarter to one third. It has the strongest influence in the automotive industry (see Chart 5.4).

For more details on marketing and advertising in general, see *Quick Answers to Marketing Questions* in the same series.

How do you manage advertising effectively?

You must begin by asking yourself, 'What do I want my advertising to achieve?' The first step is to analyse the benefits to your business that could only be gained by advertising. The Advertising Association suggests that you try ticking the boxes in Chart 5.5 that apply to your business now.

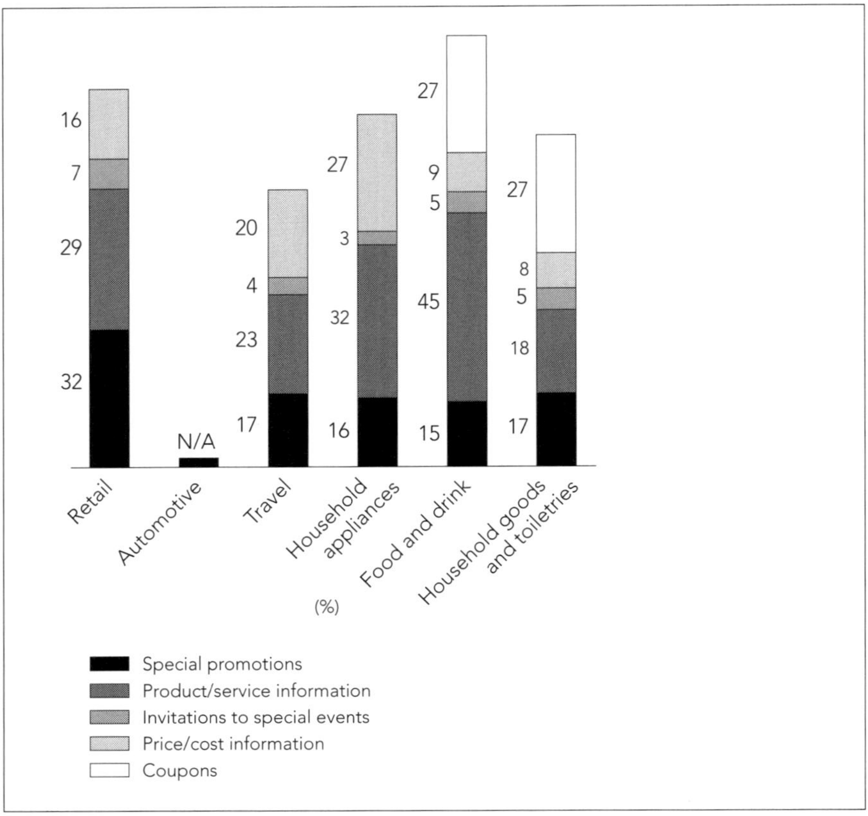

Chart 5.3 What information should companies provide?

(*Source: DMIS Intelligence Sector Reports*, Direct Mail Information Service, 1997)

The conclusion drawn from this exercise is that different types of advertising may be required. Advertising needs to be tailored to its precise audience.

(*Source: Advertising Means Business – A Practical Guide to Advertising*, The Advertising Association, 1997)

How do you choose appropriate advertising media?

Research provides us with statistics which show how receptive customers are to the different sorts of advertising. Direct marketing is one option.

- The average householder responds to direct mail 3–4 times a year.
- 43% of business people consider direct mail 'very useful' or 'quite useful'.

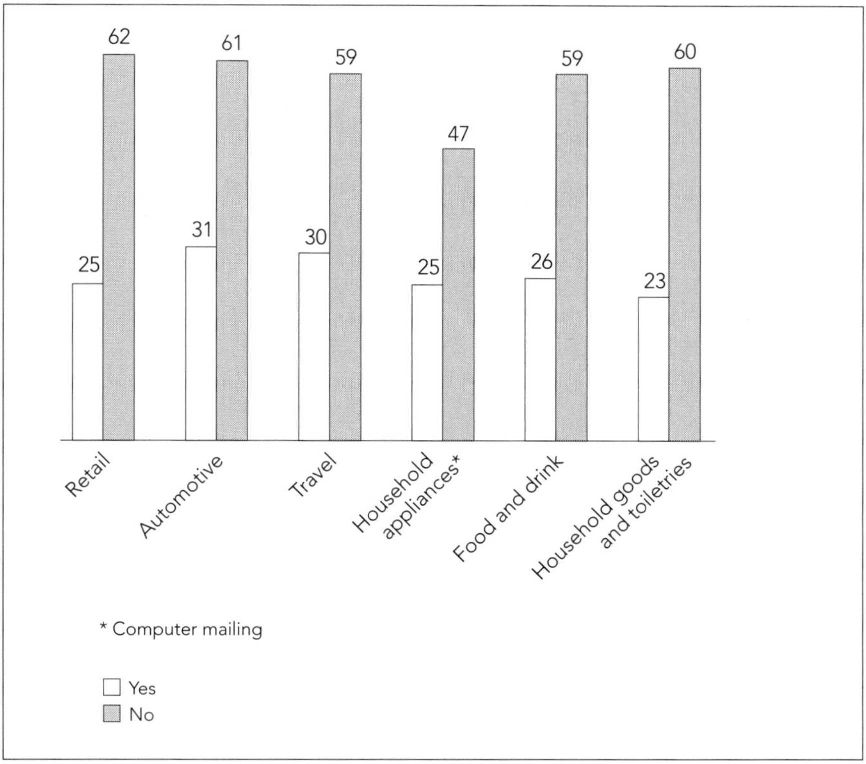

Chart 5.4 Likelihood to purchase

(*Source: DMIS Intelligence Sector Reports*, Direct Mail Information Service, 1997)

1 People who always buy from a competitor and don't know us. ☐

2 People who buy from a competitor, know us but have never bought from us. ☐

3 People who mainly buy from a competitor, but know us and buy from us occasionally. ☐

4 People who mainly buy from us, but occasionally from our competitors. ☐

5 People who buy from us and never from our competitors. ☐

Chart 5.5 Who could use your products or services now?

- 58% expect companies who trade with them to mail them about special offers.
- 55% of customers would like to be mailed by any firm they have used when new literature becomes available.

Press advertising is another option, and there are more than 4,000 publications in the UK to choose from. Press advertising provides flexibility, is cost-effective, and is measurable as you can include a response option.

Radio and TV advertising may seem expensive, and will be for prime time, but budget packages are worth considering. Local radio and TV will transmit some adverts outside peak times, and these may well be appropriate for specific categories of viewer.

Or consider using an agency. Their expertise costs money, but this may well be outweighed by the additional income they generate. Make sure though that you check the agency's credentials carefully.

(*Source: Advertising Means Business – A Practical Guide to Advertising,* The Advertising Association, 1997)

How much advertising can you do yourself?

There is a lot of effective advertising which you can do yourself. Start with your sign. A catchy slogan – 'WEE-MIX, YOU LAY. Just enough readymix for your job' – gets you remembered.

Simple A-boards outside premises will attract customers. Try to think of ingenious ways to remind them of your name at a time when they need you, like the enterprising plumber who calls with stickers to go on the central heating boiler 'for when you need me'. Distributing leaflets within a certain local area is also a very good way of advertising the product or service you are offering.

Local press and radio are fairly cheap ways of advertising in many areas. Even the cinema, or adverts on buses, may come within your price bracket.

(*Source: Start-up Guide,* NatWest Bank plc in conjunction with the Foundation for Small and Medium Enterprise Development, University of Durham, February 2000)

How do you encourage word-of-mouth advertising?

Whatever your business, word of mouth is likely to be very important, especially if you are offering a personal or specialised service. You can encourage word of mouth by:

- satisfying your customers with work well done;
- having a good relationship with your customers;
- building up a good reputation and protecting it by sorting out any problems quickly;
- getting your name mentioned in trade magazines, by local press and radio, or possibly through community public relations activities.

Generating word of mouth is not easy, but if you can do it you will have created advertising money can't buy – the most effective advertising of all.

(*Source: Start-up Guide*, NatWest Bank plc in conjunction with the Foundation for Small and Medium Enterprise Development, University of Durham, February 2000)

How powerful are point-of-sale signs?

Tests carried out by a large American supermarket produced the following results.

- Stores using simple hand-written signs with 'As advertised' on them to promote products on shelves increased their sales. This was compared to products in stores with no signs.
- Using 'New item' signs increased sales of powdered bleach by 73%.

Point of sale clearly pays – see Table 5.7.

Table 5.7 Number of sales per week

Product	Type of display	No sign	Handmade sign	Manufacturer's sign
Paper tissues	Floor display	52	75	94
Bleach	Wire basket	15	24	29
Biscuits	In dairy case	6	15	38
Sponges	Shelf extender	9	15	—
Toothpaste	Floor display	10	29	34
Doughnuts	Table display	45	105	—

Research from Progressive Grocer and Great Atlantic and Pacific Tea Company (A&P) Point of Sale Research, USA

(*Source: Start-up Guide*, NatWest Bank plc in conjunction with the Foundation for Small and Medium Enterprise Development, University of Durham, February 2000)

Customer service

What do people hope to gain by complaining?

When your customers make a valid complaint, what should you do about it? Give them a written apology? Or a refund? What are they usually after? Of course, you could ask them – and it's a very good idea to do so – but if you're planning or reviewing your complaint handling system, it might help to know what most people generally want in recompense. MORI carried out research for the Citizen's Charter Unit which looked at the reasons why people complain (see Table 5.8).

Table 5.8 Why people complain

Reason for complaint	Proportion citing reason
Improved service	39%
To get money/service eligible for	32%
To get an explanation	29%
Prevent the same thing happening to others	28%
To get an apology	11%
To tell them what I thought of them	9%
To get compensation	7%
To vent anger/frustration	6%

(*Source: MORI Research on Complaints Handling*, carried out for the Citizen's Charter Unit, 1997)

What do customers think are the most important factors in handling a complaint?

There are a lot of things you can do to handle a complaint effectively, but it can be impractical – not to mention expensive – to do them all. So which factors do the general public think are the most important in handling a complaint (see Table 5.9)?

Table 5.9 Important factors in dealing with a complaint

Factor	Important factors	Single most important
Speed of response	52%	23%
Being kept informed	46%	17%
Fair investigation	40%	19%
Having a clear procedure	34%	10%
Friendliness and helpfulness	29%	6%
Named person dealing	25%	9%
Receiving written explanation	25%	5%
Receiving written apology	25%	5%
Investigation by senior staff	15%	5%
Receiving compensation	7%	2%

(*Source: MORI Research on Complaints Handling*, carried out for the Citizen's Charter Unit, 1997)

Marketing effectiveness

What skills do you need to be good at marketing?

Small firms were asked which skills they considered most vital for effective marketing. Knowledge of the product and the market topped the bill (see Chart 5.6).

Chart 5.6 Skills needed for marketing

(*Source: Marketing and the Small Firm*, Barclays Bank plc Small Business Services, May 1997)

How do you find out if your marketing is effective?

NatWest Bank plc has designed a marketing effectiveness questionnaire. Its purpose is to help you assess how 'customer orientated' your business is. It will not tell you what you need to do to improve, but it can suggest marketing strengths in your business and areas that might need some improvement.

Base your answers on your assessment of your marketing effectiveness (not what you believe is your customers' assessment). Tick the answer that is most appropriate to your business.

Questionnaire

Customer philosophy

1 Do you recognise the importance of designing the business to serve the needs and wants of particular markets?
   - a *We sell to whoever will buy.*
   - b *We sell to specific market segments.*
   - c *Yes, we analyse customer needs and serve specific segments.*

2 Do you develop different products or services and marketing plans for different segments of the market?
   - a *Occasionally.*
   - b *Never.*
   - c *Quite often.*

3 Have you developed any advantages over your main competitors that attract customers?
   - a *We concentrate on selling the brand name or 'British made' and competing on price.*
   - b *We concentrate on providing superior quality goods and services, guaranteed reliability and unmatched customer service.*
   - c *We have not developed any advantages over our main competitors.*

Developing business

4 How much effort do you put into building business for the future?
   - a *None. We concentrate on servicing existing customers – profit is what counts.*
   - b *Some effort.*
   - c *We go for a balance between long-term and short-term.*

5 How experienced and effective is your sales person?

a *Very experienced, able to achieve one sale for every two opportunities.*

b *Some experience. All right with existing customers but does not relish cold calls.*

c *No experience, dislikes selling.*

6 How effective are your advertising and promotion in generating leads and enquiries?

a *More leads than we can cope with.*

b *Some leads, but not enough.*

c *We have to work very hard to find new leads.*

Proper marketing information

7 When did you last carry out market research studies of your customers, their buying influences and your competitors?

a *Several years ago (over 5 years or never).*

b *A few years ago (1–5 years).*

c *Recently (within the last few months).*

8 How well do you know the sales and profit potential of different market segments, customers, sales areas, products and order sizes?

a *Very well – we have detailed analysis and research.*

b *Quite well – we have information on certain parts.*

c *Not at all.*

9 How effective is your marketing information system at providing high-quality data quickly and accurately to help marketing decisions?

a *Very effective information system, constantly updated and used.*

b *Quite effective system, but sometimes not fast, accurate or complete enough to help decision making.*

c *We have no system. We rely on gathering information informally and through intuition.*

Planning strategy

10 What is the extent of your marketing planning?

a *We develop a detailed annual marketing plan and have careful long-term plans that we monitor and update.*

b *We develop a formal annual marketing plan.*

c *We do little or no formal planning.*

11 What is the quality of your current marketing strategy?

a *The current marketing strategy is not clearly defined.*

b *The current strategy is clear, and just extends our past strategy.*

c *The current strategy is clearly defined and well reasoned, with new ideas.*

12 What are the main marketing objectives?

a *To achieve short-term profits and maintain our present position.*

b *To dominate the market by significantly increasing our share of the market and growing aggressively.*

c *No real strategic long-term objectives – just survival.*

Marketing efficiency

13 What is your pricing policy and how effective is it?

a *We charge what we can get.*

b *We charge the same or less than our competitors.*

c *We charge more than our competitors to match the higher quality of our product or service.*

14 What marketing techniques do you regularly use to improve business performance?

a *We do not use marketing techniques. We just assess our past performance.*

b *We regularly use a wide range of marketing techniques, including sales platform and customer attitude surveys.*

c *We have some marketing techniques that we use when necessary.*

15 How effective is your marketing compared to that of your competitors?

a *An outsider would regard us as better than our competitors.*

b *We are about the same as our competitors.*

c *Frankly, we are not as good at marketing as our competitors.*

Score

Calculate your score by sections, then add up the total.

1	a: 0 b: 1 c: 2	**2**	a: 1 b: 0 c: 2	**3**	a: 1 b: 2 c: 0	**4**	a: 0 b: 1 c: 2
5	a: 2 b: 1 c: 0	**6**	a: 2 b: 1 c: 0	**7**	a: 0 b: 1 c: 2	**8**	a: 2 b: 1 c: 0
9	a: 2 b: 1 c: 0	**10**	a: 2 b: 1 c: 0	**11**	a: 0 b: 1 c: 2	**12**	a: 2 b: 1 c: 0
13	a: 1 b: 0 c: 2	**14**	a: 0 b: 2 c: 1	**15**	a: 2 b: 1 c: 0		

The higher the score, the more effective your marketing is. A low score overall would suggest the need for a rethink of your marketing plan. A low score in a particular section suggests that this area is a priority for improvement.

(*source:* www.natwest.com.business zone).

6

Managing your business

the questions

Time management / 134

- What is the one aspect on which you would like to spend more time?
- Do you feel time management principles and techniques help? If so, how?
- Do you find business services and equipment save time?

Financial management / 136

Cost control / 136

- Which areas of the business do you need to manage to control costs?
- How do you keep an eye on working capital?
- How do you ensure that you don't over-trade?
- How can you make sure you keep your income flowing?
- How can you make sure you are paid on time?

Credit management / 138

- Why bother with credit checking?
- Which accounts should you credit check?
- How do you check how creditworthy your customers are?
- How much credit should you allow?
- What is a risk code?
- How do you reduce risk of late or non-payment?
- When should you make your credit terms clear?

Financial records / 143

- What business records do you need to keep?
- Why do you need to keep business and personal financial records separate?

Managing your business

the answers

Problems

What are the most important problems encountered by small businesses?

Low turnover remains the most important problem for the greatest number of small firms. Government regulations and paperwork are in second place, though fewer businesses selected this category than in the previous survey. Close behind is a skills shortage. Cash flow is a particular problem for small construction firms, while small retailers are suffering from competition (see Table 6.1).

Table 6.1 Most important problem for small businesses

Respondents were asked to select, from a list of 13, the most important problem facing their business on that day. Every firm faces many problems, but this survey focused on the most important single problem facing the business at the time.

Problem	Percentage considering it most important problem
Low turnover/lack of business	26.8
Government regulations and paperwork	12.5
Lack of skilled/trained employees	12.0
Cash flow/payments/debtors	9.4
Total tax burden	7.4

Table 6.1 continued

Problem	Percentage considering it most important problem
Competition from big business	6.4
Premises/rent/rates	2.8
Internal management difficulties	2.4
Access to finance	2.1
High rates of pay	1.5
Shortages of materials, supplies, etc.	1.0
Interest rates	0.9
Inflation	0.3
Other	12.5
No response	1.9

Base: 758 small firms

(*Source: NatWest SBRT Quarterly Survey of Small Business in Britain*, Vol. 16, No. 3, September 2000)

Have government regulations become more or less onerous recently?

In the 36 surveys that Small Business Research Trust carried out between 1990 and 1998, the proportion finding government regulations a burden was higher on only two occasions than it was in September 2000. A record high of 18.9% of small firms found government regulations their most important problem in June 2000; the percentage has dropped since, but in 2000 was at record levels (see Chart 6.1).

Does the most important problem vary with the size of the company?

Table 6.2 indicates that while an overwhelming number of sole traders find lack of turnover a problem (43.3%), the major problem for firms employing 50 people or more is a lack of skilled/trained employees.

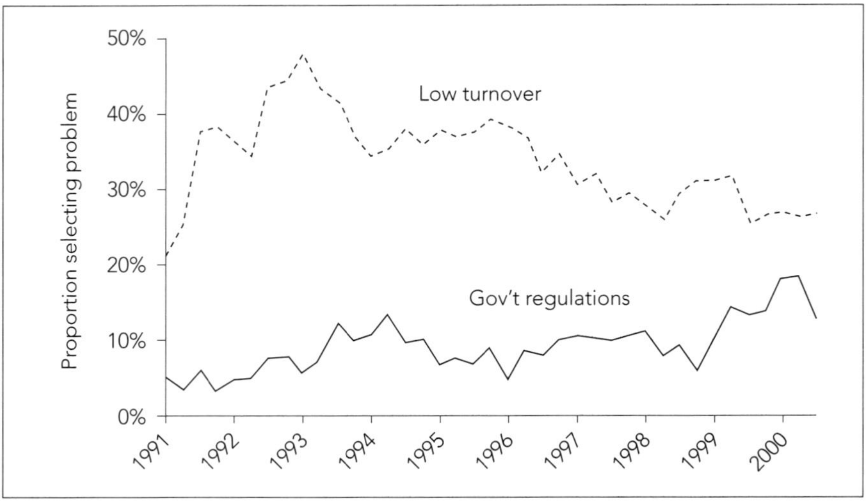

Chart 6.1 Percentage of businesses selecting government regulations or low turnover as their most important problem, 1991–2000

(*Source: NatWest SBRT Quarterly Survey of Small Business in Britain*, Vol. 16, No. 3, September 2000)

Table 6.2 Most important problem by employment size band

Employment size band	1	2	3–4	5–9	10–14	15–24	25–49	50+	All
Inflation	1.0%	0.0%	0.0%	0.6%	0.0%	0.0%	0.0%	0/0%	0.3%
Interest rates	1.0%	2.5%	0.8%	0.6%	0.0%	1.5%	0.0%	0.0%	0.9%
Access to finance	3.1%	2.5%	3.2%	1.1%	2.7%	2.9%	1.6%	0.0%	2.2%
Lack of skilled/ trained employees	2.1%	8.3%	8.8%	7.9%	12.3%	22.1%	17.5%	18.2%	10.3%
Total tax burden	8.2%	4.1%	7.2%	6.2%	13.7%	8.8%	3.2%	3.0%	6.9%
Low turnover/lack of business	43.3%	37.2%	32.0%	23.7%	20.5%	23.5%	30.2%	18.2%	29.7%
Competition from big business	10.3%	5.8%	6.4%	9.6%	4.1%	4.4%	4.8%	6.1%	7.0%
Gov't regulations and paperwork	6.2%	9.9%	15.2%	13.6%	17.8%	8.8%	20.6%	15.2%	13.1%
High rates of pay	0.0%	0.0%	0.8%	2.3%	0.0%	1.5%	1.6%	3.0%	1.1%
Shortages of materials, supplies, etc.	0.0%	0.8%	0.8%	1.7%	1.4%	1.5%	0.0%	0.0%	0.9%
Internal management difficulties	2.1%	1.7%	1.6%	2.8%	4.1%	1.5%	4.8%	3.0%	2.5%
Cashflow/payments/ debtors	5.2%	7.4%	7.2%	12.4%	8.2%	11.8%	6.3%	6.1%	8.6%

Table 6.2 continued

Employment size band	1	2	3–4	5–9	10–14	15–24	25–49	50+	All
Premises/rent/rates	2.1%	4.1%	4.0%	5.6%	1.4%	1.5%	1.6%	0.0%	3.3%
Other	12.4%	13.2%	11.2%	10.2%	13.7%	10.3%	7.9%	24.2%	11.9%
No response	3.1%	2.5%	0.8%	1.7%	0.0%	0.0%	0.0%	3.0%	1.5%
Base	97	121	125	177	73	68	63	33	758

(*Source: NatWest SBRT Quarterly Survey of Small Business in Britain*, Vol. 16, No. 3, September 2000)

Management skills

Are you cut out for management?

How do you decide whether you are cut out for management? One way to find out is to ask those who manage what qualities are needed. Small business managers were asked what they thought the most important attribute for managing a small firm was. Surprisingly, delegation skills came lower on the list than perseverance and adaptability (see Table 6.3).

Table 6.3 Attributes for managing a small firm

Attribute	Proportion considering this most important
Ability to determine priorities	22%
Perseverance	19%
Adaptability	19%
Ability to motivate others	12%
Communication skills	10%
High stress tolerance	7%
Ability to delegate	4%
Ability to learn from mistakes	3%
Creativity	1%
Emotional stability	1%
Self-analysis	1%
Negotiation skills	1%

(*Source: Quarterly Small Business Management Report No. 3*, September 1993, Lloyds Bank/Small Business Research Trust)

What decision-making styles do owner-managers choose?

Are you inclined to be consultative? Do you empower your staff? Or would you prefer to keep control of all decisions rather than just the most important ones? The Small Business Research Trust surveyed owner-managers about their decision-making styles, and found that the majority did consult (see Table 6.4).

Table 6.4 Decision-making styles

Style	Percentage choosing this style
Obtain employees' views, then decide	53%
Take decisions, then 'sell' them	20%
Take decisions, to get things done	26%

- Managers in the very smallest firms selected the authoritarian 'take decisions' more often than those in other firms.

(*Source: Quarterly Small Business Management Report No. 3*, September 1993, Lloyds Bank/Small Business Research Trust)

Delegation

Which tasks are not delegated?

If your style is naturally democratic and you trust your employees to take responsibility, what are you most likely to delegate? Is it an issue of continuing to do what you are best at? Or is the decision to delegate made more on the basis of where the buck stops? The latter seems to be the guiding principle: 70% of managers keep responsibility for drafting proposals for finance, yet only 17% undertake stock checks.

Tasks least likely to be delegated

1 Personally draft proposals for raising finance.
2 Handle important order enquiries.
3 Undertake staff appraisals.
4 Draft employment contracts/letters.
5 Design company brochures.
6 Prepare sales figures.
7 Personally evaluate major suppliers.

8 Prepare regular management accounts.
9 Open all company mail.
10 Personally draft quality control procedures.
11 Personally test prototypes.
12 Prepare statutory returns.
13 Formulate training programmes in detail.
14 Man company's stands at exhibitions.
15 Formulate equipment maintenance schedules.
16 Undertake stock checks.

(*Source: Quarterly Small Business Management Report No. 3*, September 1993, Lloyds Bank/Small Business Research Trust)

Which tasks are delegated?

Are all the routine tasks delegated? If you no longer open company mail, or formulate equipment maintenance schedules, are you alone? Respondents were asked which tasks were delegated – multiple answers were allowed (see Table 6.5).

Table 6.5 Which tasks are delegated?

Prepare statutory returns	68%
Undertake stock checks	65%
Open all company mail	61%
Prepare management accounts	56%
Prepare regular sales figures	46%
Formulate equipment maintenance schedules	45%
Formulate training programmes in detail	43%
Personally draft quality control procedures	38%
Draft employee contracts/letters	31%
Handle important order enquiries	26%
Personally test prototypes	25%
Man company stands at exhibitions	21%
Undertake staff appraisals	21%
Personally draft proposals for raising finance	10%

(*Source: Quarterly Small Business Management Report No. 3*, September 1993, Lloyds Bank/Small Business Research Trust)

Time management

What is the one aspect on which you would like to spend more time?

Do you feel weighed down by the pressures of work? Do you feel you need to take a break? Do you feel you're not getting your priorities right? If you do, you're not alone. Nearly 20% of managers admitted that planning and setting of objectives are their major concern. A third of respondents wanted to concentrate more on new business development because it is essential to small businesses (see Table 6.6).

Table 6.6 Which aspect managers would like to spend more time on

Aspect on which you want to spend more time	Proportion citing this aspect
New business development	34%
Planning/setting objectives	19%
Personal training/development	14%
Representing organisation externally	7%
Staff training	5%

(*Source: Finding The Time. A Survey of Managers' Attitudes to Using and Managing Time*, Karen Cole, Institute of Management, March 1995)

Do you feel time management principles and techniques help? If so, how?

You are probably familiar with time management principles. Do you find them a helpful concept? Do you feel that you prioritise well? Responding managers seemed fairly well organised and disciplined in terms of controlling their working day (see Table 6.7).

Table 6.7 Managers' time management

Discriminate between urgent and important tasks	91%
Find it easy to prioritise their daily tasks	84%
Run their meetings in a time-efficient manner	82%
Delegate tasks (upwards or downwards) in a time-efficient manner	82%
Achieve daily priorities	70%
Remember to review their long-term work goals (percentages indicate those who were confident of each skill)	55%

(*Source: Finding The Time. A Survey of Managers' Attitudes to Using and Managing Time,* Karen Cole, Institute of Management, March 1995)

Do you find business services and equipment save time?

You probably have at least one piece of equipment that you swear by. When it comes to introducing new equipment, though, it is often difficult to choose. There is such a plethora of services – and equipment – at a manager's disposal. The choice is obviously personal, but what do other managers think? Online databases, a desk fax machine and a portable laptop computer were regarded as key aids by those who had them (see Table 6.8).

Table 6.8 Choosing new equipment and services

Percentage who found them:	Very helpful	Fairly helpful	Not very helpful	Not helpful at all	Don't use/NA
Online databases	28	30	7	2	33
Desk fax	23	21	7	4	44
Portable laptop computer	23	16	4	1	44
Mobile phone	22	18	4	2	54
Email	18	16	10	4	52
Car phone	18	11	3	2	66
Local/domestic delivery services	12	33	11	4	40
International express distribution	11	20	7	4	58
Electronic diary	11	13	13	8	55
Internal messengers	8	24	10	4	54

Table 6.8 continued

Percentage who found them:	Very helpful	Fairly helpful	Not very helpful	Not helpful at all	Don't use/NA
Pager	7	10	5	4	74
Voice mail	6	8	5	3	78
Video conferencing	4	8	5	3	78

(Source: *Finding The Time. A Survey of Managers' Attitudes to Using and Managing Time*, Karen Cole, Institute of Management, March 1995)

Financial management

Cost control

Which areas of the business do you need to manage to control costs?

You need to be in control of the cash, or 'working capital' as it is known, which is generated by your sales and profits.

- Is the cash coming quickly enough?
- What's happening to it when it's in the business?
- Is there a danger that you'll need more than you've got?

(*Source: Setting Up and Running Your Business*, Barclays Bank plc, June 2000)

How do you keep an eye on working capital?

Working capital is the term used to describe the short-term financial resources used by your business for everyday trading purposes. It's the lifeline of your business, and it consists of:

- *debtors* – the money owed to you by customers to whom you have sold on credit;
- *creditors* – the money owed by you to suppliers from whom you have made purchases on credit;
- *stock* – the value of materials you have purchased for immediate resale or for conversion into finished articles;
- *cash or overdraft* – the money you hold as cash or in a bank account.

All of these have to be carefully controlled if your business is to prosper.

(*Source: Setting Up and Running Your Business*, Barclays Bank plc, June 2000)

How do you ensure that you don't over-trade?

Over-trading is one of the main reasons that small businesses fail. If your level of sales becomes too high, and you don't have sufficient working capital, you may simply run out of money, often with fatal results. Sales alone do not make a successful business. You need enough cash as well.

One of the most important ways to ensure you have sufficient cash in your business to fund growth or to reduce the need for borrowing is to collect money from customers as quickly as possible.

(*Source: Setting Up and Running Your Business*, Barclays Bank plc, June 2000)

How can you make sure you keep your income flowing?

Here are a few tips (dealt with in more detail below).

1 Check your customers' ability to pay.
2 Set out your terms of trading, and state clearly when you expect payment.
3 Set up a system which ensures your invoices go out promptly and shows when payment is due.
4 Keep clear and accurate records so that you can deal with any customer queries quickly.
5 Collect your payment on time by having a clear collection process.
6 Put sufficient funds aside in a high-interest account to cover your tax liability, as this is collected several months after you make the sales.

(*Source: Setting Up and Running Your Business*, Barclays Bank plc, June 2000)

How can you make sure you are paid on time?

Getting the cash is even more important than making the sale, and a large bill can cause concern and worry. Here are some tips to ease the pain:

1 Agree payment methods in advance with clients.
2 Spread the load – send out a series of smaller invoices.
3 Accept stage payments.

4 Negotiate the best terms you can get – for example, with a big order, suggest 50% with acceptance of order, 30% on delivery, 20% within 14 days of delivery.
5 Offer an incentive for prompt payment, such as free delivery.
6 Offer a discount for prompt payment.
7 Ask your customers to set up standing orders for staged payments.
8 Ask your customers to set up direct debits.
9 Charge interest on late payments.
10 Keep your word. Set up a credit control system and stick to it. Don't feel you might upset a 'good' client relationship by chasing.

(*Source:* www.clearlybusiness.com, 'Accounting and Tax – Make Sure You're Paid on Time')

Credit management

Why bother with credit checking?

If you knew a customer was about to go bust, would you allow 30 days' credit? If you knew a customer paid others late, would you expect payment on time? It makes sense to find out.

When you allow customers time to pay, it should be a conscious decision. There are two powerful reasons for managing credit risk.

1 Commercial – it makes future sales more reliable.
2 Financial – profit is increased by fewer bad debts and lower borrowings.

(*Source: Better Payment Practice – A Guide to Credit Management,* Department of Trade and Industry, January 1998)

The main reason to check credit is, of course, to avoid late payment or non-payment of invoices. Well over one-third of Britain's small firms say that slow payment of invoices is a problem. The proportion complaining of slow payment problems has fallen consistently, yet it remains a burden to a substantial number of small businesses, as Chart 6.2 shows.

In order to quantify the intensity as well as the extent of payment problems, firms were asked what proportion of their invoices were overdue. Table 6.9 shows that the average proportion of invoices overdue is 21.9%.

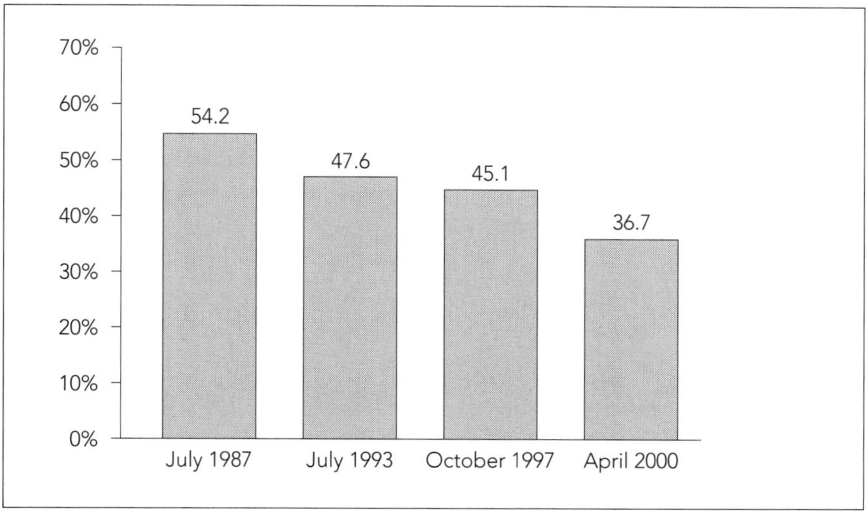

Chart 6.2 Proportion of respondents who say that slow payment of their invoices is a problem

(*Source: NatWest SBRT Quarterly Survey of Small Businesses in Britain*, Vol. 16, No. 2, June 2000)

Table 6.9 Proportion of invoices which are overdue

	Replies	%	Cumulative %
100%	10	1.2	1.2
Over 90%, less than 100%	5	0.6	1.8
Over 80%, up to 90%	15	1.8	3.6
Over 70%, up to 80%	22	2.7	6.3
Over 60%, up to 70%	21	2.5	8.8
Over 50%, up to 60%	38	4.6	13.4
Over 40%, up to 50%	60	7.3	20.7
Over 30%, up to 40%	47	5.7	26.4
Over 20%, up to 30%	88	10.6	37.0
Over 10%, up to 20%	84	10.2	47.2
10% or less	212	25.6	72.8
None	225	27.2	100.0
Responses	827		
Average (mean)	21.9%		
No response	39		

(*Source: NatWest SBRT Quarterly Survey of Small Businesses in Britain*, Vol. 16, No. 2, June 2000)

Which accounts should you credit check?

Use the 80/20 rule to identify the few accounts which buy most of your sales (list accounts in descending order of value until they add up to 80% of the total). Give those a full credit check, and do only brief checks on the smaller ones. Always check customers by size of debt, not alphabetical order, so you never suffer a large bad debt through lack of time.

(*Source: Better Payment Practice – A Guide to Credit Management*, Department of Trade and Industry, January 1998)

How do you check how creditworthy your customers are?

There are four main methods.

1 *Status reports from credit agencies*. These cost, but give you full customer details, financial results, payment experience of other suppliers, county court judgments, registered lending etc. and a recommended credit rating.

2 *Bank references*. There is a fee for this service – and references will only be given with the written permission of the customer. Ask specific questions such as 'Do you consider XYZ Ltd good for £5,000 per month on 30-day terms?' Banks use only standard terms, and anything less than 'good for your figure' is a guarded warning. Remember the bank's loyalty will be to its customer, not to you. Use this only for small-value decisions.

3 *Trade references*. Use only referees selected by you, and not by the customer. Customers are not going to offer names of dissatisfied suppliers. Make it easy for the respondent with a printed form, tick-boxes and prepaid envelopes, as shown in the example on page 141.

4 *Company accounts*. Companies House requires public limited companies and their large private subsidiaries to state in days the average time taken to pay their suppliers, and to publish this figure in their director's report. The Federation of Small Businesses publishes league tables of the average payment time of public companies.

It is also possible to search the Register of County Court Judgments, the Register of Individual Voluntary Arrangements (Insolvency) and the Bankruptcy Lists for a small fee per search.

(*Source: Better Payment Practice – A Guide to Credit Management*, Department of Trade and Industry, January 1998)

Name and address of business		
How long known?	years	less than a year?
Terms: 30 days	60 days	longer (specify)
Sales per month: £1,000	£1,000–£5,000	over £5,000
Payments prompt?	up to 60 days late?	very late?
Name of payments contact		
Other useful information		
Thank you for helping. We will reciprocate at any time.		

How much credit should you allow?

You can:

- buy an opinion from a credit agency;
- get an opinion from a credit insurer;
- make your own calculation.

To set your own credit limit, there are two approaches.

1 *A credit limit to support sales levels.* If references are good enough, the credit limit would be twice the monthly sales figure for that customer.

2 *A maximum amount you are prepared to be owed* regardless of current sales levels. A popular calculation is the lower of 10% of net worth or 20% of working capital (net current assets).

Method 1 needs constant revision as sales grow but is a useful trigger for rechecking risk at intervals. Method 2 is better as sales staff have automatic scope to sell up to the credit limit, which needs less frequent revision.

(*Source: Better Payment Practice – A Guide to Credit Management,*
Department of Trade and Industry, January 1998)

What is a risk code?

A risk code indicates the likelihood of being paid late, and therefore how closely you need to watch the account. For example:

A = No risk – those with the best credit references and excellent payment records.
B = Average.
C = High risk – those who have become slow payers or have county court judgments against them.

You may have to take on some 'C' accounts if you can't get enough business from 'A's and 'B's. If you identify your 'C' customers, you can put more sales effort into 'A's and 'B's to put your business on a sounder footing. Remember to review these codes over time.

(*Source: Better Payment Practice – A Guide to Credit Management*, Department of Trade and Industry, January 1998)

How do you reduce risk of late or non-payment?

As well as from credit checking, there are other ways in which you can reduce the likelihood of late payment, or protect yourself against the consequences. Possible measures include:

- part pre-payment;
- legal expenses insurance;
- special payment terms;
- prompt payment rebate schemes;
- retention of title;
- credit insurance;
- third-party guarantees;
- stakeholder accounts/secure deposits;
- cash discount;
- contra or offset against payables;
- debt factoring.

(*Source: Better Payment Practice – A Guide to Credit Management*, Department of Trade and Industry, January 1998)

When should you make your credit terms clear?

You should make your credit terms clear at every available opportunity.

- *In sales negotiations*. It is professional, not anti-selling, to say 'We allow 30 days to pay – does that give you any problems?' Discuss it, don't duck it.
- *On an order acknowledgement*. Stressing your payment terms as a condition of sale supersedes any buyer's terms. Send this to a responsible, named person.
- *On an account application form*. Include a paragraph for the buyer to sign, agreeing with your stated payment terms and conditions of sale.
- *On invoices*. Show the payment terms boldly on the front. Also show the due date, e.g. 'Payment terms: 30 days from invoice date – payment to reach us by 14 March 200X.'
- *On statements*. Repeat the terms and indicate debts past due dates.

(*Source: Better Payment Practice – A Guide to Credit Management*, Department of Trade and Industry, January 1998)

Financial records

What business records do you need to keep?

To begin with, you may be able to manage with a handful of files. The basic categories of records you will need to keep are:

- sales invoices to your customers;
- purchase invoices from your suppliers;
- records of petty cash expenditure;
- tax returns;
- VAT returns;
- bank statements.

There is a wide range of paper or computer-based bookkeeping systems specially designed for small businesses. Even if you decide to set up a computerised bookkeeping system, you will still need to keep files of the original paperwork.

(*Source: Setting Up and Running Your Business*, Barclays Bank plc, June 2000)

Why do you need to keep business and personal financial records separate?

The best way of knowing what's going on in your business is to keep your personal and business financial records apart, particularly if you are a sole trader. If you have separate business and personal accounts, it will be easier to find the information when you come to complete returns for the Inland Revenue and for HM Customs and Excise.

How do you use a cash book?

This records your daily receipts and payments, the names of the parties involved, and the way each transaction is settled (cheque, standing order, direct debit, credit card). The records in your cash book should match your bank (and/or credit card) statements, so it will be useful to check these weekly or monthly.

(*Source: Setting Up and Running Your Business*, Barclays Bank plc, June 2000)

How do you use a sales ledger?

Sales ledgers are records of all sales. Sales invoices can be split into 'sales unpaid' and 'sales paid'. If you number your invoices sequentially, you will find it easier to identify each one. Once an invoice is paid, write or stamp the date of payment on the invoice, update the sales ledger, and refile it under 'sales paid'.

Normally you record sales on the left-hand side, and details of payment received on the right. This allows you to maintain a balance of monies owed. It will also enable you to see how quickly you were paid. Check through the 'sales unpaid' entries/file regularly – to spot any late invoices.

(*Source: Setting Up and Running Your Business*, Barclays Bank plc, June 2000)

How do you use a purchase ledger?

Your purchase records can be very similar to those for sales, with separate files for paid and unpaid invoices. Details of invoices go on the left-hand page, details of payment on the right.

Always ask for an invoice or receipt with purchases for your records.

(*Source: Setting Up and Running Your Business*, Barclays Bank plc, June 2000)

Government regulations

How many hours do small businesses spend complying with government regulations?

On average, Britain's small business owners say that they, their staff, and their professional advisors spend approximately 3.9 hours per month per person working in the business. Chart 6.3 and Table 6.10 show that the time spent varies markedly with firm size. Larger firms naturally spend a greater number of total hours on compliance, but the number of hours spent per person working in the business falls sharply as the size of the firm increases.

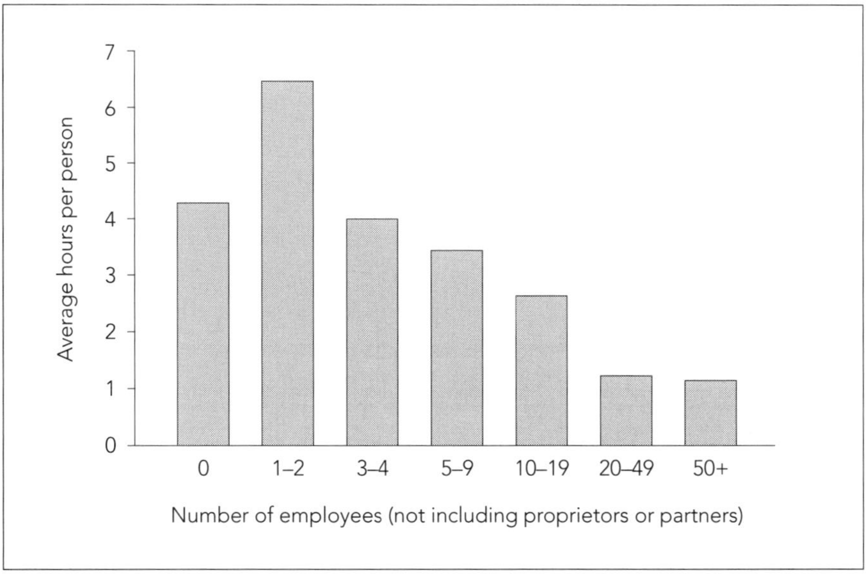

Chart 6.3 Person-hours per month per person working in the business spent on dealing with red tape – by size of business

Table 6.10 Time taken per month to deal with government regulations and paperwork – by size of business (number of people employed, not including proprietors and partners)

Number of employees	Total hours	Hours per person working in the business	Responses	No responses/ unknown
0	6.5	4.4	102	13
1–2	12.8	6.4	153	14
3–4	16.4	4.1	94	14
5–9	23.8	3.4	130	15
10–19	31.8	2.4	88	14
20–49	41.1	1.4	82	7
50+	76.7	1.3	23	9
All	22.6	3.9	672	86

(*Source: NatWest SBRT Quarterly Survey of Small Business in Britain*, Vol. 16, No. 3, September 2000)

Has the burden of compliance increased recently?

Only 0.3% of the 758 respondents to the survey said that time taken to comply had decreased significantly; 1.7% said it had decreased a little. In contrast, 31.4% said that the time taken to comply had increased significantly, and 38.0% said it had increased a little. The balance of firms saying that the time taken to deal with red tape had increased over the last year actually increased with firm size (see Chart 6.4).

Which area of red tape takes the most time from small businesses?

Taxation (including VAT, PAYE, NI and self-assessment) was cited as causing the greatest increase in compliance time for small businesses. The smaller the firm, the more dominant taxation is (see Table 6.11).

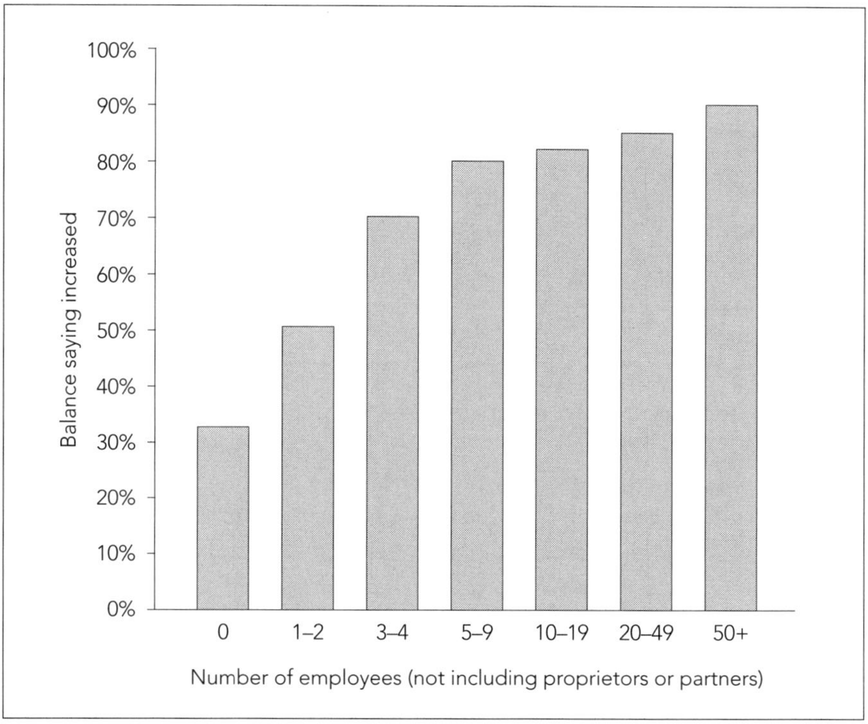

Chart 6.4 Balance saying time to deal with red tape has increased over the past year – by size of business

(*Source: NatWest SBRT Quarterly Survey of Small Business in Britain*, Vol. 16, No. 3, September 2000)

Table 6.11 'Which area of red tape has caused the biggest increase over the past year in compliance time?' – by size of business (number of people employed, not including proprietors and partners)

	0	1–2	3–4	5–9	10–19	20–49	50+	All
Taxation (e.g. VAT, PAYE, NI, self-assessment)	66.7%	69.1%	56.4%	48.7%	44.2%	39.0%	37.9%	52.3%
Non-tax employment regulations	4.4%	10.6%	12.8%	8.5%	12.8%	13.0%	20.7%	11.2%
Health and safety regulations	6.7%	6.4%	6.4%	23.1%	27.9%	24.7%	10.3%	16.5%
Environmental regulations	8.9%	2.1%	6.4%	3.4%	1.2%	3.9%	3.4%	3.8%

Table 6.11 continued

	0	1–2	3–4	5–9	10–19	20–49	50+	All
Statistical inquiries from government	6.7%	2.1%	1.3%	1.7%	4.7%	9.1%	17.2%	4.6%
Other	4.4%	6.4%	12.8%	12.8%	8.1%	10.4%	6.9%	9.5%
No response	2.2%	3.2%	3.8%	1.7%	1.2%	0.0%	3.4%	2.1%
Sample	45	94	78	117	86	77	29	526

(*Source: NatWest SBRT Quarterly Survey of Small Business in Britain*, Vol. 16, No. 3, September 2000)

Managing a family business

Combining family life with the running of a commercial business poses particular challenges. The impact of personal relations on business cannot be over-estimated. There needs to be a balance between the interests of the family and those of the business.

Do family businesses do better or worse than average?

The answer is both. Family businesses tend to have a higher than average chance of folding in the first 18 months. But those that survive are often more successful.

(*Source:* www.clearlybusiness.com, 'Your Business – How to Run a Successful Family Business')

How do you help your family business succeed?

Many of the obvious sources of conflict in family businesses can be avoided if you follow a few straightforward rules.

1. *Avoid straining personal relationships* by formalising each job position to create a clear demarcation between business and family affairs.
2. *Compile an agreed, detailed, written policy governing the way the business is run.* This should include decision making, salary setting, ownership stakes, loans to family members, succession rules, and what to do if a family member wants to leave the company.
3. *Formalise a clear procedure for the resolution of disputes.*
4. *Put in place a policy where family members can join the company only if they have acquired a specific qualification or achieved a certain level within another company first.* Families tend to grow, and it is wise to

have a written policy on how to choose which family members to recruit. Excluding some family members but not others can prove dangerous or divisive.

5 *Apply policies to all members of the family equally*, to minimise conflicts and ensure no family member feels aggrieved or singled out.

(*Source:* www.clearlybusiness.com, 'Your Business – How to Run a Successful Family Business')

Information technology

How important is IT to the small business?

David Lavarack, Small Business Services Director, Barclays Bank plc, reckons that IT is a fundamental tool for developing a business. He says:

Small businesses that use their IT more effectively will benefit from freeing up valuable time that can be used to plan and market the business more effectively ... Small businesses recognise that they need to embrace IT more fully in order to gain its full benefit ... Ever decreasing purchase costs and continuous improvements in speed and power now enable even the smallest businesses to compete against their larger counterparts on a level footing.

- Nine out of ten small businesses feel that IT has a positive benefit for their business.
- Yet only 7% say they are using it efficiently – half of the small businesses in the survey which had recently invested more than £10,000 in IT had not undertaken any training in how to use the new equipment.

(*Source: Information Technology*, Barclays Review, 1996)

How do you select appropriate office hardware?

The combinations and configurations of hardware available are legion; computer magazines offer seemingly endless advice. A good starting point is to ask yourself the following questions.

1 *Do I need to network?* A single PC may not be much use unless it is attached to similarly enabled computers. Vendors increasingly offer complete networks and cabling at reasonable cost.

2 *What about a LAN?* A LAN (local area network) solution requires no additional cables beyond your existing telephone wiring. Bear in mind that most LANs are slower than cabled networks.

3 *What print quality do I need?* Business documents need good print quality – photographic-quality images might require a better printer.

4 *Am I going to use video conferencing?* If so, choose your web camera with care. Compact cameras which plug into parallel ports and a keyboard socket suffice for most small businesses. Even if a party doesn't respond to a call, you can then record a video clip and send it as an email attachment.

5 *What about ISDN?* If you decide on ISDN, bear in mind that most ISDN terminal adapters have sockets for only one or two analogue phones. Work out how many phones, faxes and answering machines you will need, and make a decision on functionality.

(*Source:* www.clearlybusiness.com, 'Getting Online – IT for SMEs')

Which functions does your business use computers for?

Efficient use of computers will require simultaneous, not singular work functions. Yet an IT review will not hit the mark unless you understand how computers are used in your business. So how do other businesses use their computers (see Chart 6.5)?

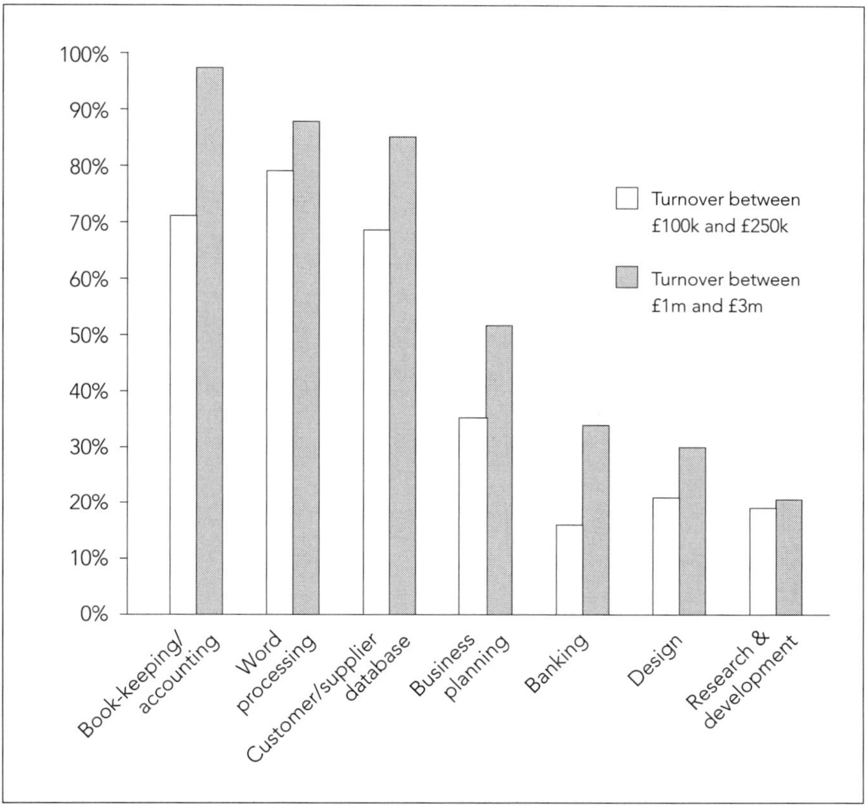

Chart 6.5 How businesses use their computers

(*Source: Information Technology*, Barclays Review, 1996)

Why do you need an IT strategy?

The IT Skills Forum is a non-profit-making consortium of 70 businesses and other organisations whose aim is to share knowledge and promote the research and education of IT throughout the UK. The Forum's research shows that:

- three-quarters of the general workforce are not using IT to their maximum advantage;
- seven out of ten users believe their IT systems are not providing any return on their investment;
- around 20% of IT spend is wasted.

(*Source: Information Technology*, Barclays Review, 1996)

7

Managing growth

the questions

Exporting / 172

- What are the most common reasons for starting to export?
- How do you find out about overseas business opportunities?
- What factors influence your decision about target countries for export?
- If you don't export, why not?

Managing change / 175

- What is the traditional approach to the management of change?
- Why does change fail?
- How can you make sure that change succeeds?

High-technology companies / 177

Business incubation / 177

- What is business incubation?
- What sorts of businesses use incubators?
- How do incubators work?

Technology transfer / 179

- What is technology transfer (TT)?
- What are the advantages and disadvantages of technology transfer?
- How do you prepare for technology transfer?

Managing growth

the answers

Introduction

Are small businesses expanding?

A major concern of all small businesses is growth. You can't stand still in the business world, so if you don't grow, you shrink. How healthy are your fellow small businesses? Are the majority expanding? The proportion of businesses that were expanding, categorised by number of employees, is shown in Table 7.1.

Table 7.1 Businesses expanding, categorised by number of employees

No. of employees	Percentage
1–4	30
5–9	41
10–19	48
20–49	55
50–99	43
100+	43
National average	**41**

(*Source: 38th Quarterly Survey of Small Firms, Quarter 2,* The Forum of Private Business)

Are small businesses with a higher turnover expanding faster?

Expansion for small firms therefore seems more likely with more employees – does a large turnover make a difference?

Table 7.2 Does turnover make a difference?

Turnover size	Percentage of firms expanding
Less than £21,000	31
£21,000–£44,000	29
£45,000–£89,000	30
£90,000–£149,000	31
£150,000–£499,000	40
£500,000–£999,000	47
National average	**41**

(Source: *38th Quarterly Survey of Small Firms, Quarter 2,* The Forum of Private Business)

What are the problems of expanding small businesses?

Perhaps you started a business a while ago, and are now looking to expand. Are the possible problems now old hat – ones that you came across at the beginning – or does expansion bring with it a new set of challenges?

Late payment and the shortage of skilled employees were significantly more important to expanding businesses than they were to the nation as a whole (see Chart 7.1).

Why do businesses grow?

If your business is beginning to grow substantially, it could be for a variety of reasons. The first, and most obvious, is that you planned to grow. Businesses can also grow because:

- the number of customers who want your products is growing;
- your current customers have increased their demand for your products;
- one factor has changed in the dynamics of your particular market – for example, a direct competitor has gone out of business.

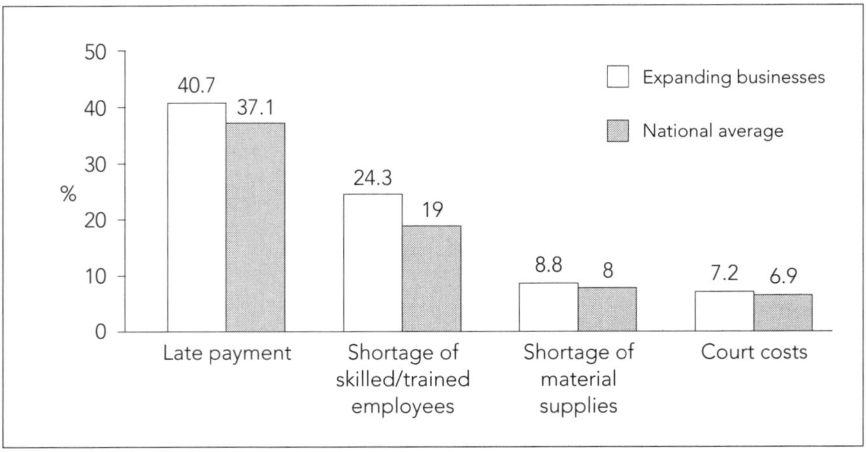

Chart 7.1 Problems associated with expansion

(*Source: 38th Quarterly Survey of Small Firms, Quarter 2,* The Forum of Private Business)

If you are planning growth, you will need to understand its implications – financially, practically and emotionally. One crucial question needs to be asked: Do you wish to grow indefinitely, or do you wish to grow slowly in order to keep personal control of the business? In answering this question, it is helpful to look at patterns of growth.

(*Source: Starting and Growing Your Own Business – Entrepreneurial Management,* Nick Morris and Bridget Rosewell, City University Business School)

The business growth life cycle

What is the business growth life cycle?

Growth is never continuous and uninterrupted – levels of growth can fluctuate, even if the overall pattern is one of steady growth. There are essentially four stages of growth, known as the business growth life cycle.

1 *Birth*

This is the stage at which most businesses climb the learning curve, due to a lack of commercial experience. 'Birth' usually starts with identifying a gap in the market and choosing a product or service. It also includes planning, finding funding, premises and staff, and the initial stages of building a customer database.

2 *Survival*

This is the 'testing' stage for most businesses, in more than one sense of the word! Trial and error plays a part, the market for your product or service becomes clearer, and the product is therefore refined/redefined. It's also the stage at which you start being an employer, with all the teething problems that may bring. And however well you have planned your business, you're likely to experience the worst cash flow problems during this phase, as the limited size of the business means limited resources.

3 *Growth*

Most of the teething problems have disappeared by this stage. You have a definite customer database and a clearly defined product or range of products. You are looking at new markets, with sufficient experience, resources and confidence to expand.

4 *Changes in management control*

Growth means more staff, and more responsibility. Key tasks will need to be delegated; some business functions may be outsourced. Successful adaptation to this stage will require different skills – how to train staff, how to delegate, how to make sure accurate management information is still available.

(*Source: Starting and Growing Your Own Business – Entrepreneurial Management,* Nick Morris and Bridget Rosewell, City University Business School)

Implications of growth

What are the implications of growth?

It's certainly important to understand the practical implications of growth. If you do not look at all the implications, there is a genuine risk that your cash flow and budgeting will not be accurate. An increase in demand for your products may result in:

- increased staff levels – requiring more training, and the introduction of reporting lines and management structures;
- the need for new premises – to house increased production or a second branch of the business;
- a further increase in sales – to fund the increase in staffing or new premises;

- a decision to expand the market geographically – either to increase the national customer base or to export.

(*Source: Starting and Growing Your Own Business – Entrepreneurial Management,* Nick Morris and Bridget Rosewell, City University Business School)

For more details on staff issues, please see Chapter 8.

Premises

Where do most small businesses work?

If you really want to understand the implications of growth in terms of premises, it is useful to know where small businesses work. One way of answering this is to look at where people work. A considerable number of small business people work from home (making relocation more likely once the business takes off). Even if your small business is conducted in commercial premises it may prove too small once you begin to grow (see Chart 7.2).

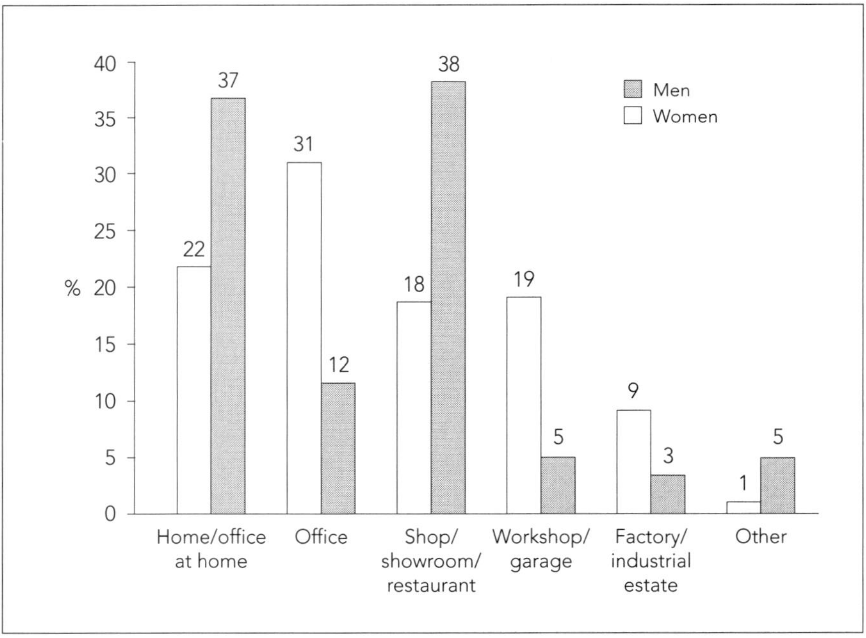

Chart 7.2 Where people work

(*Source: Starting up in Business*, Barclays Research on Small Business Characteristics, Barclays Bank plc, 1995)

Financial

What are the financial implications of growth?

You may well need finance on a scale that goes beyond grants, business loans and bank lending. This will take you into the realms of finding venture capital or a 'business angel' (see Chapter 4 for definitions and advantages and disadvantages).

Only 2% of firms seeking venture capital manage to raise it. The major handicap appears to be that small businesses are not investment-ready. Many entrepreneurs are either unwilling or do not know how to meet investors' requirements. Result: they are ineffective at convincing venture capitalists or business angels to invest.

(*Source:* www.clearlybusiness.com, 'Your business – how to attract a business angel')

Are you investment-ready?

You will have a better chance of finding informal venture capital if you can answer the following questions positively.

1 Can your business achieve significant growth over the next three to five years?

2 Can you demonstrate that your business has a unique selling proposition?

3 Do you have a strong management team?

4 Are you prepared to raise finance by selling some shares in your company to an outside investor?

5 Can you benefit from an angel's hands-on management skills in your business?

6 Are you prepared to forgo some flexibility in decision making and to justify your major actions to outside scrutiny?

You need to think carefully about your business and targets before you approach an angel. Work out how much money you are asking for. Be realistic. Don't ask for half a million when you only need £100,000. Develop a solid sales plan.

(*Source:* www.clearlybusiness.com, 'Your business – how to attract a business angel')

How do you find the right investor for your business?

More and more small businesses are turning to private equity investors as a source of long-term finance. But how does a business find the right individual? Here are a few tips.

1. Be certain that private equity finance is appropriate for you, and that you understand exactly what it entails.
2. Create a profile of the type of investor you want and the added value they should bring to the business.
3. Do you want a hands-on executive or a non-executive?
4. The business plan must be based on a sensible proposition and consistent assumptions. Wild projections do not impress!
5. Use informal networks, for example accountants, solicitors and personal and other business contacts, as well as formal business angel networks. Some charge – check out their success rates and fee structures.
6. Business angels see many propositions, are hard to convince and are under no pressure to invest. The first two pages of your business plan must persuade them to read on or ask for a meeting.
7. Be prepared to give a professional presentation of your venture. Focus on its innovative nature, the market growth potential, investor returns and why your team can succeed.
8. Investors will carry out their own due diligence – know your markets well and be prepared to provide detailed and defensible financial and market information.
9. Take up references on your investor, checking financial resources and business and investment experience. Will you require further investment? Does your investor have sufficient funds? Will additional investors be accepted?
10. Start searching early – finding the right investor can take many months. Don't wait until your cash position becomes desperate.

For more information, contact the National Business Angels Network on 0207 329 2929.

(*Source:* www.natwest.com, 'Innovation and growth – ten tips on finding private equity finance')

What tax changes result from growth?

On the whole, the tax situation doesn't change unless the type of business changes.

1 *Income tax*

(i) If you operate as a sole trader, you will pay normal rates of income tax on the whole of your profits.

(ii) If you operate as a partnership, the amount of income tax charged on your profits will depend on the income tax rates paid by the individual partners on their income.

(iii) If you are employed by your company, you will pay income tax on your salary.

2 *Capital Gains Tax (CGT)*

(i) This is the tax you pay if you make a profit of more than £7,100 (currently), after allowing for inflation, when disposing of a capital asset such as land, investments or property.

(ii) You can offset capital losses against capital gains when calculating your liability.

(iii) You may be liable to pay CGT on the sale of your home if you have claimed the cost of running it as a business expense.

3 *Inheritance tax*

(i) You will need to take note of inheritance tax if the value of your business is an important part of your estate. This tax is currently paid if your estate is worth more than £231,000.

(ii) Any assets you have transferred to someone else less than seven years before death are included in this calculation.

4 *Corporation tax*

(i) If you change to running a limited company, it is important to know that corporation tax is levied on a limited company's profits. Profits are total sales less allowable expenses, plus investment income.

(ii) The more common expenses are costs of goods and materials, wages and employer's NI contributions, pension contributions, marketing and advertising costs, premises costs, finance costs, cost of bad debts, capital allowances for the purchase of certain fixed assets, and a range of general business expenses.

Small companies making profits of less than £300,000 enjoy a special corporation tax rate of just 20% rather than the full 30%.

(*Source: Setting Up and Running Your Business*, Barclays Bank plc, 2000)

Operations

How do you avoid 'over-trading'?

One of the main implications of a growth in sales can be 'over-trading'. This is a common problem facing many small, growing businesses. The more sales you make, the more money you will need to spend on funding materials and debtors before you are paid for the sales. If your level of sales becomes too high, and you do not have the necessary working capital to support it, you may simply run out of cash. This can be disastrous for your business, and shows that a full order book is not the only thing to strive for. Even with a profitable business and a full order book, it is imperative to have enough cash available.

(*Source: Setting Up and Running Your Business*, Barclays Bank plc, 2000)

How do you protect innovation?

Intellectual property – the right to use for gain specific knowledge that makes your idea unique – is fraught with dangers for the inexperienced. If you have an idea that is original and inventive, and has a commercial or industrial application, you should seriously think about protecting it. Here are a few pointers for innovators.

1. *Keep your idea secret* until you have decided how best to protect it – disclosure could prevent it being patented.
2. *Patenting is not always the best way.* A confidentiality or secrecy agreement may be sufficient, will be cheaper, and will keep your idea secret, which patenting does not.
3. *Seek advice early,* whether from free sources (e.g. Business Links) or from professional patent agents.
4. *Keep records of all correspondence* and other information relating to your idea.
5. *A patent is worthless unless you are able to police it adequately* and can afford to take legal action against infringers.
6. *Consider taking out intellectual property insurance.*

7 *Explore all types of intellectual property rights* – copyright, design right and trade marks – not just patents.

8 *Patents work both ways* – ensure you're not infringing someone else's patent.

9 *DIY patent applications are unlikely to give you comprehensive protection* – use a professional patent agent.

10 *Patents last 20 years*. Remember, you have to pay repeat fees every year to retain protection, and the more countries you cover, the more it costs.

(*Source:* www.natwest.com, 'Innovation and growth: ten tips on intellectual property rights')

Will you need more insurance as a result of growth?

The cost of insurance is one more overhead for any business. You'll need to offset the effects of premiums on your current or projected profits against the potential impact of various unforeseen events.

One way to consider the issue is to imagine yourself faced with a particular problem, for example a fire, or theft of your computers, or illness of a key member of your team, or the loss of something in transit. This concentrates the mind on how vital it is to protect your business against that situation, whatever the cost.

Some insurance is compulsory, such as motor insurance and employer's liability insurance. The other forms of insurance may or may not be required because of growth.

- *Material damage* – protects buildings, contents, stock against perils (storm, flood, fire, theft, subsidence, burst pipes, etc.).
- *Business interruption* – provides cover for a reduction in turnover or loss of trading profits following damage to your business assets at your premises. Cover is available for damage at key suppliers' or customers' premises, or at neighbouring premises preventing access to your premises if these affect turnover or profit.
- *Public liability* – covers your legal liability to members of the public for bodily injury or damage to their property arising from work that you carried out in connection with your business.

- *Products liability* – covers your legal liability to members of the public for bodily injury or damage arising from products supplied by you.
- *Professional liability* – covers your legal liability for professional errors and omissions while carrying out your business.
- *Key person insurance* – helps to protect your business from loss of profit if a key employee dies or becomes seriously ill.
- *Share protection insurance* – helps to protect business continuity by providing funds to purchase the business interests of a deceased or seriously ill partner or director.
- *Loan protection insurance* – helps to repay loans or personal guarantees if a business owner dies or becomes seriously ill.
- *Money/goods in transit insurance* – covers losses to specified limits. 'In transit' covers carriage of goods by own vehicles, by carrier or by other means.

(*Source: Setting Up and Running Your Business*, Barclays Bank plc, 2000)

Franchises

One possible way to expand is to franchise out your business idea to willing franchisees. This will require a great deal of preparation, but it is well worth considering.

What are the advantages to the franchisor?

If you are considering establishing franchises, what are the benefits?

- The system gives franchisors the ability to expand an existing successful business more rapidly than by using their own capital.
- Day-to-day administrative/staffing problems sometimes associated with company-owned chains are greatly reduced.
- The franchisor gains wider buying opportunities, and is in a better position to acquire national accounts.

(*Source: The Two Partners of Franchising*, Peter Stern, *Franchise World Directory*, 1998)

What are the drawbacks to the franchisor?

This sounds so rosy, but there have to be drawbacks. What are they? Standards of product and service have to be maintained – if one outlet fails, it can do irreparable damage to the whole chain – and communications may become a problem. The secret of success is to select franchisees with care.

(*Source: The Two Partners of Franchising*, Peter Stern, *Franchise World Directory*, 1998)

What factors should a prospective franchisor consider?

The franchisor's eight key success factors

1. Is there sufficiently wide-scale market demand?
2. Is the product/service competitive and franchisable?
3. What, if any, is the competition?
4. Has the product got staying power or is it a passing fad?
5. Can a distinctive, attractive image be created?
6. Can a simple framework be established?
7. Can effective controls be established?
8. Is there sufficient depth of management to recruit franchisees and to lead and develop the franchise?

If the answers are all positive, then at least one pilot scheme should be launched and run for a minimum of 12 months. In many cases, it would be wiser to run several pilot schemes in tandem for a longer period.

(*Source: The Two Partners of Franchising*, Peter Stern, *Franchise World Directory*, 1998)

What preparations do you need to make for a successful franchise?

- A well-written prospectus
- Protection of intellectual property rights through registered trade marks and copyrights.
- Drawing up of a franchise contract to include licensing, terms, fees, rights and advertising policy.

(*Source: The Two Partners of Franchising*, Peter Stern, *Franchise World Directory*, 1998)

How much will it cost to establish a franchise?

To get to breakeven stage might take £75,000–£100,000; a major operator might exceed £250,000.

(*Source: The Two Partners of Franchising*, Peter Stern, *Franchise World Directory*, 1998)

How can a franchisor expand abroad?

There are several options:

- direct franchising;
- establishing a subsidiary in each country which then sells franchises;
- expansion via company-owned outlets;
- sale of a national or regional licence to someone abroad, allowing that person to develop the franchise.

The fourth option is the most popular. The franchise should always be pilot tested in each new country.

(*Source: The Two Partners of Franchising*, Peter Stern, *Franchise World Directory*, 1998)

How widespread is franchising?

If you're thinking of getting into franchising, it's worth knowing how mainstream it is nowadays.

- Annual sales relating to franchising in the UK total £6.4 billion.
- 541 business-format franchisors have created 26,800 separate businesses, and more than 264,000 people are employed in franchising.
- 94% of franchisees claim profitability.

(*Source: 1997 NatWest/BFA Franchise Survey*, NatWest UK and the British Franchise Association)

For more details on franchising, see Chapter 4.

New suppliers

All businesses have suppliers, if only for office stationery. When you decide to grow, it inevitably has an impact on your supplier relationships. The Small Business Research Trust undertook a survey which found that respondents emphasised the importance of working closely with suppliers, actively managing the relationship.

How does your company learn about new suppliers?

Most businesses are at both ends of the supply business – they are supplier and purchaser. If you are seeking to supply, it helps to know the best way to approach other companies. If you are expanding your purchasing, it is worth looking at how other companies learn about new suppliers.

How do you learn about your suppliers? Word of mouth, through advertising, or through direct mail? Bear in mind the breadth of supplies that the average business requires. Supply proves to be a people business – the most common sources of information are personal recommendation and contact by salespeople (see Table 7.3).

Table 7.3 Finding suppliers

Source of information	Percentage
Personal recommendation	51
Salespeople visiting/telephoning	49
Media advertising	19
Direct mail	18
Other	9

- Other methods include trade shows and reference books.
- Retailers and wholesalers rely more than other sectors on visits by salespeople (65%).
- Business services and manufacturing are more likely to rely on personal recommendation.

Business services seemed to be the most receptive sector to direct mail approaches.

(*Source: Quarterly Small Business Management Report*, No. 1, Vol. 2, 1994, Lloyds Bank/Small Business Research Trust)

Does your company check the financial status of its new suppliers?

If you do, you are unusual. While a supplier's failure can have a drastic negative effect on a firm, few firms seem to take the trouble to vet their suppliers' financial status by, for example, using a credit reference agency.

- Only 16% of respondents said they checked supplier status.

(*Source: Quarterly Small Business Management Report, No. 1, Vol. 2*, 1994, Lloyds Bank/Small Business Research Trust)

How many suppliers does your firm have?

The average small firm seems to have a surprisingly large number of suppliers – about 80 on average. Broken down into categories, these are shown in Table 7.4.

Table 7.4 Categories of suppliers

Supplier type	Average number
Goods/services for resale	31
Components/raw materials	21
Transport and storage	4
Office suppliers/equipment	3
Other equipment/capital goods	5
Financial services	3
Other	11

(*Source: Quarterly Small Business Management Report, No. 1, Vol. 2*, 1994, Lloyds Bank/Small Business Research Trust)

Do you stick with the same suppliers?

Growth might mean rethinking your supplier strategy. Do firms chop and change frequently? Overall, the average length of time with a supplier is six years, suggesting that firms stay loyal to good suppliers. Larger, older firms stay with their suppliers for longer (see Table 7.5).

Table 7.5 Staying loyal to suppliers

Supplier type	Average number of years
Goods/services for resale	6.3
Components/raw materials	6.2
Transport and storage	5.5
Office suppliers/equipment	4.9
Other equipment/capital goods	5.1
Financial services	8.2
Other	8.2

(*Source: Quarterly Small Business Management Report, No. 1, Vol. 2,* 1994, Lloyds Bank/Small Business Research Trust)

Why do small firms stay loyal to their suppliers?

Why do firms stay loyal to their suppliers, despite the challenges of growth? Is it because the suppliers provide excellent service? The answer would appear to be more complicated than that. A surprisingly small percentage of small firms rated their suppliers 'good' or 'very good' (see Table 7.6).

Table 7.6 Why do small firms stay loyal to suppliers?

Supplier type	Percentage of 'good' and 'very good'
Goods/services for resale	13
Components/raw materials	11
Transport and storage	14
Office suppliers/equipment	15
Other equipment/capital goods	9
Financial services	16

About half of respondents rated at least one supplier 'average' or worse. The reasons given for keeping such suppliers were those given in Table 7.7.

Table 7.7 Reasons for keeping 'average' suppliers

Reason	Proportion citing reason
Lack of competing alternatives	48%
Good quality	32%
Geographical proximity	32%
Good credit terms	14%
No time to find an alternative	9%

This suggests that while overall firms think there is plenty of competition among suppliers, the main reason why firms stick with a supplier they perceive as giving poor value is lack of competition.

(*Source: Quarterly Small Business Management Report, No. 1, Vol. 2,* 1994, Lloyds Bank/Small Business Research Trust)

Exporting

What are the most common reasons for starting to export?

Are you considering exporting? Do your competitors export? For many firms, the decision to export means embarking on another learning curve, so it will help to understand the reasons why firms export. The Association of British Chambers of Commerce looked at reasons for exporting in 1995, and discovered that the motivation was often a personal link:

1 expansion into new markets;

2 personal experience of a particular country;

3 visit overseas by a director or manager of the business;

4 personal contacts;

5 improving quality.

An unsolicited overseas order and an approach from a potential supplier came much further down the list. At the bottom came 'suggestion from government or trade organisation'.

(*Source: Internationalisation for World Class Strategies,* Association of British Chambers of Commerce, 1995)

How do you find out about overseas business opportunities?

For all you know, there could be customers in Portugal or Peru who are just crying out for your product. Chart 7.3 shows where other businesses go to gather information about overseas business opportunities.

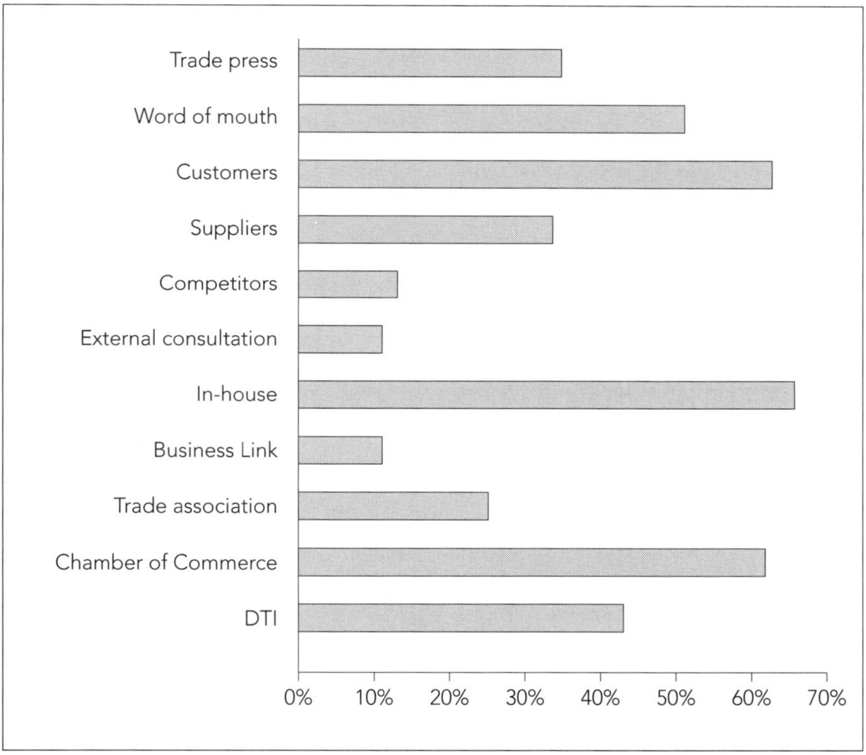

Chart 7.3 Source of information about export business opportunities

(*Source: Internationalisation for World Class Strategies*, Association of British Chambers of Commerce, 1995)

What factors influence your decision about target countries for export?

You may, of course, have decided on a particular national market because of personal links. Some respondents in this survey admitted that this was the case. However, the vast majority were prepared to consider several countries, but felt that several regulatory factors influenced their decision.

- Just over 50% felt that trade barriers would influence their choice of target countries.
- 25% felt that the cost of export credit insurance would influence their decision.
- More than 10% were concerned about intellectual property, the level and cost of regulations within target countries, and labour costs.

Regulatory factors were not as important to potential exporters as other factors – 80% of respondents admitted they were influenced by the economic stability of the country, while between 50 and 60% were concerned about political stability, market size and market growth. Language was a barrier to more than 30%.

(*Source: Internationalisation for World Class Strategies*, Association of British Chambers of Commerce, 1995)

If you don't export, why not?

The same survey looked at firms that chose not to export. More than 80% of these had considered it at some stage, but decided against it. If you find yourself in this category, it may be of interest to know why other firms have also rejected the idea. Do any of these reasons apply to you?

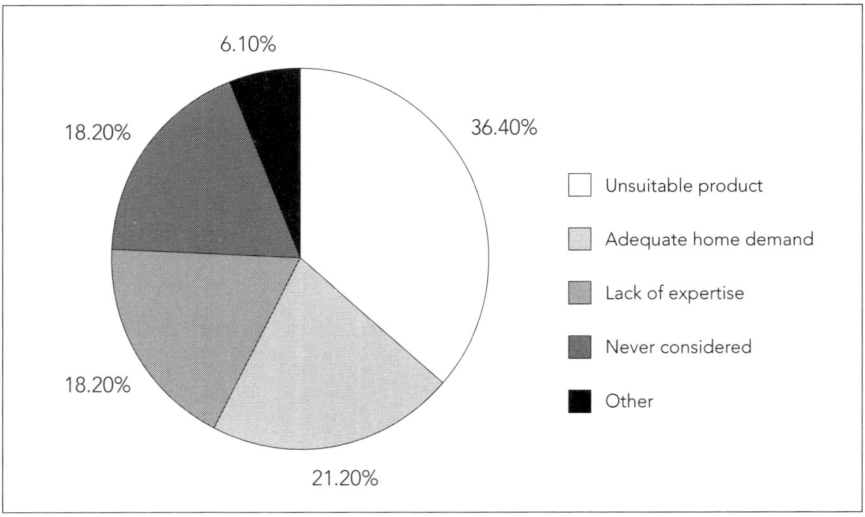

Chart 7.4 Main reason for not exporting

(*Source: Internationalisation for World Class Strategies*, Association of British Chambers of Commerce, 1995)

Managing change

What is the traditional approach to the management of change?

For many organisations, a typical change management programme follows a predictable pattern.

1. Senior management announces a new corporate quality/engineering/process improvement programme.
2. Company-wide half-day training workshops are arranged to bring everyone up to speed.
3. Cross-functional committees are quickly set up to meet and discuss 'the way forward'.
4. Resources are allocated, desks are duly moved, PCs are plugged in at a new abode.
5. And somewhere along the line, the reasons and focus for change get lost …

(*Source: Bulletpoint*, Sample Issue 2000, Bulletpoint Communications Ltd)

Why does change fail?

The causes of failure for corporate change efforts are varied, but the vast majority come from within the company.

- *Misunderstanding of what change is.* Change is a journey, not a destination. If change is viewed as an event, it will be just an event.
- *Lack of planning and preparation.* Management may suffer from tunnel vision, looking to the end result.
- *Change programme has no clear vision.* If you don't know where you are going, how can you expect to get there?
- *Goals are set, but too far in the future.* Enthusiasm will not be generated by a seven-year plan with no short-term wins.
- *The quick-fix option.* Change means more than a quality poster, a half-day seminar, or a management message in the company newsletter.
- *Poor communication.* Giving information gradually is risky – the grapevine may get there before you.

- *The legacy of change.* Years of streamlining and right-sizing may have created a sceptical, risk-averse culture.
- *'The way we do things round here.'* Having enjoyed success in the past, managers may believe that it is because of, not in spite of, the way they do things.
- *Fear of failure.* Will business suffer in the short term? Will the workforce morale wane? Worst of all, will we, as managers, be blamed?
- *Employee resistance or ill-prepared employees.*
- *Disregarding the domino effect.* If you implement a new programme, the reward system must be altered to match the new performance-driven environment.

(*Source: Bulletpoint*, Sample Issue 2000, Bulletpoint Communications Ltd)

How can you make sure that change succeeds?

Following a few basic principles can at least help ensure that change is not doomed to failure from the start.

1. *Be clear on what kind of change is required.* A major shake-up or a moderate process improvement? Slow or rapid change? Decide which is best from customer, competitive and company viewpoints.
2. *Plan, plan, plan.* Schedule steps that must occur throughout the process, setting out clearly defined objectives and responsibilities. Focus on detail.
3. *Pre-empt resistance.* Hook into what people have got to gain or lose by changing.
4. *Set short-term goals.* The war will be won by winning the battles along the way. Reward wins. Focus on improvement, not fault-finding.
5. *Prepare employees.* Tackle training and development prior to initiating the change programme to give staff confidence.
6. *Communicate.* Ensure communication is two-way – establish feedback sessions or suggestion slips.
7. *Set your sights on the specific objective.* For example, is the aim to be the first to the market with X product, or to gain Y market share, or to cut back on lead time by Z days?

8 *Prepare for the unpredictable.* Continued adaptation is a necessity. An organisation prepared for uncertainty is better placed to optimise the opportunities which change creates.

(*Source: Bulletpoint*, Sample Issue 2000, Bulletpoint Communications Ltd)

High-technology companies

Business incubation

The Enterprise Panel was set up by HM Treasury to identify whether there are greater benefits to be gained in the UK from the principles of business incubation. Its objectives were to reduce the failure rate in young technology companies, and increase the success rate of the small percentage of such companies that can hope to achieve substantial growth.

The panel's report, *Growing Success – Helping Companies to Generate Wealth and Create New Jobs Through Business Incubation*, contains a variety of case studies that prove that the principle works. Incubators provide hands-on support in a 'hot house' environment where business innovation and growth flourish. The report also looks at how this successful principle can be extended.

What is business incubation?

Business incubation is a process or 'tool' which can deliver stronger new businesses, create jobs and produce firms developing new ideas and technology. Incubators (technology parks, centres for innovation, development agencies offering specific resources) offer a specialist service to selected groups of small firms – usually those with high growth potential. They can help develop fast-track companies that become real wealth and employment generators.

(*Source: Growing Success – Helping Companies to Generate Wealth and Create New Jobs Through Business Incubation*, The Enterprise Panel, October 1996)

What sorts of businesses use incubators?

The key features of successful client businesses are innovation, growth potential and quality or flexibility of management, rather than any association with high technology. While the type of technology being developed is relevant, the critical factor in incubator success is in selecting and developing those businesses which have the right management skills to deliver a product or process with a clear commercial edge and scope to grow. Such businesses can be and often are those using or developing high technology, but they can also be those which involve innovations in existing or even declining industries.

(*Source: Growing Success – Helping Companies to Generate Wealth and Create New Jobs Through Business Incubation*, The Enterprise Panel, October 1996)

How do incubators work?

There are a number of examples in the UK of *technopoles* – these tend to be science parks. Two of the more established ones are Aston Science Park and the University of Warwick Science Park. Their objectives are similar, although Warwick places more emphasis on technology transfer.

By offering good-quality accommodation and business support services, they aim to create and foster growth companies which will commercialise new and/or existing high technology, thus creating local employment and wealth. Aston and Warwick are both located on city council property, and development has been supported by the next-door universities and in the first instance bank finance (Lloyds and Barclays). Later developments have drawn significantly on EU finance.

Both incubators have identified finance for their clients as a key requirement of start-up businesses. Each has set up a scheme for access to venture capital, and made a priority of seeking access to EU initiatives and finance.

In terms of achievements, Warwick and Aston can point to the growth of the number of businesses, the number of jobs and the size of their parks. Each can identify a significant number of businesses occupying space on the park which have graduated from the incubator centre. The business profile of each local area has been significantly changed by the growth of the science parks and their development as regional foci.

(*Source: Growing Success – Helping Companies to Generate Wealth and Create New Jobs Through Business Incubation*, The Enterprise Panel, October 1996)

Technology transfer

What is technology transfer (TT)?

Technology transfer – exploiting your technology by licence or outright sale, and acquiring technology from external sources – offers technology-based small businesses an alternative way of commercialising their ideas.

(*Source:* www.natwest.com, 'Innovation and growth – ten top tips on technology transfer')

What are the advantages and disadvantages of technology transfer?

Potential benefits include:

1 Improved cash flow.

2 Rapid return on R&D outlay.

3 Reduced costs.

4 Rapid penetration of new markets.

There are two main disadvantages.

1 TT is a long-term strategy, not a quick fix. Objectives must be set and a plan constructed.

2 TT can be time-consuming and costly in the early stages. Commitment is essential, as is ongoing monitoring and control.

(*Source:* www.natwest.com, 'Innovation and growth – ten top tips on technology transfer')

How do you prepare for technology transfer?

Here are a few pointers:

- Intellectual property rights issues must be addressed before you begin.
- Keep a record of development costs from the outset. You'll need a realistic figure on which to build a negotiating position.
- Understand your target markets and use external expertise if necessary.
- Be aware of competitor developments and changes in the target marketplace. Check patent positions etc. to ensure you are not wasting your time.

- TT specialists are a cost-effective resource to assist in the identification of potential partners and in negotiations. Ensure they are specialists in the market/country or technology you're involved in, and that they have a track record of success.
- Think of the effect on your corporate and management culture. New technologies bring change and the need for new skills.
- Check out potential licensees to ensure they have the right technical, commercial and organisational strengths.
- Keep yourself informed of developments in your licensee market. Build close, long-term relationships with your licensees.

For more information on technology transfer, contact one of the Regional Technology Centres around the country or your local Business Link.

(*Source:* www.natwest.com, 'Innovation and growth – ten top tips on technology transfer')

Interview with an entrepreneur

Dr Chris Evans is a 'serial entrepreneur'. He has established 14 technology companies in a range of sectors and now has his own biotechnology venture capital fund, Merlin Ventures. Here are some key extracts from an interview with him.

- 'The motivation to move from the laboratory was to make money for myself rather than for others.'
- 'The key success factors for a technology small business are as follows – *money* and *management*. A brilliant team will attract money. Technology is important, but not the key!'
- 'The right people are those who deliver promises, overcome obstacles, are committed to the business, hungry for success and work as a team.'
- 'Selling technology products is difficult – you have to be tough, determined, imaginative and creative. You must get your product right first time – customers and financiers are pretty unforgiving.'
- 'There is no shortage of cash – the problem lies in quality of management, the projects and how they are presented to the sources of finance.'

- 'The proposition must be well researched and sold to potential supporters – management is critical. Bring in partners to establish credibility, be prepared to take advice from the experts.'

(*Source:* www.natwest.com, 'Innovation and growth: interview with an entrepreneur')

Best practice

Best practice benchmarking

What is best practice benchmarking?

Best practice benchmarking comes in many forms, but essentially it will always involve:

- establishing the things that make a difference, in the customer's eyes, between an ordinary supplier and an excellent supplier;
- setting standards in each of those things, according to the best practice they can find;
- finding out how the best companies meet these challenging standards;
- applying both other people's experience and their own to meet the new standards and, if possible, to exceed them.

(*Source: Best Practice Benchmarking*, Department of Trade and Industry, 1995)

Fit for the Future

What is 'Fit for the Future'?

'Fit for the Future' is the CBI's national best practice campaign. It seeks to encourage companies to work together and to share their learning. The campaign will:

- promote the best practice message more widely between organisations;
- network like-minded individuals and organisations to swap ideas;
- signpost companies to valuable sources of information and advice;
- help raise the profile of best practice activities.

(*Source: Fit for the Future*, CBI Campaign Literature, October 2000)

Why is 'Fit for the Future' important?

If British companies adopted only the average best practice levels of leading competitors, the UK's gross domestic product would increase by £300 billion. Jack Welch, Chairman and CEO of General Electric, understands the importance of best practice:

We believe companies that can learn, share that learning and act quickly on it, have a fundamental and sustainable competitive advantage. If you believe that, then nothing is more suitable for your intense support than the 'Fit for the Future' best practice campaign.

(*Source: Fit for the Future*, CBI Campaign Literature, October 2000)

How does the 'Fit for the Future' campaign work?

The 'Fit for the Future' campaign was launched in December 1998 by the Secretary of State for Trade and Industry and the Director General of the Confederation of British Industry (CBI). The overall strategic direction of the campaign is provided by a high-level steering group which includes some of the leading names in British industry, all recognised as champions of best practice in their own right. 'Fit for the Future' operates through a network of more than 50 partners – companies and intermediaries – that are committed to the aims and activities of the campaign. These partners include:

- companies which spread the message through their best practice activities, for example their supply chains;
- support organisations that actively promote best practice transfer via their products and services, such as seminars, national awards, accreditation schemes, and benchmarking programmes.

All 'Fit for the Future' partners share their best practice experiences at every opportunity.

(*Source: Fit for the Future*, CBI Campaign Literature, October 2000)

8

Staff

the questions

Human resource policy / 203

- What is human resource management?
- How do you apply human resource management to a small business?
- How can you improve your human resource management?

Absence / 205

- What is the average level of sickness absence?
- What is the average direct cost of sickness absence?
- What are the main causes of sickness absence?
- What are the benefits of monitoring absence?
- Do disciplinary procedures help to reduce absence?
- How many companies give return-to-work interviews?
- Do return-to-work interviews cut down on absences in future?
- How many companies reward good attendance?

The minimum wage / 208

- What is the law regarding the minimum wage?
- When are these rates payable?
- What are the penalties for breaking the minimum wage law?

Health and safety / 209

- Why is health and safety such an important issue?
- What are the most frequently asked questions about health and safety?
- What are the most common accidents at work?

Staff

the answers

Company directors

How does the law define 'company director'?

Along with the impressive-sounding title of 'company director' go some hefty responsibilities. If you become a director, you must carry these out by law, so it's vital to know what you should and should not do, otherwise you risk prosecution and even imprisonment.

You do not have to be called a director to be covered by the legal rules on directorship. Often in a small company there may be no formal agreement as to your title, but if you attend and vote at a board meeting, even if it is on a director's behalf, the law regards you as a director of the company. It helps to avoid misunderstandings if people have formally agreed titles.

(*Source:* www.clearlybusiness.com, 'Keeping it legal: company directors – What do they actually do?')

What do company directors agree to do?

- As company director you are expected to do your reasonable best for that company.
- You also owe your company 'fiduciary' duties, so you must always act honestly and with the best interests of the company at heart.
- If you have a specific professional qualification, you are expected to

have higher standards when you are employed in that area than someone who is not qualified. For example, if you qualified as an accountant you would be expected to have a better understanding of the company's finances than a personnel director.

- You can hold directorships of more than one company.

(*Source:* www.clearlybusiness.com, 'Keeping it legal: company directors – What do they actually do?')

What are a company director's key responsibilities?

1. *It is the directors' responsibility to prepare the company accounts.* You might delegate this to a firm of accountants or bring in a part-time accountant to do the job. Copies of the accounts must be submitted to the Registrar of Companies.
2. *You must not borrow from the company in excess of strict statutory limits.* Directors can, and often do, lend money to their companies – this is quite legal.
3. *You must keep up to date with the law as it affects your business.* This includes current Health & Safety at Work legislation.
4. *As an officer of the company, you are deemed to have authority to act on the company's behalf.*

(*Source:* www.clearlybusiness.com, 'Keeping it legal: company directors – What do they actually do?')

What happens when things go wrong?

Although you can and should be insured against liability for debts or 'wrongful trading', you can still be found personally negligent when things go wrong. Check the exceptions to your insurance policy. Generally, however, if a court is satisfied that a director has acted honestly and reasonably, it will lift any personal liabilities.

If, however, you act prematurely in advance of becoming a director of a company, you may be personally liable for any deals you enter into.

Directors often guarantee a company's overdraft. If you have to wind up your company, be careful to pay off the creditors before or at least in parallel with any bank loans or overdraft facilities so that you aren't seen to favour your own interests. Take independent advice before signing any such guarantee.

If you even suspect that your company is in financial difficulties and you go on trading, you can be prosecuted. This is known as 'wrongful trading'. If, on the other hand, you do all you can to minimise the company's losses, the likelihood is that the courts will clear you of liability. The correct course of action should be to alert the other directors and try to bring about a recovery, if necessary by calling in outside help.

Only resign your position as a last resort when you have tried all these reasonable means to avoid liquidation. You are not automatically barred from being a director of another company because one you used to work for went into liquidation. If, however, you set up another business under the same or a very similar name, you run the risk of being held personally liable for its debts, even if you are a limited company. You may be barred from being a director or controlling a company if you are prosecuted and struck off.

(*Source:* www.clearlybusiness.com, 'Keeping it legal: company directors – What do they actually do?')

Working methods

As your business develops, you will need to recruit help. Before you take on staff, however, it is worth looking at your company's working methods.

Do you really need someone in-house to do this job?

Could you buy in (or outsource) from an external specialist supplier, or do you actually want an employee? Design, product maintenance, IT, market research and payroll administration are just a few of the increasing number of specialised services available.

External specialist suppliers may find it easier to recruit high-quality staff than companies which use specialist skills only in a support role.

(*Source: Mind the Gap. How to Fill the Skills Gap and Improve Your Recruiting – A Guide for Small Businesses*, Department for Education and Employment, 2000)

Could you reorganise work to suit people with different skills?

You may be able to get the same results with fewer people, or find staff easier to recruit if you:

- use new, user-friendly plant, equipment and software;
- break down some skilled tasks into jobs which more people could train to do;
- give people the freedom to decide their own working methods – this can help take some elements out of the process.

You could also consider redesigning the product or service so that people with different skills can provide it:

- using standard or bought-in components to replace ones made in-house;
- replacing IT designed in-house with off-the-shelf packages;
- using new materials that people with different skills can use more easily.

(*Source: Mind the Gap. How to Fill the Skills Gap and Improve Your Recruiting – A Guide for Small Businesses*, Department for Education and Employment, 2000)

How do you make sure skilled staff concentrate on skilled jobs?

Routine tasks often take up time that you, or other skilled staff, could put to better use. Use your resources more effectively by:

- restructuring work so that specialist staff use their skills all the time;
- reviewing how you handle paperwork, inspection and supervision.

(*Source: Mind the Gap. How to Fill the Skills Gap and Improve Your Recruiting – A Guide for Small Businesses*, Department for Education and Employment, 2000)

Recruitment

To create a good team, you need to recruit carefully. So define the role precisely, take a systematic approach to finding the right person, construct an attractive package and a fair yet tight contract, and offer structured induction and training.

First steps

What are the first steps in recruitment?

The first steps are to work out how to 'sell' the job to potential applicants.

1 *Begin by writing a full job description.* A job description is as much a selling document to candidates as a checklist for you. So you need to define the experience you require and any other personal attributes necessary. It's often good to mention any additional languages that are useful but not essential.

2 *Sell the benefits.* The right pay package is important. However, responsibility, autonomy and self-development or training opportunities are also important to senior staff.

(*Source:* www.clearlybusiness.com, 'Managing people – how to find the best staff for your business')

How do you find the right candidate?

- The grapevine is often an effective (and cheap) way of finding the right staff, so tell contacts you are looking.
- If it's junior staff you require, contact your Training & Enterprise Council and ask about Modern Apprenticeships.
- Traditional methods also include advertising in the press. Make sure that you sell the benefits of working for you, but spend a lot of time filtering responses.
- Don't be put off by recruitment agencies' high placement fees. Many are open to some tough negotiation. Also think of the cost in the context of your time saved.

(*Source:* www.clearlybusiness.com, 'Managing people – how to find the best staff for your business')

Unless you already know a suitable candidate, you will have to contact your local JobCentre or careers office, or advertise. If you decide to advertise the position yourself, remember to include as much detail as possible about your business. State clearly how applications are to be made, and give a closing date. Remember, it's against the law to advertise a job and then select people in such a way that it discriminates against disability, a particular gender or race.

(*Source: Starting a Business – Taking a Closer Look,* HSBC Bank plc, 1999)

How do you screen and shortlist applicants?

Ask all applicants to fill in an application form (which you will need to design) or submit a full curriculum vitae (CV) (*source: Starting a Business – Taking a Closer Look*, HSBC Bank plc, 1999).

When shortlisting candidates, be ruthless. It will save you a lot of wasted time. Make sure you choose only five candidates at the most. Reject anyone who doesn't meet your full list of necessary skills and attributes, whatever else their attractions.

(*Source:* www.clearlybusiness.com, 'Managing people – how to find the best staff for your business')

How do you conduct interviews effectively?

Choose your degree of pressure. For example, a two-person, or more, interview panel is more demanding to test reactions under stress. Describe the role, the business and its aims briefly. Then shut up and listen carefully to the answers to questions such as, 'Describe a typical day/week at your previous employment.' Let the candidates reveal themselves.

1. *Check qualifications and experience*. Make no assumptions – check behind every claim. Ask for specific extra detail about previous jobs and school achievements. Things to look out for include any long gaps in the applicant's work record.
2. *Give practical tests*. Don't hesitate to give practical tests to assess book-keeping, numeracy or use of English. Candidates for secretarial positions should be asked to demonstrate typing, shorthand and dictation skills. Consider psychometric or handwriting tests for senior positions.
3. *Check previous employment record*. Ask how many sick days they have had in the past year; you can request a medical report if you wish.
4. *Hire the right person for the job*. It sounds obvious, but sometimes people find themselves hiring just because they like the interviewee or have a rapport with them. Look for people who complement you or your team and bring new skills.

(*Source:* www.clearlybusiness.com, 'Managing people – how to find the best staff for your business')

How important is it to follow up references?

References can give many indications about a prospective recruit. The Institute of Manpower Studies (now the Institute for Employment) researched employers' reasons for taking up references. The percentages in Chart 8.1 indicate the proportion of respondents who felt that the reason given for using references was a 'very important' one.

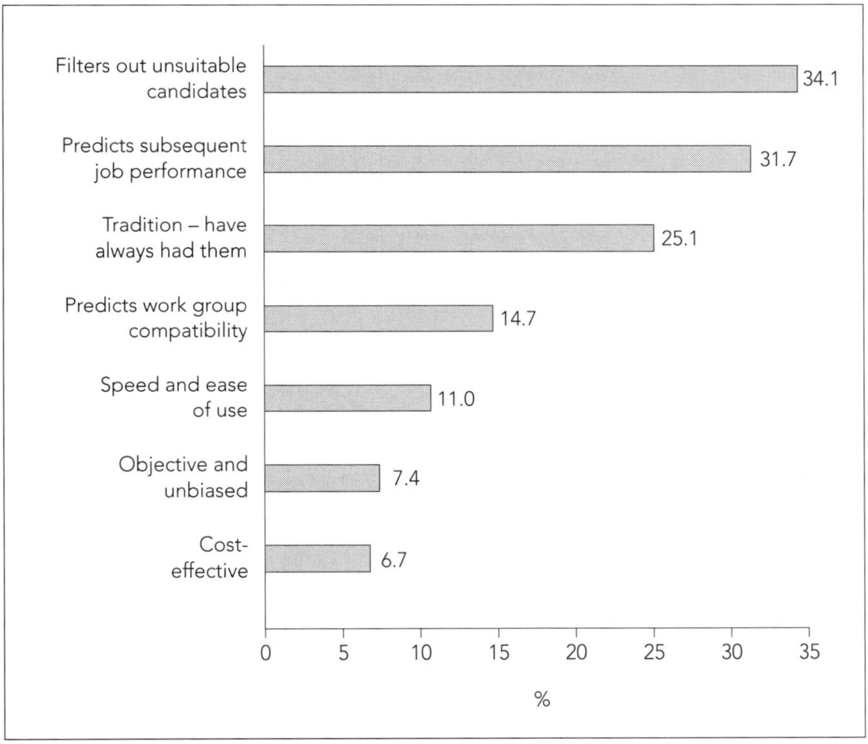

Chart 8.1 Reasons for taking up references

(Source: *Employee Selection in the UK*, Institute of Manpower Studies)

What questions should you ask a referee?

Examples of the kinds of questions you need to ask include:

1 What was the job title and exact role of the candidate before they left?

2 How long did they work for you?

3 What were their areas of responsibility?

4 How good were their administrative and/or time management skills?

5 How good were their interpersonal and managerial or supervisory skills?

6 Do they have any strong characteristics?

7 Do you remember any particular achievements or projects that stood out while they worked for you?

8 Would you hire them now?

Make any job offer conditional on references, and check the latter first to avoid embarrassment or worse.

(*Source:* www.clearlybusiness.com, 'Managing people – how to find the best staff for your business')

What do you need to know about hiring and firing?

You need to acquaint yourself with all the current legislation. You must take out employers' liability insurance to cover your business against any claims for injury and accident at work.

(*Source: Starting a Business – Taking a Closer Look*, HSBC Bank, 1999)

It is a criminal offence to employ anyone, full or part-time, aged 16 or over, who does not have leave to work in the UK and/or who is not entitled to work here. There are 13 types of document that are acceptable as proof of entitlement. They include a documented P45, a P60, a birth certificate issued within the UK or the Republic of Ireland, a work permit or a British passport showing that the holder has the right of abode or readmission to the UK. Protect yourself by insisting on seeing one of them. Temporary National Insurance numbers are not acceptable. Keep a copy of the document concerned.

(*Source:* www.clearlybusiness.com, 'Managing people – how to find the best staff for your business')

What should a contract of employment contain?

You must provide all employees who work eight hours a week or more with written terms and conditions of employment or give them access to written terms. This must be done within two months of starting work. The terms and conditions should give the following information:

- names of the employer and the employee;
- date the employee began work;

- job title;
- full job description;
- hours of work;
- amount and frequency of pay;
- sick pay arrangements;
- holiday entitlement;
- pension rights;
- disciplinary regulations;
- grievance procedures;
- period of notice required to end employment.

(*Source: Starting a Business – Taking a Closer Look*, HSBC Bank plc, 1999)

Recruitment practices

What are the most popular recruitment channels for different occupations?

People recruit in different ways for different jobs. So what are the most commonly used channels for different posts? The figures in Table 8.1 indicate, for several major recruitment channels, which posts were often filled through this channel. This is expressed as the percentage of vacancies of each type filled through the channel in question. (The figures are for 1992 as this survey is only undertaken every ten years.)

Table 8.1 The major recruitment channels

Percentage of engagements by occupation where first contact was through JobCentre	
Routine/unskilled	23.6%
Clerical/secretarial	16.0%
Operative and assembly	15.6%
Percentage of engagements by occupation where first contact was through paid-for local press	
Personal services	22.0%
Clerical/secretarial	22.3%
Routine/unskilled	21.1%

Table 8.1 continued

Percentage of engagements by occupation where first contact was through direct application	
Sales	27.5%
Craft/skilled service	25.1%
Operative/assembly	22.7%
Percentage of engagements by occupation where first contact was through fee-charging agency	
Managerial	11.9%
Clerical/secretarial	9.5%
Professional associate/technician	7.5%
Sales	6.9%
Professional	6.5%

(*Source: Employers' Recruitment Practices, the 1992 Survey*, Social and Community Planning Research)

How long does it take to fill a vacant post?

If you are in a hurry to fill a vacant post, the length of time that different recruitment channels will take will be crucial. Chart 8.2 shows average time (in days) from use of the successful channel to interview date.

What are the advantages and disadvantages of the main recruitment channels?

Speed may not be your top priority. Price may sometimes be your main concern, and your needs may vary considerably from case to case. So what are the advantages and disadvantages of the main recruitment the channels? (Table 8.2 also shows the percentage citing this as the main advantage or disadvantage.)

Table 8.2 Advantages and disadvantages of the main recruitment channels

Recruitment channel	Main advantage	Main disadvantage
Direct applications	Quality (39%)	Service (36%)
Word of mouth	Quality (64%)	None (29%)
JobCentre	Service (35%)	Quality (42%)
Fee-charging agencies	Service (44%)	Cost (71%)

(*Source: Employers' Recruitment Practices, the 1992 Survey*, Social and Community Planning Research)

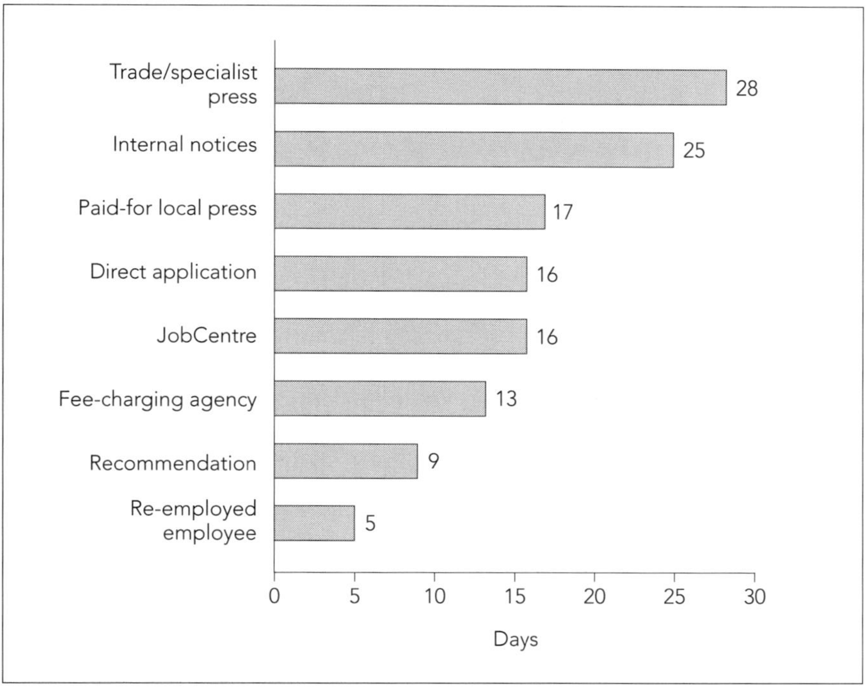

Chart 8.2 Time involved in different recruitment channels

(*Source: Employers' Recruitment Practices, the 1992 Survey*, Social and Community Planning Research)

Are small firms engines of job creation?

The government's decision to set up the Small Business Service and its continuing investment in Business Links and start-up schemes suggest that this is how they are perceived. Is this really the case? In the UK from 1989 to 1991, more than 90% of additional jobs created were in firms with fewer than ten employees, although such firms accounted for only 18% of total employment.

However, net job change over any given time period is the outcome of two distinct, separate processes. Gross new jobs result from new enterprises creating jobs and increases in jobs in existing firms. These processes are paralleled by gross job losses, due to firms closing, and reductions in jobs in those which remain in business. Small firms do create jobs, but more modestly than the raw statistics indicate.

(*Source: The Role of the Small Firm in the UK Economy: Hot Stereotypes and Cool Assessments*, James Curran, Small Business Research Trust Report, May 1999)

Do small businesses run by ethnic minorities suffer discrimination?

In 1997 Barclays commissioned research in recognition of the important role played by ethnic minority businesses within the small business sector. Ethnic minorities represent 5% of the UK population, yet around 9% of new business start-ups involve entrepreneurs from ethnic minority backgrounds. The research also found that:

- Asian small businesses continue to dominate the retail industry, and retailing accounts for 60% of all Asian-owned small businesses;
- black small business owners are the most optimistic in the country: 84% are optimistic about the future; 79% believe that ethnic minority small businesses will have an increasingly important role to play in the economy.

Yet not all the findings were positive – discrimination still remains a major concern. Nearly half of black small businesses (46%) and 29% of Asian small businesses have experienced discrimination in some form.

(*Source: Cultural Change and the Small Firm*, Barclays Review, 1997)

Do small businesses have a different recruitment style?

Much attention has been paid to the importance of local economic networks to small businesses. So is their recruitment style very different from the overall one?

- 62% of small businesses (fewer than 50 employees) recruit by word of mouth.
- As firms grow, the use of JobCentres, local press, agencies and national press increases.
- Preference for word of mouth was notably stronger in the South (71%) than in the Midlands and the North (57 and 53% respectively).

(*Source: Recruitment*, Lloyds Bank/SBRT Quarterly Small Business Management Report, Vol. 5, No. 2, July 1997)

Are small firms at a disadvantage relative to larger firms when recruiting new staff?

If you run a small business and feel that the larger firms can cream off the better staff, are you alone? No – but 70% of small firms overall claimed that they were not at a disadvantage. However, the majority of firms which felt they were least disadvantaged were in the South. The same firms made best use of word-of-mouth methods of attracting new staff (see Chart 8.3).

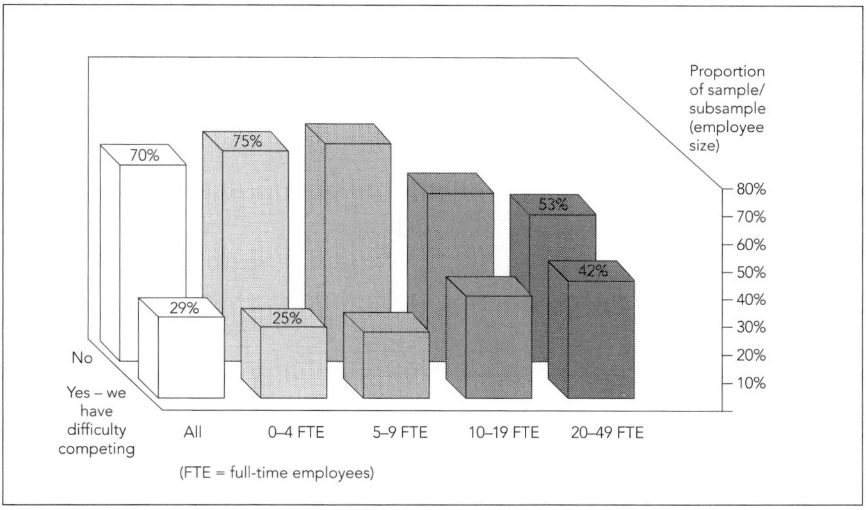

Chart 8.3 Competition between small and larger firms

(*Source: Recruitment*, Lloyds Bank/SBRT Quarterly Small Business Management Report, Vol. 5, No. 2, July 1997)

Do small firms experience problems in recruiting new staff?

If you are in the retail or distribution sectors, you are likely to find recruitment easier. Overall, the firms which experienced fewest problems recruiting staff were using local networking strategies (see Chart 8.4).

Skill shortages

Are small firms seriously affected by skill shortages?

Small firms were asked about any major effects of skill shortages (see Chart 8.5). The four main effects were, in order:

1 Having to settle for unsatisfactory employees.

2 Missing business opportunities.

3 Incurring extra training costs.

4 Vacancies remaining unfilled.

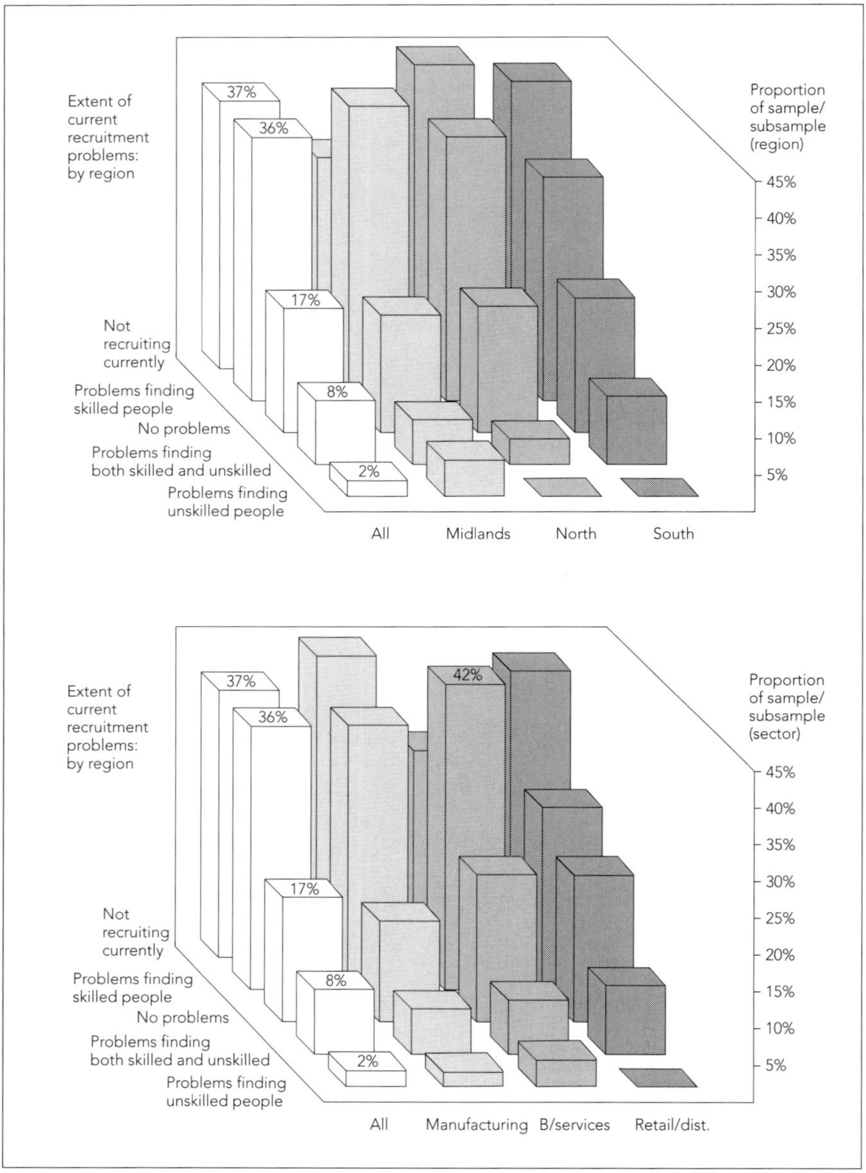

Chart 8.4 Recruitment problems

(*Source: Recruitment*, Lloyds Bank/SBRT Quarterly Small Business Management Report, Vol. 5, No. 2, July 1997)

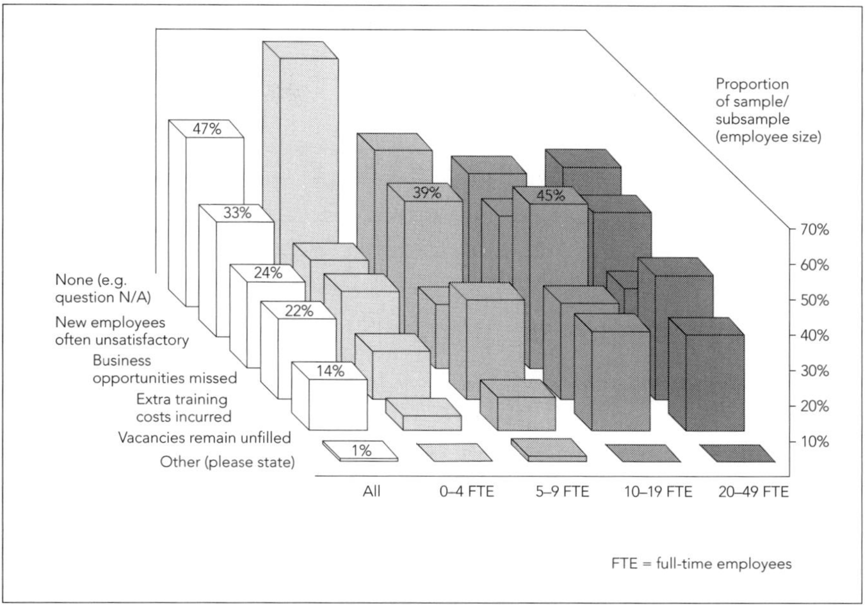

Chart 8.5 Main effects of skill shortages

(*Source: Recruitment*, Lloyds Bank/SBRT Quarterly Small Business Management Report, Vol. 5 No. 2, July 1997)

What are the reasons for skill shortages?

No doubt each firm can lay the blame at a different door. The Small Business Research Trust highlighted 'schools', 'colleges' and 'other employers' as the main reasons for skill shortages. Individual statements about skill shortages indicated particular concerns.

Basic English needs full attention at all schooling levels. Even graduates lack spelling, grammar and focused reading skills.

We are extremely worried about the quality of candidates. There is, no doubt, a decline in their educational standards and hence ability.

We have a very unsatisfactory pool of 16-year-olds to recruit every summer. [This is] not because 16-year-olds are getting less able, but as a result of school keeping even mediocre students on into the sixth form, and then on to university.

Most colleges in graphic design – our field – are out of date ... Probably the lecturers need regular in-trade refresher courses.

(*Source: Recruitment*, Lloyds Bank/SBRT Quarterly Small Business Management Report, Vol. 5, No. 2, July 1997)

Human resource management

Tax and National Insurance

Who do you have to notify once you become an employer?

Notify your local Inland Revenue office and your local DSS office as soon as you take someone on. Register with the relevant health and safety inspectorate (see below). In most cases, you will need to deduct some income tax and National Insurance contributions from your employees' salaries.

(*Source: Starting a Business – Taking a Closer Look*, HSBC Bank plc, 1999)

What paperwork is required for tax and NI?

Both the Inland Revenue and the DSS will send you all the necessary paperwork for registration, and provide you with instructions to calculate income tax and NI contributions. They will also tell you how and when these should be paid to the Inspector of Taxes.

Each year you will need to complete a P60 form for each employee. This is a certificate summarising pay, tax, and NI contributions. You will also need to fill in a P35 (a year-end payroll summary) and a P14 year-end return. The Inland Revenue will automatically supply you with these forms and will tell you how to complete them.

(*Source: Starting a Business – Taking a Closer Look*, HSBC Bank plc, 1999)

Do the costs of compliance with tax and NI pose a problem for many small businesses?

The cost of compliance with tax and NI can become a substantial burden for small businesses. Chart 8.6 shows the cost of compliance with income/corporation tax, PAYE and NIC by turnover band. The percentage of turnover is particularly high for those businesses with a smaller turnover.

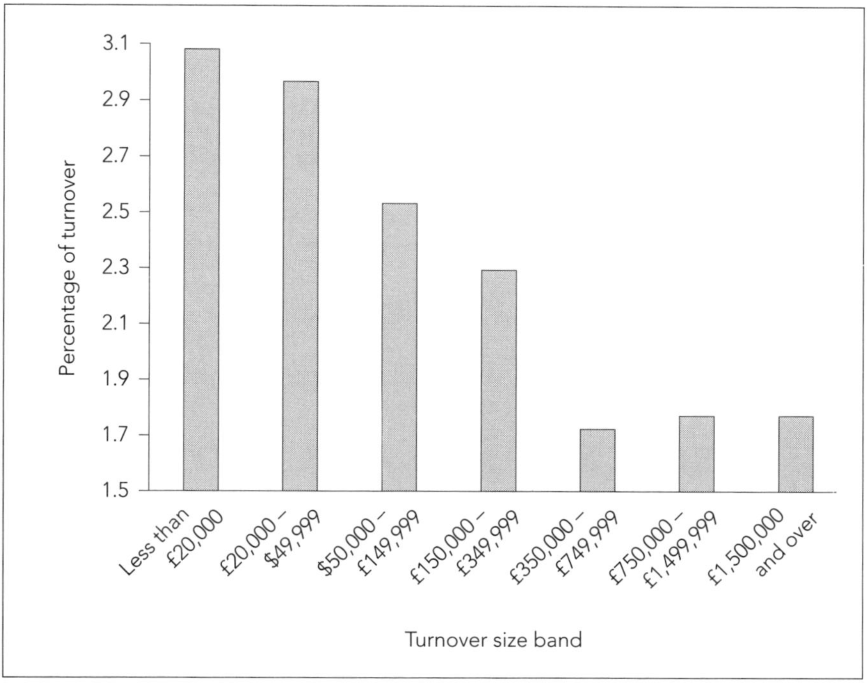

Chart 8.6 Average cost of compliance with income/corporation tax, PAYE and NIC as a proportion of turnover, by turnover size band

(*Source: Compliance Costs*, NatWest SBRT Quarterly Survey of Small Businesses in Britain, Vol. 12, No. 1, March 1996)

Human resource policy

What is human resource management?

Human resource management is concerned with the effective use of the skills of people. They may be salespeople in a store, clerks in an office, operators in a factory, or technicians in a research laboratory. In a business, human resource management starts with the recruiting and hiring of qualified people and continues with directing and encouraging their growth as they encounter problems and tensions that arise in working towards established goals.

In addition to recruiting and hiring, some of the responsibilities of a personnel manager are:

1 To classify jobs and prepare wage and salary scales.

2 To advise employees.

3 To deal with disciplinary problems.
4 To negotiate with labour unions and service union contracts.
5 To develop safety standards and practices.
6 To manage benefit programmes, such as group insurance, health, and retirement plans.
7 To provide for periodic reviews of the performance of employees, and for recognition of their strengths and needs for development.
8 To assist individuals in their efforts to develop and qualify themselves for more advanced jobs.
9 To plan and supervise training programmes.
10 To keep abreast of developments in human resource management.

(*Source:* www.bizmove.com/personnel, 'Introduction to personnel management')

Q How do you apply human resource management to a small business?

Human resource management is a balancing act. At one extreme, you hire only qualified people who are well suited to the firm's needs. At the other extreme, you train and develop employees to meet the firm's needs. Most expanding small businesses fall between the two extremes, i.e. they hire the best people they can find and afford, and they also recognise the need to train and develop both current and new employees as the firm grows.

It normally falls to the owner/manager to fulfil most of the personnel functions:

- assessing personnel needs;
- recruiting personnel;
- screening personnel;
- selecting and hiring personnel;
- inducting new employees to the business and providing for their training and development;
- deciding compensation issues.

(*Source:* www.bizmove.com/personnel, 'Introduction to personnel management')

How can you improve your human resource management?

By answering the following questions honestly, and then 'filling in the gaps' or remedying the problem.

Human resource management audit questionnaire

1 Does the business have a plan for forecasting long-term personnel needs?
2 Are there guidelines for hiring personnel, or are employees hired based on gut feelings?
3 Are there job descriptions for all positions?
4 What do employees like about their jobs?
5 What do employees dislike about their jobs?
6 Why do employees leave the organisation?
7 Is there an active training programme? Is it based on an assessment of where the firm is now or where it should be in the future?
8 Are a variety of training programmes available?
9 How is morale in the firm?
10 Do employees really believe what you have to say?
11 Are all employees treated fairly?

(*Source:* www.bizmove.com/personnel, 'Introduction to personnel management')

Absence

Absence can be a particular problem for small businesses. Losing two members of staff to illness is likely to have more effect if you employ five people than if you employ 50. The costs of absence also have a proportionately greater effect on a smaller business. So it helps to understand the patterns and cost of absence.

What is the average level of sickness absence?

Sickness absence is a fact of life for all organisations, but for some it can be a real problem. How can you tell if the amount of working time you lose every year to sickness absence is par for the course or a matter for genuine concern? The national average amount of time lost through sickness absence in 1999 was 3.4% of working time, averaging just under 7.8 days in the year per worker.

- The average length of time lost to sickness absence in 1999 was 9.2 days for full-time manual employees.
- The corresponding figure for full-time non-manual employees was 6.5 days' sick leave.
- Absence among non-manual workers is at its lowest level for five years.
- The results show that the UK has one of the lowest absence levels in the European Union.

(*Source: Focus on Absence Survey*, Confederation of British Industry and PPP Healthcare, CBI Publications, June 2000)

What is the average direct cost of sickness absence?

Naturally, the cost of losing an employee for a few days varies greatly depending on who the employee is. It is very hard to measure the loss in work not done, or delayed, and other indirect costs. Workplace absence cost British business £10.5 billion in 1999, according to the same CBI/PPP Healthcare survey. This averages out as £438 per worker.

(*Source: Focus on Absence Survey*, Confederation of British Industry and PPP Healthcare, CBI Publications, June 2000)

What are the main causes of sickness absence?

Just over a third of sickness absence has nothing to do with genuine ill health according to a May 2000 survey by the Institute of Personnel and Development. The IPD surveyed 1,684 organisations, together employing 2 million people, and found the highest absence levels were in the NHS and the food, drink and tobacco industry.

- The most common reasons for time off work were minor complaints such as colds and headaches.
- For manual workers, the second most cited problem was back pain.
- For non-manual workers, the second most cited reason was stress.

(*Source: IPD Survey of Sickness Absence*, May 2000)

What are the benefits of monitoring absence?

If you are introducing or reviewing absence-monitoring procedures, the first thing on your mind will probably be to reduce absence levels to an acceptable minimum. However, there can be many other consequences of the procedure that could be beneficial to your business, and which might be worth bearing in mind. The main ones cited by respondents to one survey were:

- reducing absence levels, naturally;
- raising awareness of the issue of absence control;
- increasing line managers' responsibility for management of sickness absence;
- ensuring consistency in the assessment of absence, and fairness in the treatment of those concerned, especially the genuinely ill.

(*Source: Sickness Absence Monitoring and Control – A Survey of Practice,* IRS Employment Trends, September 1994)

Do disciplinary procedures help to reduce absence?

When absence levels are high, you may feel that some action has to be taken. Taking disciplinary action is a possibility, but will it actually help? Most employers seem to think so, with 82% saying they believe that disciplinary procedures have a high to medium impact on absence levels.

(*Source: Counting Costs to Keep Competitive,* Confederation of British Industry, 1994)

How many companies give return-to-work interviews?

The majority of employers, whatever the size of the business, seem to think that return-to-work interviews are an effective way of controlling absence. How many companies actually conduct such interviews? Is it a standard policy or one that is used only rarely?

- According to one survey, 76% of organisations use a return-to-work interview after some or all periods of absence.
- In more than 90% of cases, this is conducted by the line manager or supervisor.

(*Source: Sickness Absence Monitoring and Control – A Survey of Practice,* IRS Employment Trends, September 1994)

Do return-to-work interviews cut down on absences in future?

An Institute of Personnel and Development book underlines the importance of return-to-work interviews. They enable managers to stamp out 'malingering', to understand the nature of a domestic problem if there is one, and to show that they care. However, the book also finds that ill health is still the major cause of absences – so the return-to-work interview will not solve the absence problem by itself.

(Source: From Absence to Attendance, Alistair Evans and Steven Palmer, IPD, 1997)

How many companies reward good attendance?

In a small firm, it may be much more appropriate to encourage good attendance with an incentive than to punish bad attendance. This seems like a logical approach to the problem, but is it a generally accepted strategy?

- It seems not – only 5% of companies actually offer a cash incentive for good attendance.
- In addition to this, however, some companies take attendance into account when calculating other bonuses.

(Source: Sickness Absence Monitoring and Control – A Survey of Practice, IRS Employment Trends, September 1994)

The minimum wage

It might have come into effect on All Fools' Day (1 April 1999) but the national minimum wage law is no practical joke. It applies to almost every employer, large or small, and ignorance of its provisions is not a defence.

What is the law regarding the minimum wage?

Every employee over 18 must now be paid at least the national minimum wage. The rules apply to full-time and part-time employees, to piece-workers, those who work from home, on commission or on casual work. And, since there's no upper age limit, the law applies to pensioners too.

(Source: www.clearlybusiness.com, 'Keeping it legal: the minimum wage – Are you paying enough?')

When are these rates payable?

These rates are payable for all the time that an employee is working or is required to be available to work and also the time that they spend travelling while 'on the job' and/or training. Absences, meals and other breaks do not qualify, nor does time spent commuting to and from work.

The only exceptions are those who are self-employed, non-employee directors, the armed forces and police, au pairs, volunteer workers and people in prison. In addition, apprentices under 19 are excluded, and those under 26 and on the Modern Apprentice Scheme run by the government are exempt for their first year. Some students and teachers on training courses and some other trainees on government schemes are also exempt. There is also a special pay rate which applies to some trainees. Maternity pay does not have to be paid at the national minimum wage, nor does statutory sick pay.

(*Source:* www.clearlybusiness.com, 'Keeping it legal: the minimum wage – Are you paying enough?')

What are the penalties for breaking the minimum wage law?

Non-compliance with an enforcement notice will incur a penalty, calculated for each underpaid worker for each day that an employer does not comply. In addition, fines can be imposed for committing what is a criminal offence by refusing to pay the minimum wage, or by wilful neglect or failing to keep records, or keeping or producing false records. Obstructing the inquiry team and/or refusing to answer their questions is also a crime, with the same maximum fine. The law is here to stay, and it is important that employers are not caught out.

(*Source:* www.clearlybusiness.com, 'Keeping it legal: the minimum wage – Are you paying enough?')

Health and safety

Why is health and safety such an important issue?

Getting hurt at work is not a pleasant subject to think about. The reality is that 300 people a year lose their lives at work in Britain. In addition, around 158,000 non-fatal injuries are reported each year, and an estimated 2.2 million suffer from ill health caused or made worse by work.

The mistake is to believe that these things happen in highly unusual or exceptional circumstances that never occur in your workplace. This is not the case. Some basic thinking and acting beforehand could have prevented these things from happening.

- Did you know that employers with five or more employees should have a written health and safety policy?
- Did you know that all employers and self-employed people have to assess the risks from their work activities?
- Did you know that employers with five or more employees have to record all significant findings of their risk assessment?
- Did you know that employers have to consult their employees or their employees' representatives on certain health and safety matters?
- Did you know that employers have to provide health and safety training for their employees?

(*Source: Health and Safety in Small Firms – An Introduction to Health and Safety*, The Health and Safety Executive, October 1997)

What are the most frequently asked questions about health and safety?

The Health and Safety Executive publishes 'Ten questions and answers for everyone'.

1 *What is health and safety all about?*

Preventing people from being harmed at work by taking the right precautions – and providing a satisfactory working environment.

2 *Why are there health and safety laws?*

Because health and safety at work is so important, there are rules that require all of us not to put ourselves or others in danger. The law is also there to protect the public from workplace dangers.

3 *Do health and safety laws apply to me?*

Yes. To all firms, however small; also to the self-employed and to employees.

4 *Who administers health and safety law?*

Inspectors from the Health and Safety Executive (HSE) or your local authority. For example:

- the HSE at factories, farms and building sites;
- local authorities in offices, shops, hotels and catering, and leisure activities.

5 *What do inspectors actually do?*

They visit workplaces to check that people are sticking to the rules. Mainly they help you to understand what you need to do. They enforce only when something is seriously wrong.

6 *Do I have to contact an inspector to get information?*

No. HSE operates a confidential telephone helpline called InfoLine: phone 0541 545500. Or you can write to Health and Safety Executive, Information Centre, Broad Lane, Sheffield S3 7HQ.

7 *Do I need to register my business?*

It's likely if you employ anyone – contact HSE or your local authority if you are in doubt.

8 *Do I need to have employers' liability compulsory insurance?*

It's the law if you employ anyone – and you must display the certificate.

9 *Do I need to display any posters?*

Yes, the health and safety law poster (ISBN 0 7176 13 80 1) if you employ anyone. To order a poster, ring HSE Books on 01787 881165.

10 *Do I have to report injuries at work?*

Yes, and other incidents. Reporting accidents and ill health at work is a legal requirement. The enforcing authorities use the information to see the big picture of where injuries, ill health and accidental losses are occurring and to advise on preventative action.

(*Source: Health and Safety in Small Firms – An Introduction to Health and Safety,* The Health and Safety Executive, October 1997)

Q What are the most common accidents at work?

The most common cause of injuries at work is the slip or trip. Resulting falls can be serious. They happen in all kinds of businesses, but sectors such as food and catering report higher than average numbers. It's a particularly important subject if members of the public use your premises.

The estimated annual cost to employers of all these injuries is more than £300 million, and insurance covers only part of this. Effective solutions are often simple and cheap, and can lead to other benefits.

(*Source: Health and Safety in Small Firms – An Introduction to Health and Safety,*
The Health and Safety Executive, October 1997)

For more detail on health and safety issues, and personnel issues in general, see *Quick Answers to Key People Questions* in the same series.

Motivation

If you want to employ a team of people, you will have to learn how to motivate them. To do this, you need to understand what motivates them. Although the psychology of motivation is fascinating, it is less important in business terms than the practical components of motivation: fair treatment, incentives, and personal development.

Does the average employee want to go to work?

Most British workers can't wait to get to work according to a 1997 IPD survey. They are also hard workers, who put in extra hours from choice.

- 57% of employees said they wake up in the morning and really look forward to going to work.
- Over half – 53% – said they had a lot of choice about how hard they worked, compared with 26% who said they had little or no choice.
- Many people do more than they are required to – for example, 62% help new workers, 50% stay late to help out when necessary.

(*Source: Employee Motivation and the Psychological Contract,*
IPD Employee Attitude Survey, 1997)

Do people feel they are treated fairly at work?

Fair treatment is a vital component of motivation. Encouragingly, the same survey shows that people feel they are fairly treated.

- A resounding 90% believe they are generally treated fairly.

- 79% trust their organisation to keep its promises to employees.
- 71% trust that managers will look after employees' best interests.
- 70% feel that managers have always or to a large extent kept promises about job security.

(*Source: Employee Motivation and the Psychological Contract*, IPD Employee Attitude Survey, 1997)

What occupational groups are most in need of motivation?

Motivation is one of the many issues in business that are relevant to all sizes and types of company. If you have to decide which of your staff is top priority for a motivation initiative, it would help to know who is most in need of motivation. One survey asked this question; Table 8.3 shows the proportion of each category identified by employers as being in most need of motivation.

Table 8.3 Employees in most need of motivation

Sales force	27%
Administrative and support staff	24%
Manual workers	16%
Supervisors/middle management	8%
Senior management/owners	7%

(*Source: Garnishing the Corporate Carrot, Marketing Week*, November 1990)

Incentives

What are the main reasons for operating variable pay systems?

Are you considering giving your employees a bonus, or shares in the company, or introducing an element of performance-related pay? Will this increase motivation? The CBI looked at the main reasons employers introduce variable pay systems, and discovered that they were, in order of priority:

- to motivate employees;
- to communicate business objectives;
- to retain employees.

(*Source: Counting Costs to Keep Competitive*, Confederation of British Industry, 1994)

What are the most commonly used variable pay systems?

If you do decide to introduce a variable pay system, you will be faced with the daunting prospect of choosing between the many schemes you could run. One thread which may help you through this maze is to know which are the most popular systems in use.

- Individual bonuses are common, being used by 75% of companies.
- SAYE share schemes are the next most popular – in use in 38% of companies.
- Discretionary share options came close behind, being used in 35% of companies surveyed.

(*Source: Counting Costs to Keep Competitive*, Confederation of British Industry, 1994)

Are different payment systems more effective for different goals?

An overall effectiveness rating may be helpful, but sometimes there is one particular goal that takes priority. The effectiveness of a variable pay system in another area may then prove to be only of minor concern. The Confederation of British Industry survey asked respondents to rate schemes' effectiveness on a range of objectives. The most effective schemes for each desired outcome are listed below (in order of priority again).

- More closely link pay to performance
  - Individual bonuses.
  - Spot award.
  - Team incentives.
- Encourage participation/empowerment
  - Spot awards.
  - Team incentives.
  - Profit-sharing share schemes.
- Communicate business objectives
  - Individual bonuses.
  - Skill/competency pay.
  - Discretionary options.

- Aid staff retention
  - Cash profit share/profit-related pay.
  - Discretionary share options.
  - Restricted shares.

(*Source: Counting Costs to Keep Competitive*, Confederation of British Industry, 1994)

Does team working help motivation?

If you want to introduce a team working initiative, is it likely to work better in some occupations than in others? The Institute for Employment Studies studied team working across a variety of occupations, and found it worked well across the board (see Chart 8.7).

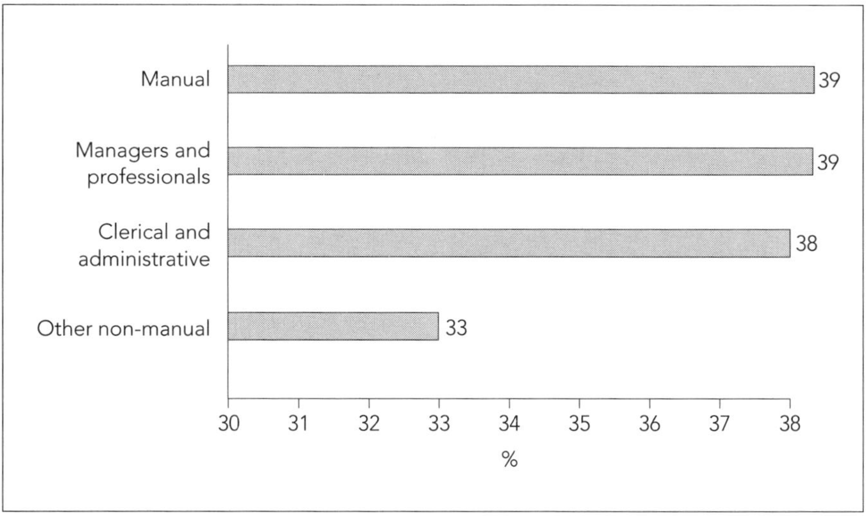

Chart 8.7 Occupations using team working

(*Source: Team Working and Pay*, Institute for Employment Studies, 1995)

Personal development

How common are formal appraisals, and how often are they used to plan training?

Most staff are evaluated in some way, but this does not have to be by means of a formal appraisal. Even if it is, there is still the question of how appraisals relate to training. If you are thinking of formalising your staff appraisals and possibly linking them to training, you might want to know how common this practice is. The figures below apply only to staff who have supervisors.

- 55% of employees with supervisors have formal appraisals.
- This varies according to job level – 60% of non-manual workers, technicians and supervisors had appraisals compared with 43% of manual workers.
- Of all employees having appraisals, 66% reported that they were used to help plan training.

(*Source: Employee Commitment and the Skills Revolution*, Policy Studies Institute, 1993)

How often are appraisals linked to pay?

An appraisal on its own will not increase staff motivation. It must be linked to increased training, or to some other reward. One obvious answer is to give bonuses and pay rises on the basis of appraisals. Do other firms do this? These figures come from the same survey but apply to all employees, with or without supervisors.

- 53% of employees said they received formal appraisals.
- 33% of these (18% of all employees) felt that these affected their earnings to some extent.
- 60% of those having appraisals (33% of all employees) felt that the outcome of appraisals could influence their job prospects, and hence their earnings, in the long run.

(*Source: Employee Commitment and the Skills Revolution*, Policy Studies Institute, 1993)

Do staff like objective setting?

Staff appear to have mixed feelings, though, about formal objective setting. The Institute of Personnel and Development reviewed this process in 1997 and found that 70% of the companies it interviewed rated it very or mostly effective. However, staff were not as enthusiastic.

- Only 45% of staff believe formal objective setting is very or mostly effective.
- 37% of respondents said that performance management is time-consuming and bureaucratic.

(*Source: IPD Survey of Performance Management Policies and Practices in the UK*, Institute of Personnel and Development, 1997)

Employee involvement

How prevalent is employee involvement in small firms?

'Employee involvement' is taken to mean an employee relations practice which management believes encourages employees' commitment to managerial goals and to the success of the enterprise.

Employee involvement is less prevalent in small firms (those with 25–100 employees) than in larger firms. For example, roughly half of small firms use some form of two-way communication between management and employees, compared with four-fifths of larger firms.

(Source: Employee Involvement in Small Firms, Policy Studies Institute, 1997)

On what issues should management consult staff?

If you want to open up more communication channels with your staff, you will have to decide what you are going to communicate. Chart 8.8 shows what issues are most commonly opened for staff consultation, together with the percentage of establishments in which managers consult on these issues.

How many employees take part in some form of employee involvement activity?

There are a variety of methods of communication and consultation – meetings, newsletters, suggestion schemes or informal communication. How widespread are the various kinds of communication and consultation? The Institute of Personnel and Development wanted to know how many employees take part in some form of more formalised employee involvement activity.

- Nearly half the workforce (45%) report that they take part directly in some form of employee involvement activity.
- These activities range from making suggestions to quality circles.

(*Source: Employee Motivation and the Psychological Contract,*
IPD Employee Attitude Survey, 1997)

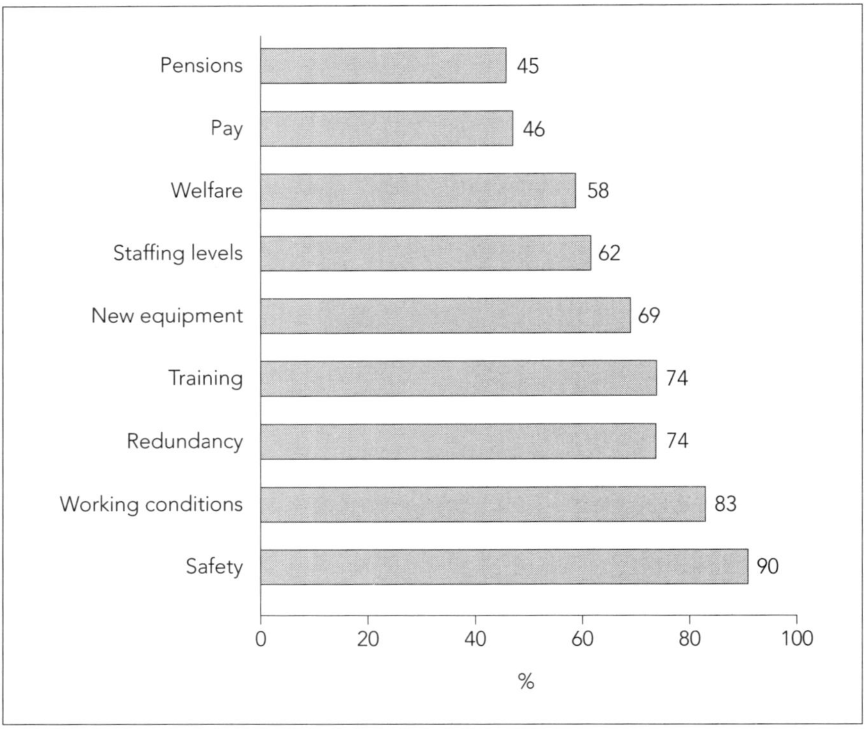

Chart 8.8 Staff consultation issues

(*Source: Communication and Consultation*, ACAS, 1990)

Training

What types of training do small businesses use?

The following figures apply to businesses with fewer than 50 employees, and are for 1998. Employers were asked if they had provided any of each form of training in the previous 12 months.

- On-the-job training was provided by 90% of employers with fewer than 50 employees.
- Some form of off-the-job training was provided by 79% of employers, mostly arranged at the location.
- Training leading to formal qualifications was provided by 61% of employers with fewer than 50 employees.

(*Source: Skills Needs in Great Britain and Northern Ireland, 1998*, IFF research for the Department of Education and Employment)

How much training does the average employee receive?

If you're operating on limited resources but want to provide enough training for your staff to feel valued, it helps to have a measure of what other employers are offering.

- Employees given training received an average of 11.4 days, equivalent to an average of 5.3 days for every employee.
- Two-thirds of those employees had a formal training plan.
- A similar number had a formal training budget.

(*Source: Skills Needs in Great Britain and Northern Ireland, 1996*, Public Attitude Surveys Ltd research for the Department of Education and Employment)

9

Getting out

the questions

Getting out

the answers

Making the decision

What are your reasons for giving up the business?

You may have a variety of reasons for giving up the business. You may have decided to terminate the business, or you may have decided just to terminate your involvement with it. The most common reasons for giving up are:

1 Financial difficulties.

2 To realise your investment.

3 Personal reasons, such as retirement, relocation, or disagreement over strategy with the rest of the management team.

Whatever your reasons, it is important to make the most of your investment. If the business is going to continue without you, it is also important that you make sure there is a reasonable deal for the staff you leave behind.

(*Source: Starting and Growing Your Own Business – Entrepreneurial Management,* Nick Morris and Bridget Rosewell, City University Business School)

Do small business owners quit because the demands of running a business are too great?

Research suggests that very few business owners quit simply because of the demands of running a business.

- Small business owners work an average of 51.5 hours a week.
- Three in ten put in more than 60 hours a week.
- The average small business owner will take only five days' holiday in their first year.
- Just under half (47%) take no holiday at all.

Over 60% of small business owners find running a business stressful, but the majority do not find it difficult to juggle their business and personal lives (see Chart 9.1).

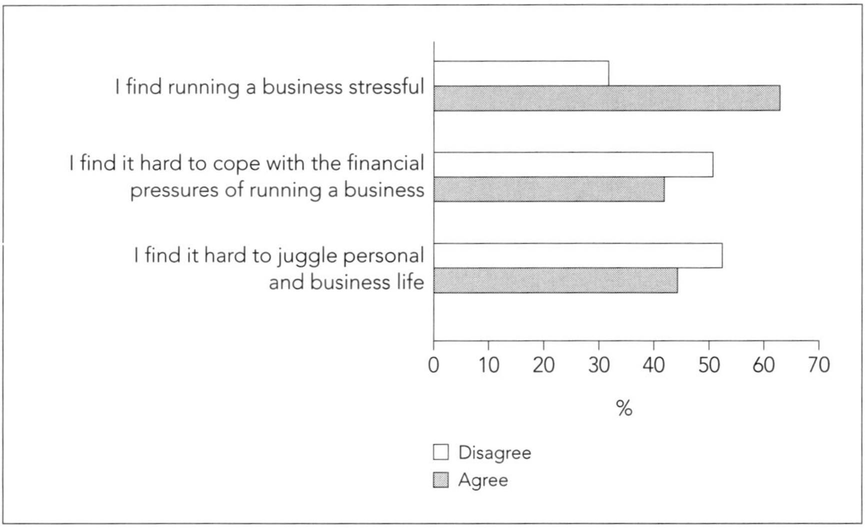

Chart 9.1 Coping with pressures of running a business

(*Source: Starting up in Business*, Barclays Research Review, 1999)

What are your options for getting out of the business?

Realistically you have two main options: to wind up the business, or to sell it. Winding up the business is commonly known as liquidation. The assets of the business are turned into cash to satisfy the debts accrued by the business. The business is then dissolved. You may have to take this path if your business has become insolvent. A voluntary dissolution is a more comfortable (and potentially profitable) route; if you are confident that you are able to pay off all debts, then it's better to take this option.

(Source: *Starting and Growing Your Own Business – Entrepreneurial Management*, Nick Morris and Bridget Rosewell, City University Business School)

Serial entrepreneurs

How many entrepreneurs have experience of running a previous firm?

It's worth looking at serial entrepreneurs (people who have set up other businesses prior to the current one) to learn from their business experience and to understand the reasons behind their decisions. There does appear to be quite a strong serial entrepreneur culture in the UK. Owners who have experience of running small firms have, on average, run two businesses prior to setting up their current enterprise.

- 13% of business starters have set up a previous business.

(Source: *Starting up in Business*, Barclays Research Review, 1999)

What did serial entrepreneurs do with their previous firms?

Some serial entrepreneurs run more than one business concurrently. However, a considerable number either sell the business or are bought out (24% and 3% respectively), suggesting that many sell the goodwill of a previous business to finance the next one.

Chart 9.2 shows what happened to serial entrepreneurs' previous firms.

Do serial entrepreneurs stay in the same line of work?

Owners who have previously run a small firm are just as likely to move into a different line of work (45%) as they are to stay in a similar one (43%). This may be because they are more likely to identify gaps in the market when they are closer to the ground running a business. Alternatively, it may be because they found the sector in which they originally set up was too competitive.

(Source: *Starting up in Business*, Barclays Research Review, 1999)

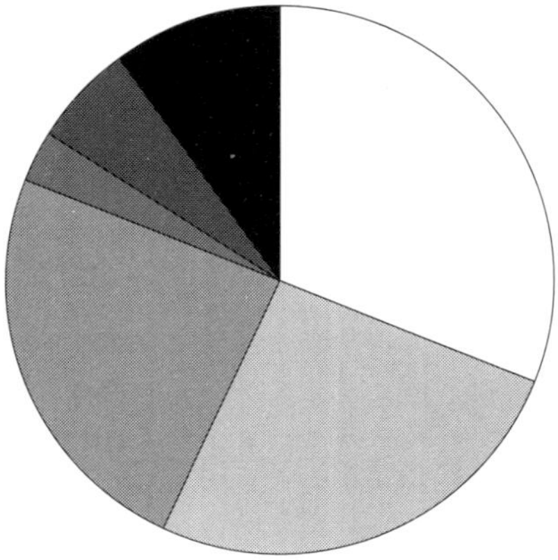

Chart 9.2 Fate of previous businesses

(*Source: Starting up in Business*, Barclays Research Review, 1999)

Insolvency

How many businesses survive insolvency?

R3 is the leading professional business recovery body. The company fills the role of a professional institute for the insolvency and business rescue profession; it also conducts research into insolvency.

R3's 9th Survey of Business Recovery shows that:

- Nearly one in five businesses survive insolvency and continue in business in one form or another.

However, there is little doubt that insolvency is a sizeable problem. Total liabilities in the sample are over £2.5 million, which extrapolates to £42 million throughout the UK, and total number of jobs put at risk through insolvency in the sample is over 31,000 – which extrapolates to some 520,000 throughout the UK.

(*Source:* www.insolvency.org, 'Welcome to R3's 9th Survey of Business Recovery')

Why do companies fail?

In nearly one in two cases, a company's insolvency was due primarily to the failings of the company's management. In the same number of cases, an insolvent company had experienced previous financial difficulty.

- In almost one in four cases, an insolvent business could have been rescued if the directors had sought advice earlier.
- But advice was sought at such a late stage that, in four out of five cases, nothing could be done to save the company by the time the insolvency practitioner had been appointed.

(*Source:* www.insolvency.org, 'Welcome to R3's 9th Survey of Business Recovery')

Are smaller companies more likely to fail than larger companies?

The answer would appear to be yes. Nearly nine out of ten cases in the sample had a turnover of less than £5 million (88.5%). Younger businesses are also more likely to fail – figures from the Federation of Small Businesses indicate that within three years of start-up, one in four businesses fails. R3's figures show that two out of five business failures occur in businesses less than four years old.

(*Source:* www.insolvency.org, 'Welcome to R3's 9th Survey of Business Recovery')

Legal processes

What are the legal processes involved with insolvency?

Insolvency proceedings are the formal measures taken to deal with company debt. There are many different types of company insolvency proceedings. Companies House produces a helpful booklet entitled *Liquidation and Insolvency* which gives a simple guide to insolvency procedures. Companies can, of course, be dissolved without insolvency proceedings. If the Registrar of Companies has reason to believe that a company is not carrying on business or is not in operation, he will strike the company off the register. Companies House produces another booklet entitled *Strike Off, Dissolution and Restoration* which outlines these procedures.

(*Source: Liquidation and Insolvency*, Companies House, www.companies-house.gov.uk)

How does voluntary insolvency work?

A voluntary arrangement is when a company makes an agreement with its creditors by proposing a 'composition in satisfaction of debt' or a 'scheme of arrangement of its affairs'. This means an arrangement, approved by the court, in which the company has formally agreed terms with its creditors for the settlement of its debts.

(*Source: Liquidation and Insolvency*, Companies House, www.companies-house.gov.uk)

How is a voluntary arrangement agreed and approved?

A voluntary arrangement may be proposed by:

- the administrator if there is an administration order;
- the liquidator if the company is being wound up; or
- the directors in other circumstances.

A meeting of creditors is then summoned; the meeting's resolutions are binding on all creditors who had notice of the meeting.

(Source: Liquidation and Insolvency, Companies House, www.companies-house.gov.uk)

Administration

What is an administration order?

This is a court order made to appoint an administrator to manage the company's affairs. Its purpose may be to:

- save the whole of the company as a going concern;
- approve a company's voluntary arrangement;
- sanction a compromise or agreement; or
- get a better price for the company's assets than might be achieved through a winding up.

(Source: Liquidation and Insolvency, Companies House, www.companies-house.gov.uk)

Who can petition for an administration order?

This can be done by the company itself, its directors, or one or more of its creditors. The administrator who is then appointed must notify the Registrar of Companies of his appointment, and advertise the order in the *Gazette* and in a newspaper in the area where the company has its principal place of business. The *Gazette* is published daily by HMSO and contains various statutory notices and advertisements.

(Source: Liquidation and Insolvency, Companies House, www.companies-house.gov.uk)

Voluntary liquidation

What kinds of voluntary liquidation are there?

There are two kinds of voluntary liquidation:

1 Members' voluntary liquidation (MVL) – this means the directors have made a statutory declaration on solvency five weeks before a resolution to wind up.

2 Creditors' voluntary insolvency (CVL) – this means the directors have not made such a declaration.

The liquidation starts when the members, in a general meeting, pass a resolution to wind up the company. This resolution must be published in the *Gazette* within 14 days of the meeting.

An MVL can be converted into a CVL if a liquidator decides that the company will not be able to pay its debts in full.

(*Source: Liquidation and Insolvency*, Companies House, www.companies-house.gov.uk)

Compulsory liquidation

What is compulsory liquidation?

Compulsory liquidation is when the company is ordered by a court to be wound up. The High Court, or a county court with appropriate jurisdiction, may order the winding up of a company. This might be on the petition of a creditor, on the grounds that the company cannot pay its debts. A company is regarded as unable to pay its debts if, for example:

- a creditor is owed more than £750;
- a creditor presents a written demand in the prescribed form;
- the company fails to pay, secure or agree a settlement of the debt to the creditor's satisfaction.

(*Source: Liquidation and Insolvency*, Companies House, www.companies-house.gov.uk)

Advice

Where can you go for help with winding up a company?

Staff at Companies House in Cardiff are able to advise on general matters. Companies House produces a series of booklets, and insolvency forms for all the above situations. If you are considering liquidation or insolvency proceedings, you should seek the advice of an insolvency practitioner or the Insolvency Service. The Insolvency Service can be contacted at PO Box 203, 21 Bloomsbury Street, London WC1B 3QW.

(*Source: Liquidation and Insolvency*, Companies House, www.companies-house.gov.uk)

Selling your business

How do you start the sale process?

Selling your business is not unlike the sale of any other product. You need to understand your product, convey its attractiveness to others, get to know the needs and wants of your prospective buyer and sell, sell, sell. As you are going to sell your business only once, it makes sense that you do it right first time. Once you have decided to commit yourself to the long, arduous process, there is a well-defined set of steps you can take to improve your chances of arranging a successful sale of your company. Questions you should ask include:

- Is the amount you eventually receive for your company more important than who buys it?
- Do you want to retain the autonomous integrity of the company?
- Would it matter if an acquirer moved your business?
- Do you feel any obligations towards your employees?

After setting your goals, you need to develop a strategy to achieve them. A well-conceived strategy will force you to define the types of acquirers you want to approach, the method of sale you want to employ and the timetable you want to set to accomplish the sale.

(*Source:* www.clearlybusiness.com 'Selling your business: the sales process')

How do you prepare for the sale?

It is important that a complete descriptive memorandum is prepared on your company before going to market. A memorandum provides potential acquirers with the relevant data they need to make a rational, informed decision on whether or not to pursue the acquisition of your company and also indicates a sincere and professional approach to the sale process.

- Avoid going into excruciating detail on all possible aspects of your operations in the descriptive memorandum. Given most people's short attention span, this could be as big a mistake as not having a prospectus on your company.
- Misleading, inaccurate or incomplete data included in the memorandum will undermine your credibility and could eventually jeopardise any deal that you negotiate.
- You must provide a detailed analysis of your company, including a list of your largest customers and suppliers (by volume), your employees (by compensation and length of service) and your facilities. Any potential acquirer will demand this information before bidding on your company, so it makes sense to provide it to them at the outset.

(*Source:* www.clearlybusiness.com, 'Selling your business: the sales process')

How long does the average sale take?

A typical sale, if properly conducted, should take from six to nine months to complete. Establish an anticipated schedule at the outset and continually monitor your progress against this timetable.

Markets are constantly changing and so too might your company's operating performance or prospects. You must be nimble enough to adapt your plans with changing conditions. By taking a planned but flexible approach to selling your company, you will go a long way towards ensuring a successful deal...

(*Source:* www.clearlybusiness.com, 'Selling your business: the sales process)

How do you close the deal?

Once you have negotiated a price, structure and terms, and have then codified your agreement in a letter of intent, you are on the home stretch. However, you still have to preside over the prospective buyer's due diligence process and negotiate and execute the purchase agreement. The two processes generally occur simultaneously, primarily because it is in everyone's best interest to close on an agreed deal as soon as possible.

But there are some key points to remember about the purchase agreement.

1 'Due diligence' refers to the process by which a prospective buyer both verifies all previously provided data and undertakes a full review of all other relevant information prior to legally committing to a deal. While each prospective buyer will want to examine differing aspects of your business in differing degrees of detail, due diligence enquiries generally focus on the following:
   - corporate organisation and ownership;
   - products, including the manufacturing process and markets;
   - customers and suppliers;
   - sales and marketing;
   - facilities and equipment;
   - management and employees;
   - reporting and control systems;
   - financial results and balance sheet.

2 A purchase agreement is a legal document that sets out all of the agreements and understandings between the buyer and the seller of a business. It not only covers the price, terms and structure of the deal but also details all the other legal and financial aspects of the transaction. Most purchase agreements cover the following areas:
   - the price, terms and structure of the deal;
   - representations and warranties, which refer to binding claims each party makes with respect to their company and the transaction;
   - covenants, which outline the obligations of each party during the period between the signing and the closing;
   - conditions to the closing – that is, the conditions under which either the buyer or the seller has the right to terminate the agreement without being liable for damages;
   - indemnification, which establishes the liability of each party for problems that are discovered after closing.

The closing of the deal is the actual event in which a transaction is consummated through the execution of all documentation and the transfer of title or stock in exchange for a like transfer of funds. In most instances, the closing day will be as hectic and chaotic as any you will ever have encountered. Every group that is a party to the deal will be at the closing, along with their respective advisors.

(*Source:* www.clearlybusiness.com, 'Selling your company: closing the deal')

How do you make sure the sale runs smoothly?

Well in advance of the closing day, your legal advisor should provide you with the litany of documents you will need to bring to the closing, including the stock certificates, Articles of Incorporation, corporate minute book, and tax records. You also need to give yourself and your advisors adequate time to compile and prepare all necessary exhibits, schedules and other information you will need for the purchase document.

It is important to remember that you are not just executing documents at the closing; you are also transferring your entire business to another party. It is advisable to meet with your legal team a few times before the actual closing so that you are familiar with all of the various documents and your obligations at the closing.

(*Source:* www.clearlybusiness.com, 'Selling your company: closing the deal')

Retirement

Unless you decide to sell the business or wind it up, you will eventually be faced with another issue – retirement. Planning is crucial here: an unplanned retirement can cause succession and financial problems.

What are the main pitfalls to avoid when retiring?

Good retirement planning requires careful consideration of all the following:

- the form of your business – if you are a sole trader and intend to pass the business on to the family, look carefully at capital gains tax issues. If the company is a partnership, retirement planning will need to be joint;

- pension planning;
- tax planning – as well as capital gains tax liabilities, you may incur corporation tax and income tax if assets and funds are removed from the company.

(*Source: Starting and Growing Your Own Business – Entrepreneurial Management*, Nick Morris and Bridget Rosewell, City University Business School)

How many businesses are passed to a family member on retirement?

It is estimated that nearly three-quarters of all UK businesses are family owned. BDO Stoy Hayward carried out research into the length of family business life cycles, and discovered that the average life cycle of a family business is 24 years – which coincides with the average tenure of one owner.

- Only 30% of family businesses in the UK reach a second generation.
- Less than two-thirds of those businesses survive through the second generation.
- Only 13% survive through the third generation.

(*Source:* www.ffi.org, 'Facts on family business in the UK')

How often is the succession planned?

If you are trying to make sure that your business is in safe hands when you retire, are you among the minority or are succession planning issues treated carefully by most small businesses? Research into family businesses by the Centre for Family Enterprise in Glasgow showed a fairly even split.

- All family businesses surveyed whose principal intends to retire within the next five years were asked about their succession planning.
- 50% had nominated a successor to the owner/manager.

(*Source:* www.ffi.org, 'Facts on family business in the UK')

Do small business owners regret setting up in business?

Nine out of ten small business owners do not regret setting up in business. For many, the most important piece of advice they could give to others thinking of doing it is: 'Go for it.'

(*Source: Starting up in Business*, Barclays Research Review, 1999)

appendix 1

How to read statistics

This book is packed with statistical figures – percentages, average marks out of ten, tables, graphs, charts – and after a while it can become difficult to take in so much information in this form. There are also various conventions and standard formulae that are used to analyse and present such statistics. So it seemed worthwhile to give brief descriptions and explanations of these in case you haven't come across them before, or not for a long time, and might benefit from some clarification of what it all actually means.

This appendix, then, is intended to clarify some of the types of statistical data that can be found in the *Quick Answers* series. Of course, it may come in handy any time that you are presented with some statistics and would like to refresh your memory of what exactly they are telling you, or not telling you. It is also intended to clear up some of the confusions that can be caused by the use of technical terms, particular formats and so on.

Charts, graphs and matrices

There are many charts included in this book, and each has been picked to present the data in the most convenient way. It is therefore worth mentioning the particular properties and uses of each chart, so that you will know at a glance what is being presented.

Bar chart

This is one of the most common types of chart. It shows figures (usually quantity or percentage) for various items. For example, it might show what percentage of people in an office have each of the following items of fruit in their fruit bowl at home:

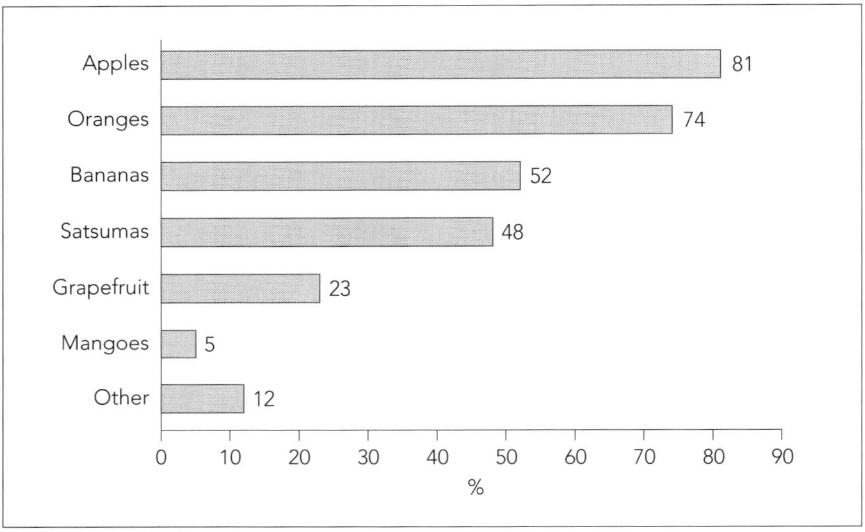

As with this chart, the highest number (and hence longest bar) should come at the top, with the others decreasing in order. Certain categories are exceptions to this rule, by always coming at the end. The most common of these are 'other' and 'none' (which may occur, for instance, in a survey of what the people in the office had for breakfast). The figures in this example do not add up to 100%, of course, since many people have more than one type of fruit in their fruit bowl.

Column chart

This looks very similar to a bar graph, but the blocks go up rather than across. Despite this similarity, the column chart is used in a significantly different way from a bar chart. It is used in instances where the different columns progress along a sequence. Typical examples of this are when the figures apply to different times (1990, 1991, 1992, etc.), different scores (strongly agree, agree, not sure, disagree, strongly disagree), and different age groups (16–19, 20–23, 24–35, 36–39). This last example is important since the groupings given are not equal. The column for people aged 24–35 is likely to be much larger than for the other groupings, since it covers a much wider range of people. This sort of distortion is worth looking out for in general (although in this series we have avoided it wherever possible), and has a certain amount of effect every time there is an open-ended group (e.g. age 40+).

Since the different categories in a column chart follow a sequence, the relative heights become much more important. For instance, let's see a graph of the number of people in the office with apples in their fruit bowls for each of the last four weeks.

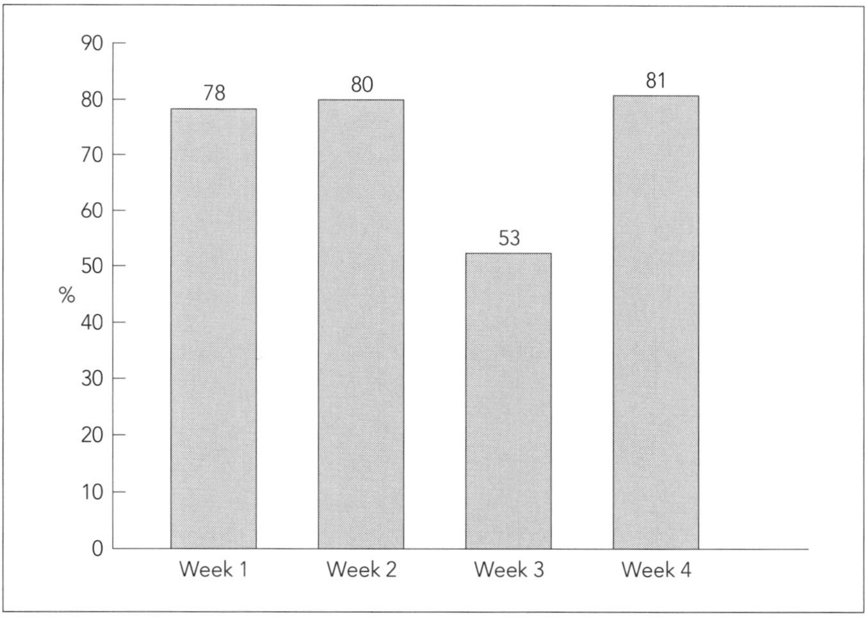

Perhaps there was a major deadline at work at the end of Week 3 and no one had time to go shopping. It is variations like this that are the main point of information in most column charts.

Pie chart

A pie chart is used in similar cases to a bar chart, but has one special property. This is that the figures in it *must* add up to 100%. Of course, the figures may be given as quantities rather than percentages, but there are no overlaps or omissions – the total sample is divided up completely between the various sections of the chart. For example, let's look at one fruit bowl, and see how many pieces of each type of fruit there are in it:

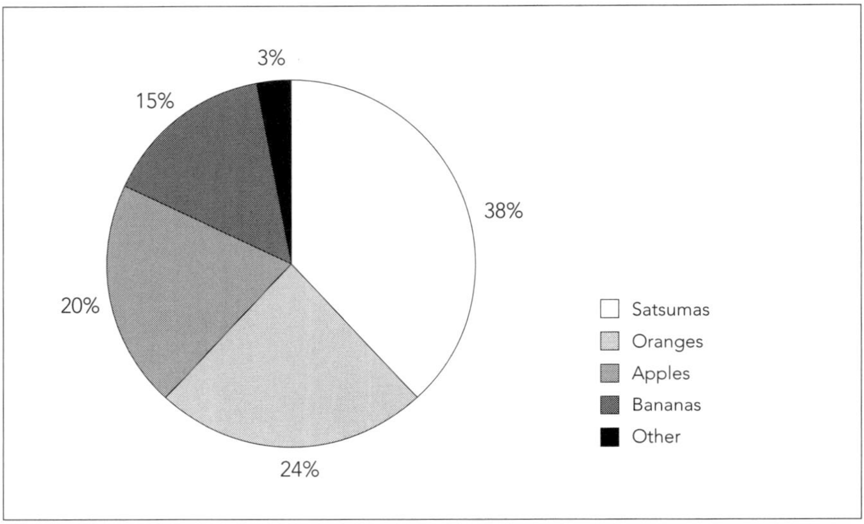

The largest segment should start at 12 o'clock and be measured clockwise from there, with subsequent segments being progressively smaller. In this way, the chart not only shows which figure is largest, but also visually conveys the relative sizes of the sections very effectively. Of course, it can be confusing if you try to fit 18 segments into a pie chart, so these are generally used only when there are six sections or fewer. Also, since the main strength of a pie chart is to convey relative sizes, there may be times when a bar chart is used instead, since this is not the main significance of the figures.

Line graph

A line graph is used almost exclusively to show changes over time, and also sometimes to show changes according to age group. As we have seen, column charts can also be used for this purpose. The main differences between these two charts are:

- column charts are useful only when there are relatively few figures – otherwise you end up with too many columns and they are hard to read;
- column charts tend to be used to show specific variations rather than general trends.

So a line graph is used for time-series comparisons when there are many figures, and usually when there is a general trend rather than a horizontal line with a few kinks in it. An example would be an analysis of the number of apples I have eaten each week for the past three months.

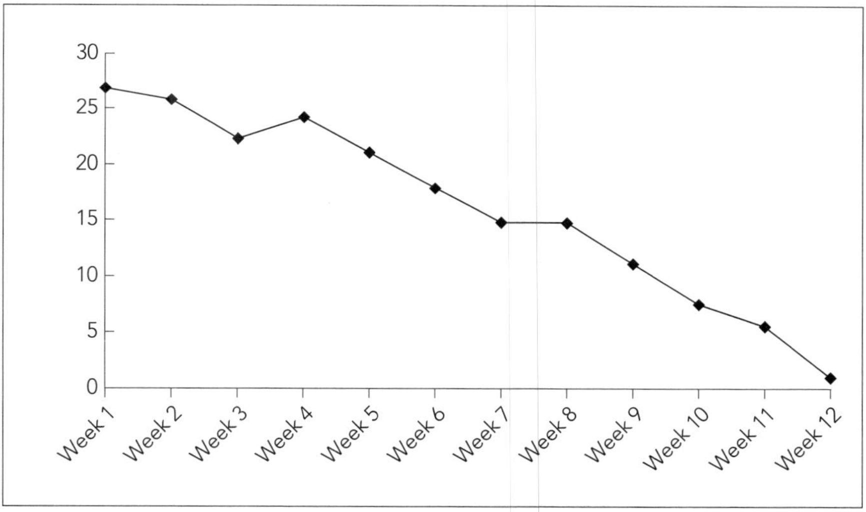

I am now completely sick of apples. What this chart conveys most effectively is the rapid decline in my apple addiction, rather than the number of apples that I ate in any given week.

Scatter chart

Scatter charts are used to show correlation – that is, the relationship between two factors. In this way, they could be used to show the relationship between the value of the pound and my tendency to eat apples. There is unlikely to be any real relationship here – both of these factors will vary without having any effect on each other. However, the relationship between the number of apples I eat and the number of bananas I eat may be very strong.

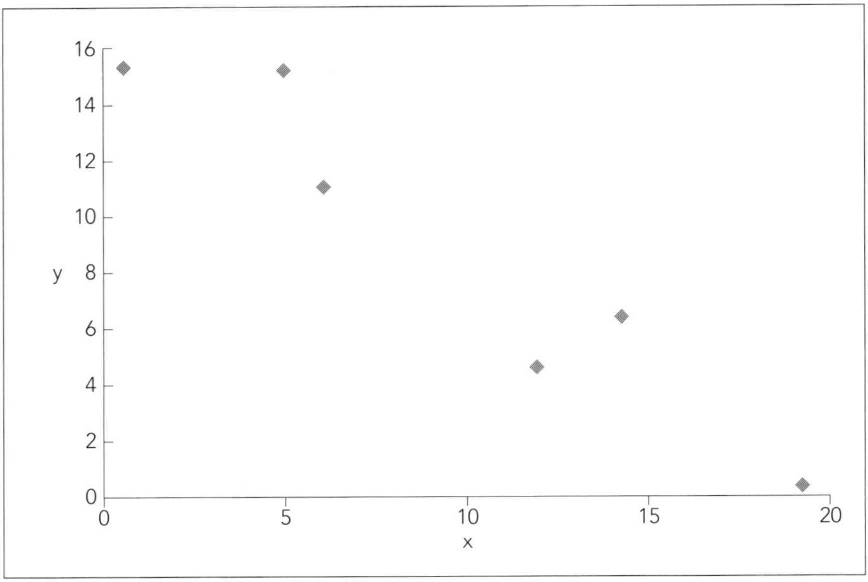

This shows that as my consumption of apples decreased (as shown by the values on the vertical Y-axis) my consumption of bananas increased (as shown by the value on the horizontal X-axis). So when I eat 15 apples, I eat one banana; when I eat one apple I eat 19 bananas. This can be seen from the fact that the points on the graph go in something approximating a straight line from the top left to bottom right of the chart. If I tended to eat as many apples as bananas on any day, the line would go from the bottom left to top right. If there were no correlation, they would not form any noticeable line. Scatter charts are quite uncommon, but are the most appropriate chart for showing this sort of correlation.

Matrix

Matrices vary from the other charts described here in that they are not necessarily dependent on numerical figures. The axes are normally shown crossed, giving a dead centre at the point where they cross. This divides the chart into quarters, and the main information given is which quarter each item is in. In some matrices, items are not positioned any more specifically than this, while in others they are given a precise place on the chart.

Suppose, for instance, that I generally eat fruit either because it tastes nice or because it is filling, and I want to know how well each type of fruit fills each of these criteria. If I were interested only in taste then I might give marks out of ten and show the results on a bar chart, but I want a chart that will show me both figures at once as the following one does.

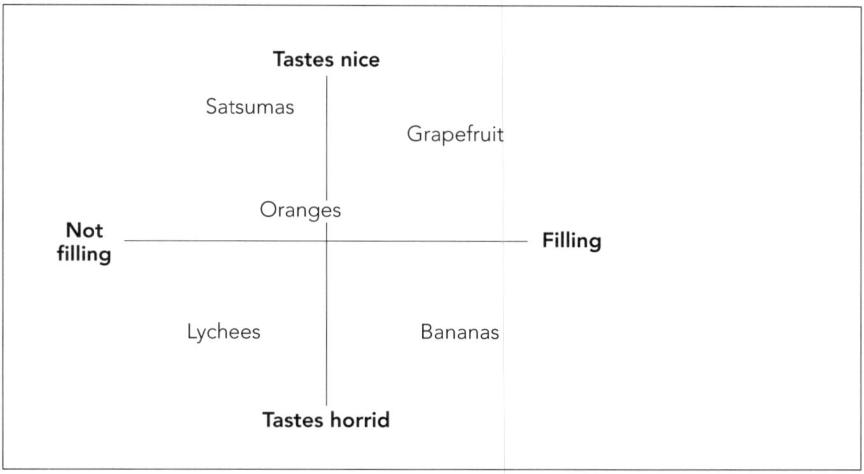

This chart tells me that if I want something filling, and I don't care about the taste, I should have a banana (the most filling item), or if I want it to taste nice as well, then I should have a grapefruit (not as filling, but much nicer). It also tells everyone exactly what I think of lychees. I could have given marks out of ten on each axis, which would have given each fruit a precise point on the graph, or I could have simply put each fruit in one of the quarters and not been any more specific than this. The matrix shown here is a compromise between the two.

So matrices are useful for showing how a variety of items rate according to two different variables (e.g. taste and fillingness).

Indexing

One particular statistical convention that may be used occasionally in these books is indexing. This is a relatively uncommon way of quantifying information, so it is probably worth giving a brief explanation of it for anyone who may not have come across it before.

Indexing is used when there are no absolute figures available, only relative ones. The information therefore shows the relationships between these figures. However, this cannot be done with percentages or quantities, since the data do not exist in this form. So how can the information be presented? The solution is to take an arbitrary figure as the standard, or as the maximum, then rate other figures relative to this.

Suppose I want to rate how much Alice, Bruce, Cynthia and David enjoy eating apples. I am not asking for scores out of ten from each of them; I am trying to measure their actual enjoyment, so there is no absolute measurement that I can apply. However, I may still have meaningful and useful information to give on this topic. One way that I can present this is to say that Cynthia seems to be fairly ambivalent about eating apples, while the others have stronger feelings one way or the other. So I take 100 as the amount of pleasure Cynthia experiences from eating an apple. Using this, I now have a scale on which to judge the pleasure of my four subjects.

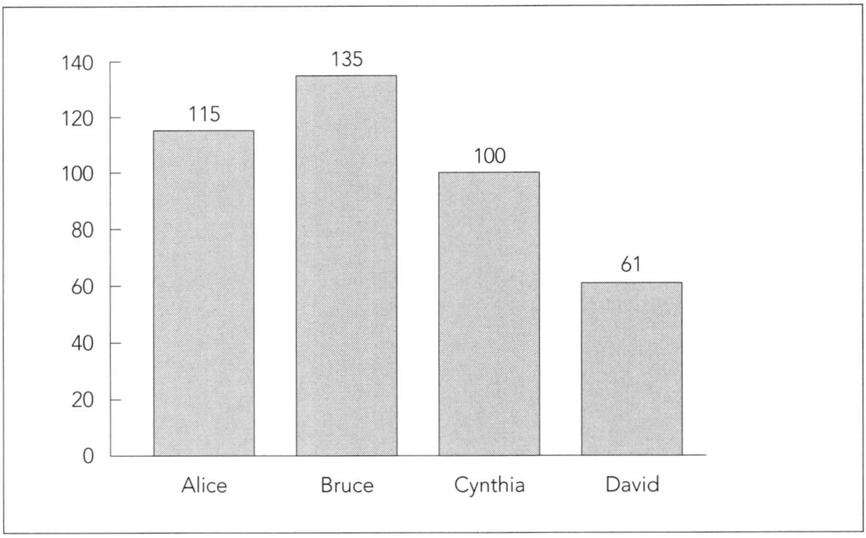

Note that the '100' here does not measure anything specific such as the volume of 'Mmmm' noises or number of endorphins released in the brain. And rather than having 100 as the most neutral point, I could have had it as the maximum enjoyment. This choice was entirely arbitrary; it was simply necessary to provide a way of presenting the data, and the data show only the relationship between these four people's enjoyment of eating apples, and cannot be related to anything beyond this.

Averages

Most of us can remember from school that there are three different kinds of average, even if we can't quite recall what all of them are. Since they are used in these books, it might be wise to recap. Imagine that 35 of us have fruit bowls, and I want to know the average number of apples in each bowl. My three options are:

1. Mean average: the total number of apples divided by the total number of fruit bowls (this is the most commonly used type of average, and the one that we generally mean when we don't specify which sort of average we are talking about).
2. Median average: the halfway point between the highest (9) and lowest (0) number of apples.
3. Mode average: the single number of apples that occurs more frequently than any other.

I'll give you an example. The following column chart shows the number of fruit bowls containing each quantity of apples; five bowls have no apples in them, one contains one apple, and so on.

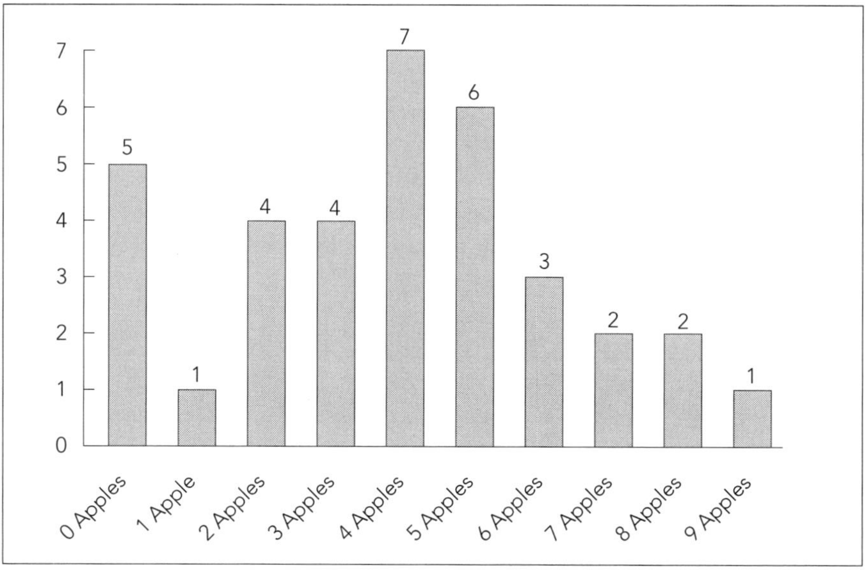

- Mean average number of apples (136 apples divided by 35 fruit bowls): 3.9
- Median average number of apples: 4.5
- Mode average number of apples: 4

Figures that seem to contradict each other

In books like *Quick Answers to Marketing Questions* and the rest of the *Quick Answers* series, there are many figures which refer to similar things. In some cases these figures may appear directly to contradict each other. In fact, we have taken great pains to ensure that no contradictory figures are included in any of the *Quick Answers* series, but there are often subtle differences between statistics which are easy to overlook, and may give the impression that they cannot both be correct.

For example, suppose we are examining the composition of a particular fruit bowl which contains four satsumas and a grapefruit. We may say that:

- the contents of the fruit bowl are made up of 20% grapefruit;
- it is also made up of 50% grapefruit.

For the sake of this example, these figures are obviously deliberately unhelpful, but they may both be correct. The first, in fact, applies to the composition in numbers of fruits (four satsumas and one grapefruit), and the second applies to the composition in weight (since four satsumas weigh the same as one grapefruit). Naturally, we will explain such differences whenever there are potentially confusing figures like this in any of the *Quick Answers* series, but if you are only looking up one piece of information, or if you are in a hurry and concentrating more on the figures than the text, it is easy to miss such slight but crucial differences.

In order to minimise the likelihood of this happening, and make it easier to spot the reasons for such discrepancies in this book or elsewhere, we will briefly explain some of the main reasons that such apparent contradictions can occur.

Differences in the sample

Even if two surveys ask exactly the same question, it is exceptionally unlikely that they will be asking the same people. For this reason, results will always vary slightly between different surveys. Often surveys will deliberately be asking different people about the same thing – one survey may ask all workers, for instance, and another may be asking only managers. This may produce substantially different results, and these differences may even be the main point of interest in the figures.

The differences are sometimes even more subtle than this. For instance, one survey may ask workplaces if they operate a certain policy, and another may ask the workers if their workplace operates the policy. If the policy is most often operated by large workplaces with many employees, then the proportion of workers answering 'yes' is likely to be higher than the proportion of workplaces answering 'yes'.

Differences in survey characteristics

Sometimes differences may be less deliberate. One survey may have covered more large companies than another, for instance, and in many cases this will lead to different results. This does not mean that one was a survey of large companies and the other a survey of small companies; it simply means that their balance of companies of different sizes was not the same. Similarly, one survey may have been conducted by interview and another by postal questionnaire, and this will also have an effect on the results.

Another factor that may lead to differences is the time of the survey. Figures of change over time can be very useful information in their own right, but since any two surveys are likely to vary in many ways (such as what exact question was asked, who was asked, and so on), it is often misleading to compare results from two totally different surveys conducted at different times.

To avoid this type of confusion, the figures in this book have been selected as the most reliable ones of all that were available. However, there may be times when two different surveys cover the same topic but ask slightly different questions, in which case both will be included, in order to provide as much useful information as possible. In such cases, it is worth remembering that the two surveys were very probably conducted at different times and in different ways, and while both are informative and valid, they are unlikely to have produced exactly the same results.

Differences in conceptual structure

Many decisions are made when designing a survey, and this is another area where surveys can vary. If I am conducting a survey into how many people eat apples often, I will have to define 'often'. Is it once a week, twice a week, or once a fortnight? Naturally, the choice I make in defining this term will affect what figure I arrive at at the end of the survey.

Similarly, I may be surveying how many apples people eat in a week. If I am doing this on a tick-box questionnaire, I will have to choose what categories to provide a box for – it may be 0–3, 4–8, 8–11, 12+, or it may be 0, 1–5, 6–10, 11+. It will be very hard to tie together the two sets of figures that I receive, and each grouping has its own strengths and weaknesses.

Similarly, I may be surveying people's favourite fruits, and listing them either by colour, or by price, or in groups such as citrus, tropical and so on. Again, I may not be able to compare the different results that I receive in any meaningful way. Each set of results will tell me something that I want to know, but will fail to tell me something else. So each set of results simply has to be taken on its own merits, and the inherent differences borne in mind when taking the results together.

Not adding up to 100%

In this book, and elsewhere, percentage figures are often given which do not total 100%. At times this may be confusing, particularly when you want to be sure that you have complete and reliable information. Of course, there are many legitimate reasons why this can occur, and it is worth running through these quickly so that, when such a situation occurs, you will be able to see why it has happened.

More than 100%

Rounding

Some of the figures that are given as whole-number percentages may originally have been calculated to one or two decimal places. This level of detail is often unnecessary, and can complicate the information that is being given; hence the figures have been 'rounded' to the nearest whole number. This process can occasionally produce figures which total 101% or 102%, although it is rare to create any more of a disturbance than this.

For example, the composition of my fruit bowl (by weight) is:

Apples:	30.6%
Oranges:	32.8%
Bananas:	36.6%

This makes a total of 100%. However, I would like to make these statistics easier to read and take in, so I want them as whole numbers. Since the numbers after the decimal places are all greater than 5, this means that all these numbers will be rounded up, giving this composition:

Apples:	31%
Oranges:	33%
Bananas:	37%

This totals 101%. This is an unfortunate, but unavoidable, effect of rounding. Although it can be disconcerting, the only way to treat it is simply to accept that it happens, but that it causes only very minimal distortion of the statistics, since the total of the percentages very rarely comes to more than 102%.

Multiple answers

Let's consider the example given earlier in this appendix of the proportion of people with each given fruit in their fruit bowl:

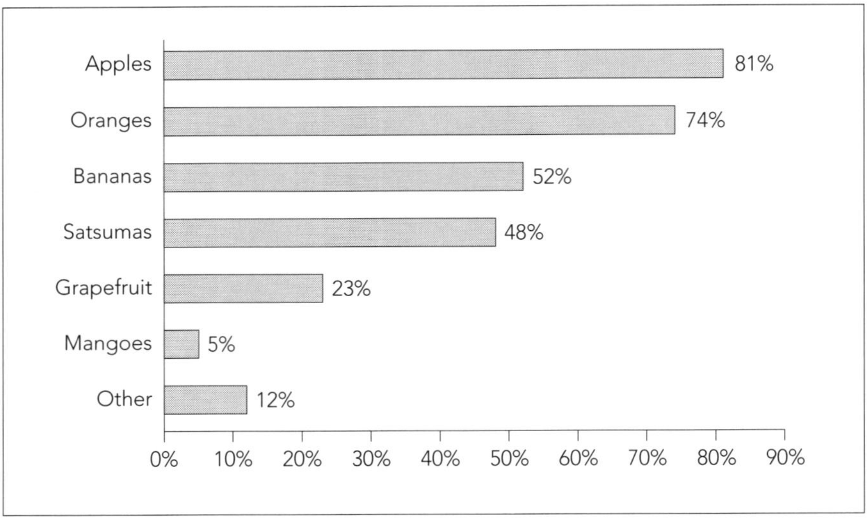

The total here is obviously much greater than 100%. The simple reason for this is that many people have more than one fruit in their bowl. Questions like this, for which each individual can give more than one answer, often end up with figures that total more than 100%. So long as we do not find that 117% of people have apples in their fruit bowl, then the data are perfectly correct.

Overlapping categories

I have found that my fruit bowl contains (by quantity) 50% tropical fruit and 70% citrus fruit. These figures seem hard to reconcile, but of course there is an explanation for this. This explanation involves grapefruit, which I class both as a citrus fruit and as a tropical fruit. My fruit bowl contains five satsumas, three bananas and two grapefruit. Hence there are seven citrus fruits (satsumas and grapefruit) and five tropical fruits (bananas and grapefruit).

It is often useful to collect information in groupings which do not have overlaps, so as to provide a total figure of 100%. However, it may also be that two particular groups are of interest (e.g. tropical and citrus fruits), and that these groups have an overlap. If so, the figures for these groups, when added together, may total more than 100%.

Less than 100%

Rounding

The effects of rounding, as discussed previously, can produce figures which total less than 100%. On re-examining my fruit bowl, I have discovered its composition (by weight) to be:

Apples:	31.3%
Oranges:	32.4%
Bananas:	36.3%

This, again, totals 100%. After rounding, however, the figures are:

Apples:	31%
Oranges:	32%
Bananas:	36%

These figures add up to only 99%. Again, there is nothing that I can do about this rounding error, except to acknowledge that it is unavoidable, and that it causes only minimal distortion of the statistics.

Omitted categories

The most obvious categories which could be relevant here are 'Not answered' and 'Don't know'. If I ask everyone in my office whether they have apples in their fruit bowl at home, I may find that:

- 72% do have apples;
- only 25% do not have apples.

But what about the other 3%? Well, maybe they didn't know, or maybe they just didn't want to say. Maybe they all, in fact, do have apples at home, and maybe none of them does. We simply can't say, and essentially we have to ignore them.

Sometimes figures for D/K or N/A are given, showing how many people did not respond to the question, and at other times they are not. Many survey questions, however, do not receive a full quota of answers, but the number not responding is usually fairly low and, as with rounding, does not undermine the other data to any appreciable extent.

Of course, other categories can be omitted when data are presented – any category can. If I ask my workmates what their favourite fruit is, I may find that:

- apples are favourite for 43%;
- bananas are the next most popular, cited by 31%;
- oranges are preferred by only 14%;
- 4% did not know or did not answer.

This gives a total of 92%. So what about the other 8%? Well, some of them preferred mangoes, others went for satsumas or guava – there were various answers. However, the proportion that opted for each was so low that it did not seem worth including them. The information that I was trying to convey was how popular the most popular fruits are, not a full breakdown with details of fruits that were favourite with only 0.3% of people.

Although the *Quick Answers* series tries to be as comprehensive as possible, it is designed for practical use, and hence some figures may have been omitted in this way when they were not significant or relevant, and would serve only to confuse the data provided. Such detail may also have been omitted in the source literature from which the statistics were gathered. For these reasons, categories may sometimes have been omitted, giving figures that add up to less than 100%. In these cases, the data are indeed not comprehensive, but the figures that are given are no less valid for it.

appendix 2

Contact addresses

ACAS – The Advisory, Conciliation and Arbitration Service
www.acas.org.uk
020 7210 3613

The Advertising Association
www.adassoc.org.uk
020 7828 2771

Barclays Bank plc Small Business Services
www.barclays.com or
www.barclays.co.uk
54 Lombard Street,
London EC3P 3AH

British Chambers of Commerce
To order publications: BCC Publications, Manning House,
22 Carlisle Place, London SW1P 1JA
020 7565 2033

The British Venture Capital Association
www.bvca.co.uk
022 7240 3846

Business Names Register
National Business Names Registry
For free information pack, call
0121 678 9000

Chartered Institute of Marketing
www.cim.co.uk
01628 427500

Clearlybusiness.com
www.clearlybusiness.com

Companies House
Crown Way, Cardiff CF14 3UZ
www.companieshouse.gov.uk
02920 380184

Confederation of British Industry (CBI)
www.cbi.org.uk
020 7379 7400

Department of Trade and Industry
www.dti.gov.uk
Order from: HMSO 01603 723008

The Dryden Press
www.dryden.hbuk.co.uk
020 7267 4466

The Enterprise Panel c/o UK Business Incubation
0121 357 0433

ESOMAR
www.esomar.org.ne
+31 20 664 2141

Fit for the Future Campaign
www.fitforthefuture.org.uk
0870 600 2513

The Franchise Business
www.franchisebusiness.co.uk

Health and Safety Executive
www.hse.gov.uk
020 7717 6000 or for publications, contact:
HSE Books
01787 881165
Information and Advisory Services, call 0151 951 4000

HSBC Bank plc
www.hsbc.co.uk
0845 6060 000 (Economic Review and Factsheets)
020 7260 7213 (Business Marketing Department)

IFF Research Ltd
www.iff.com
020 7837 6363

Inland Revenue
www.inlandrevenue.gov.uk
020 7438 6692

The Insolvency Service
PO Box 203, 21 Bloomsbury Street, London WC1B 3QW

Institute of Directors
www.iod.org.uk
020 7836 1233

Institute for Employment Studies
www.employment/studies.co.uk
01273 686751

Institute of Management Foundation
www.inst-mgt.org.uk
01536 204222, fax 01536 201651

Institute of Manpower Studies
see Institute for Employment Studies

Institute of Personnel and Development
www.cipd.co.uk
020 8263 3240

Lloyds TSB Bank plc
www.lloydstsbbusiness.com
0800 056 0056

NatWest UK
National Westminster Bank plc (Business Banking)
www. natwestuk.co.uk or
www.natwest.com
020 7454 6869

NatWest Franchise Section
020 7920 5966
To order the NatWest/BFA Franchise survey, contact:
British Franchise Association, Thames View, Newtown Road, Henley-on-Thames, Oxfordshire RG9 1HG
01491 575903, fax 01491 573517

The Policy Studies Institute
www.psi.org.uk
020 7468 0468
Publications to be ordered from:
Grantham Book Services, Isaac Newton Way, Alma Park Industrial Estate, Grantham, Lincs. NG31 9SD
01476 541080

R3
www.insolvency.org.uk
020 7831 6563

Small Business Research Trust
www.oubs-sbrt@open.ac.uk
(Open University Business School)
01908 655831

The Small Business Service
www.sbs.gsi.gov.uk
(statistics) or
www.businessadviceonline.org
08456 045678

Virgin Publishing
www.virginbooks.com
020 7386 3300